The Flower of Friendship

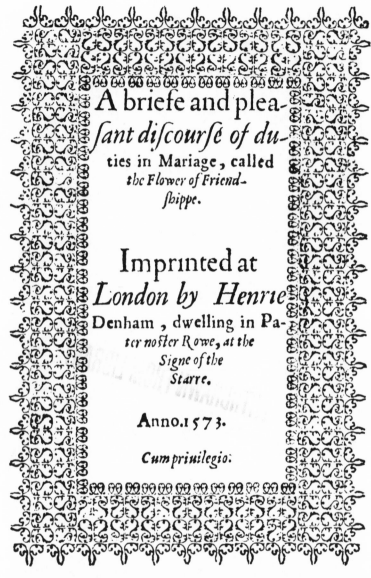

A briefe and plea-
sant difcourfe of du-
ties in Mariage, called
the Flower of Friend-
fhippe.

Imprinted at
London by Henrie
Denham , dwelling in Pa-
ter nofter Rowe, at the
Signe of the
Starre.

Anno.1573.

Cum priuilegio:

1. Title page from the 1573 edition. All the extant title pages of editions from 1568 to 1573 have this form. This one is in the best condition. Reproduced by permission of The Master and Fellows of St. John's College, Cambridge.

The Flower of Friendship

A RENAISSANCE DIALOGUE CONTESTING MARRIAGE

BY EDMUND TILNEY

Edited and with an Introduction
by VALERIE WAYNE

CENTER FOR
SCHOLARLY EDITIONS
AN APPROVED EDITION
MODERN LANGUAGE
ASSOCIATION OF AMERICA

Cornell University Press

Ithaca and London

First published 1992 by Cornell University Press.

International Standard Book Number 0-8014-2454-2 (cloth)
International Standard Book Number 0-8014-9705-1 (paper)
Library of Congress Catalog Card Number 92-52776

Printed in the United States of America
*Librarians: Library of Congress cataloging information appears
on the last page of the book.*

⊗ The paper in this book meets the minimum requirements of the
American National Standard for Information Sciences—Permanence
of Paper for Printed Library Materials, ANSI Z39.48-1984.

This book is
for Sarah
with deep love

Contents

Illustrations

Acknowledgments

This small book is the product of many changes. Over the ten years, off and on, that I have been engaged with *The Flower,* the critical climate in the profession has altered almost as much as the home in which I find myself; and though I am delighted that the chill of Chicago, of formalism, of the reverence for history has given way to the warmth of Honolulu, of feminism, and the reassessments of history, that past was still the nurturing occasion for this present. So I begin with a quite traditional acknowledgment to William A. Ringler, Jr., who directed my work at the University of Chicago a long time ago and was so generous with his extensive knowledge of Renaissance texts. I remember his help on this project up to his death in 1987 with real affection.

The obligation to work in excellent libraries was another pleasure of preparing this edition, and I am grateful to the staffs of the Beinecke Library at Yale, the Bodleian Library, the British Library, the Folger Shakespeare Library, the Huntington Library, the Newberry Library, the library of St. John's College, Cambridge, the Pierpont Morgan Library, and the Regenstein Library at Chicago for their kind assistance. Research grants from the Huntington Library in the summer of 1982 and more frequently from the University of Hawaii at Manoa enabled the work to continue.

But it is friends who consistently sustained it—Elizabeth McCutcheon, who encouraged it from the beginning, and especially Craig Howes, who never ceased his rigorous critique and determined belief in the project. I am also very grateful to those who offered their comments on the final revision: Catherine Belsey, Joseph Chadwick, Kathy E. Ferguson, Elizabeth Hageman, Janis Butler Holm, James L. Kastely, Cristina Malcolmson, and Gary Pak. Many others provided material help along the way, including Cristina Bacchilega, Nigel Bawcutt, Tom Berger, Stephen Booth, Dana Devereux, Kathleen Falvey, Robert Hoopes, Ann Rosalind Jones, Arthur Kinney, Carole Levin, Barbara Lewalski, Robert Bernard Martin, Cornelia Moore, Christopher Ricks, John Rieder, Gordon Schochet, William Streitberger, Richard Strier, and Frank Whigham. Joseph Chadwick and Harold Irving shared their expertise in sixteenth-century Spanish. Josephine Roberts prepared a more thorough review of the editing than was even required by the MLA's Committee on Scholarly Editions, thereby improving the quality of the text. Bernhard Kendler was a shrewd and benevolent editor at Cornell University Press. While this edition was in press I discovered how much book production depends upon the labor of unseen women. Those whom I can acknowledge for their help by name include Laura Moss Gottlieb, Amanda Heller, Mary Lash, and especially Carol Betsch, who was always genial and generous.

I recall with thanks the support offered in earlier stages of this project by David Callies, with whom I learned a lot about marriage. The flowering of the book I associate with productive years on my own and now, happily, with Richard Tillotson, a fine writer and a delightful companion. It is dedicated with admiration to my daughter, Sarah, whose grasp of the subject treated here seems always to have been subtle and seasoned. How unnecessary to make procreation a duty when its consequence can be such a joy.

V. W.

The Flower of Friendship

Introduction

The history of ideologies of marriage in Renaissance England does not readily make a coherent narrative. Those historians and critics who in recent years have tried to establish the difference between Catholic and Protestant or Anglican and puritan views, or have assumed such differences in order to determine their effects upon social roles within the family, have repeatedly encountered strong dissenting arguments from other scholars. Although such dispute is salutory evidence of the increased attention now being given to the issues of gender, marriage, and the family in the past and the present, it may also suggest a lack of consistency within ideological and social practice that the ordered narratives of scholarship prefer to deny. Faced with so many apparent inconsistencies, some critics have turned to conduct books as a means of grounding their arguments. Since it is the very purpose of conduct books to enunciate ideologies, those who have consulted these texts have often assumed that here, if not in the realities from which they were considered separate, one could find some agreement on "what people thought" as well as some clear difference between the views of one religious group and those of another. Yet Margo Todd has made a persuasive case

[1]

for what she calls "the humanist/puritan consensus" in household theory in the late sixteenth and early seventeenth centuries, a consensus that she sets off against both Catholic and conformist Anglican doctrines of the period.[1] Even the conduct books that we believed were constructed along the lines of religious affiliation instead disrupt our easy categorization of them.

What reason have we also to assume that when conduct books address such entangled issues as love and power, public and private duty, there should be convincing clarity and a single line of argument? When skilled writers address these subjects in literature, tropes such as paradox, hyperbole, and oxymoron configure their texts. Perhaps we hope that the problems become simpler when they are addressed by writers of lesser skill attempting to articulate in a didactic mode an ideology that has already become dominant; but as Raymond Williams points out, a dominant ideology is never either total or exclusive: "Within an apparent hegemony . . . there are not only alternative and oppositional formations . . . but, within what can be recognized as the dominant, effectively varying formations which resist any simple reduction to some generalized hegemonic function." Williams uses Gramsci's approach to hegemony as a localized maneuver and his model of social practices as continually open to conflict and contestation to distinguish among residual, dominant, and emergent ideologies existing in one cultural moment; Williams also notes the presence of divergent elements associated with a dominant ideology that it tries to "control or transform or even incorporate."[2] This approach to cultural analysis can be applied to conduct books to show how they attempt to create consensus and enforce or forestall social change by advising dutiful behavior. When we examine those texts for the diverse and contradictory elements from which they construct their apparent order, we

[1] Margo, Todd, *Christian Humanism and the Puritan Social Order* (Cambridge: Cambridge University Press, 1987), p. 238.

[2] Raymond Williams, *Marxism and Literature* (Oxford: Oxford University Press, 1977), pp. 119, 113.

make visible the conflicting forces within societies that they try to regulate through prescriptive instruction and, in some cases, narrative form.

In this introduction I have three aims as I apply such an approach to *The Flower of Friendship*. The first is to argue for the relevance of humanist thinking about marriage and women to this text and to sixteenth-century English culture. Historians such as Margo Todd and Kathleen M. Davies have taken issue with Christopher Hill, Lawrence Stone, and others who stress puritan over humanist influence in attitudes toward marriage. As Todd puts it, "In the sixteenth century, the assertion that companionship is pre-eminent among the ends of marriage was an innovation of Christian humanism, rather than of puritanism."[3] *The Flower of Friendship* participates in a large group of continental and English texts that adapt and transform *Conjugium,* one of Erasmus's colloquies on marriage, and the interrelationship among these texts provides still more evidence for continuity among humanist, Protestant, and puritan approaches to marriage. Some fictional characters in Tilney's dialogue are explicitly named after the humanists he drew upon for his advice—Desiderius Erasmus, Juan Luis Vives, and Pedro di Luxan.

My second aim is to demonstrate the presence of what Williams calls residual, dominant, and emergent ideologies of marriage within Tilney's text and to examine the contradictions that operate within the dominant mode. *The Flower* includes characters who reject marriage as well as those who serve as advocates for it. Tilney marks two of these oppositional characters as residual by giving them medieval antecedents. A third advises unambiguously egalitarian relations between husbands and wives which constitute an emergent view. Those who speak for the dominant ideology also claim that their companionate view of marriage is egalitarian, but with a crucial difference: the dominant ideology constructs marital equality on the basis of women's

[3] Todd, p. 100.

[3]

sexual control and men's wealth, with those criteria functioning as the gendered determinants of class. Related contradictions occur when those advocates celebrate love between marital partners in order to endorse male authority and female self-sacrifice, and when they evoke women's sexuality only to require its repression and control. Tilney's text shows that humanism takes seriously the problems of marriage and of women, but its ideology of companionate marriage still tries to legitimate the hierarchies of class and gender which sustained the Tudor religious and social order. Yet the commodification of women's virtue offered as part of the dominant ideology could also permit it to function in support of social mobility by according women's sexual control the value otherwise granted to their wealth or social status.

My third aim here is to show how and why the emergent view of marriage that *The Flower* releases is not contained by its dominant ideology. When the character Isabella offers an emergent view, she exposes the central contradiction of Renaissance humanists who combined claims for women's spiritual and rational equality with requirements that wives be subordinate in marriage. The rupture occurs when the character Erasmus is brought to speak for man's "absolute aucthoritie, over the woman in all places" (1177):[4] then the equation between companionate and egalitarian marriage collapses quite suddenly. Moreover Isabella, who disrupts the dominant ideology, is associated through her name and her situation with Queen Elizabeth I, whose position on marriage was often at odds with that of her Parliament and her people, particularly around 1568. Isabella's disruption opens the text up to reproducing some of the instabilities and contradictions within Renaissance ideologies of marriage which were compelling public and private dilemmas at the time it was written and read.

[4] All references to Tilney's *Flower of Friendship* in this introduction will be cited by line numbers from the accompanying critical text.

[4]

Introduction

Until the second volume of the revised *Short-Title Catalogue*
appeared in 1976, only three editions of *The Flower of Friendship*
were generally thought to exist; now we know that seven editions were published between 1568 and 1587, three of these
within the first year of issue.[5] This new information suggests that
Tilney's text achieved the kind of popularity we would associate
with a very topical book. Only three other Renaissance texts on
marriage appeared in more English editions: Heinrich Bullinger's
Christen State of Matrimonye of 1541 (which is often mistakenly
treated as different from Thomas Becon's *Golden Boke of Christen
Matrimonye*), John Dod and Richard Cleaver's *Godlie Forme of
Householde Government* of 1598, and Erasmus's *Encomium matri-
monii* in its English translations, particularly that published in
Thomas Wilson's *Arte of Rhetorique* from 1553 to 1585.[6] The

[5] See the textual notes to this introduction and *A Short-Title Catalogue of Books
Printed in England, Scotland, and Ireland and of English Books Printed Abroad, 1475–
1640*, ed. Katharine F. Pantzer et al., 2d ed. rev. and enl., vol. 2 (London:
Bibliographical Society, 1976), nos. 24076–24077a.5; see also vol. 1 (London:
Bibliographical Society, 1986). Hereinafter cited as *STC*.

[6] Bullinger's text appeared in thirteen editions, Dod and Cleaver's in nine.
Encomium matrimonii was published in Erasmus's *De conscribendis epistolis* (1521) as
A ryght frutefull epystle . . . in laude and prayse of matrymony in Tavernour's
translation of [1536?], in the eight editions of Wilson's *Rhetoric*, and in Aurelius
Brandolinus's *Lippi Brandolini, De ratione scribendi*, bk. 3, (1573). Richard Whit-
ford, *A Work for Householders* [1530?], also appeared in seven editions. The other
texts on marriage that I consulted for this comparison were (in chronological
order) William Harrington, *Commendations of Matrimony*, 4 editions; Heinrich
Cornelius Agrippa, *Commendation of Matrimony*, trans. David Clapham, 2 edi-
tions; Juan Luis Vives, *Office and Duetie of an Husband*, 1 edition; George
Whetstone, *An Heptameron of Civill Discourses*, 2 editions; Henry Smith, *Prepara-
tive to Marriage*, 4 editions; William Perkins, *Christian Oeconomie*, trans. Thomas
Pickering, 1 edition; Robert Snawsel, *Looking Glasse for Maried Folkes*, 3 editions;
Alexander Niccholes, *A Discourse, of Marriage and Wiving*, 2 editions; William
Whately, *Bride-Bush*, 3 editions; William Gouge, *Of Domesticall Duties*, 3 editions;
Thomas Gataker, *A Good Wife God's Gift*, 3 editions; Thomas Taylor, *A Good
Husband and a Good Wife*, 1 edition; and Daniel Rogers, *Matrimoniall Honour*, 2
editions. All of this information comes from both volumes of the *STC*. For the
purposes of this comparison I could not include texts in which marriage is
addressed as a subject within a larger work or collection, or in which a separate
essay on marriage appears in a collection of works on more diverse subjects,

presence of the *Encomium* in Wilson's *Rhetoric* and in Erasmus's own *De conscribendis epistolis* shows how consciously rhetorical a text the Erasmian letter is. *The Flower* also extends Erasmus's figurative adaptation of marital issues to create a narrative from prescriptive advice, for Tilney uses the fictional frame of Italian conversazione found in Castiglione's *Courtier* and Boccaccio's *Filocopo* for his text. *The Courtier* was certainly a more popular dialogue in the Italian original, but even the printings of its English translation ran to only four editions, as did those of *Filocopo,* while the translation of Guazzo's *Civil Conversations* appeared in only two.[7]

Conduct books for men are often read on the assumption that the information they provide "seems to contribute directly to our understanding of political life," whereas comparable books for women are "rarely . . . allowed to contribute to our notion of cultural history."[8] Yet by 1568, since a queen was on the English throne, the conduct of marriage had more far-reaching consequences for the English people than the conduct of a gentleman. Tilney roots his adaptation of Italian conversazione quite specifically in English soil: Master Pedro observes that such pastimes as those found in Boccaccio and Castiglione "are practised at this day in the English court" (94–95), and one member of the dialogue is named Lady Isabella (Spanish for Elizabeth) so she may

---

although some of the most important texts on marriage were published in these forms. Erasmus's *Colloquies* and Vives's *Instruction of a Christen Woman* are examples of the first instance, *Christian Oeconomie* as it appears in collections of William Perkins's works of the second.

[7]Castiglione, *STC* 4778–81; Boccaccio, *STC* 3180–82; Guazzo, *STC* 12422–23.

[8]Nancy Armstrong and Leonard Tennenhouse, eds., *The Ideology of Conduct: Essays on Literature and the History of Sexuality* (London: Methuen, 1987), pp. 4, 3. Susan Amussen argues that our current distinction between private and public "is necessarily false when applied to the experience of early modern England," and that "the analogy between the household and the state was available to all those interested in authority and the enforcement of order," in *An Ordered Society: Gender and Class in Early Modern England* (Oxford: Basil Blackwell, 1988), pp. 2, 37.

serve as Tilney's figure for Queen Elizabeth. The woodcut from a 1498 edition of Boccaccio's *Decameron* shows how these courtly dialogues would have been conducted: they occurred after a meal in the garden or arbor of a large estate, with the participants seated formally in a semicircle.[9] (See figure 5, page 72.) After the two-day *conversazione* in *The Flower,* Lady Isabella, turning to the narrator, Tilney himself, "required me for hir sake, to penne the whole discourse of this flagrant *Flower.* For quoth she, your quiet silence both these dayes, assureth mee, that you have well considered thereof" (1429–32). These passages establish a strong connection between the narrative and its social conditions. It is possible that Tilney and Elizabeth participated in such a pastime as that recounted here, and (or) that Elizabeth asked Tilney to prepare the text as we have it. We do know that Tilney dedicated all editions of *The Flower* to "the Noble and most vertuous Princesse, Elizabeth." Henry Denham, who published the first six editions, had a royal patent from the queen, and Elizabeth's coat of arms appears on the verso of each extant title page of the texts that he printed.[10]

[9]For an extended discussion of the social customs associated with conversazione and other courtly pastimes, see Thomas Frederick Crane, *Italian Social Customs of the Sixteenth Century and Their Influence on the Literatures of Europe,* Cornell Studies in English, no. 5 (New Haven: Yale University Press, 1920).

[10]Although it is not clear from all available evidence that Denham had the patent of a royal printer as early as 1568, the title pages of all texts of *The Flower* that he printed (excluding the first edition's title page, which is not extant, and the last edition, which was printed by Abel Jeffs) show the words "cum privilegio" following the date. R. B. McKerrow notes that "about the year 1574 Henry Denham acquired the patent of William Seres for printing the Psalter, the Primer for little children and all books of private prayer in Latin and English." R. B. McKerrow, ed., *A Dictionary of Printers and Booksellers in England, Scotland, and Ireland . . . 1557–1640* (London: Bibliographical Society, 1910), p. 89. His consistent use of "cum privilegio" before that date suggests he probably had an earlier patent as well.

J. D. Y. Peel has examined the coat of arms from Tilney's text and determined that heraldically it is a version either of Elizabeth's arms or of Edward VI's. Denham used the same coat of arms in his [1568?] edition of Elizabeth's own translation of Margaret of Angoulême's *Godly medytacyon of the christen sowle* (*STC*

¶To the Noble and moſt
Vertuous Princeſſe Eliza-
beth, by the grace of God, of Englande,Fraunce, and Irelande Queene,defen-
der of the fayth.&c. Be long life,
quiet raigne, and perfit
health.

HEN I CON-
ſider, moſt noble
Queene & Soue-
raigne that with-
in your Maieſties
ſacred breſt, wiſe-
dome, adourned
with Noble ver-
tues,is only harbored.From whence as
from a pure Fountaine,doth flow, the
deedes of a Noble heart, waying therewithall your Maieſties highe dignitie,
and the lowneſſe of my eſtate,with my
ſimple ſkill : I ſtoode as one diſmayde,
not daring to aduenture to put this
my baſe ſtyle to the hearing eyther of
your maieſties reuerent eares,or to the

A.2.   iudge-

2. Elizabeth I's coat of arms on the verso of the title page and the
beginning of the dedication to her, from the 1573 edition. Reproduced
by permission of The Master and Fellows of St. John's College, Cambridge.

17320.5), bordered at the top by references to Elizabeth and Henry and at the
bottom by maxims spelling out "Lizabeth Regina" through the first letter of each
maxim (sig. E4ᵛ). Since the royal arms in *The Flower* appear on A1ᵛ opposite the
dedication to Queen Elizabeth on A2, there can be little doubt that they are meant
to be the arms of Elizabeth.

It was not uncommon for printers to use the royal arms in books that they had a
royal patent to print; frequently they even incorporated these arms into their

Introduction

The author of this text also had a personal interest in the queen, for he was her distant cousin. Edmund Tilney was connected to the Howards through two of his great-aunts, both of whom had been wives of Thomas, duke of Norfolk, the grandfather of Anne Boleyn and Catherine Howard. The inscription on Tilney's restored monument at St. Leonard's Church, Streatham, requires no fewer than twenty-five lines to enumerate his connections by lineage with powerful English families.[11] According to W. R.

---

printers' devices, and Denham is known to have done so. See R. B. McKerrow, *Printers' and Publishers' Devices in England and Scotland, 1485–1640* (London: Bibliographical Society, 1949), especially Introduction, p. xvi. However, Denham's 1566 edition of Anthonie Rushe's *President for a Prince,* which was also dedicated to the queen, his 1570 edition of Thomas Kirchmeyer's *Popish Kingdom,* and his editions of Thomas à Kempis's *Imitation of Christ* ranging from 1568 to 1585 show no royal arms. Books that do show the royal arms and are dedicated to Queen Elizabeth include Lewys Evans, *The Castle of Christianitie,* printed by Denham in 1568; William Turner's *Herbal,* printed by Arnold Birckman in 1568; and Jan Van der Noot, *A Theatre for Wordlings,* printed by Henry Bynneman in 1569. The dedicatory epistles to each of these texts proclaim personal gratitude to the queen: for her clemency in allowing Evans, a religious dissident, to renounce his folly; for her help on four occasions with her letters patent after Turner had met her eighteen years earlier at the duke of Somerset's house; and from Van der Noot for the queen's reception of exiles from France and Holland. Denham's [1568?] edition of Margaret of Angoulême's text, which Elizabeth herself translated, displays her arms prominently within the text itself; the title page for this edition is, however, no longer extant.

I would infer from the present research that Denham did have a royal patent as early as 1568 and that his use of the royal arms on the same opening as the dedication to the queen reinforces her association with the text. Yet Denham was probably not required to seek permission from the queen for such a use, so there is no official endorsement implied by their presence. In coming to these conclusions, I am very grateful for the assistance of J. D. Y. Peel in heraldry, Nigel Bawcutt on printers, George Walton Williams on printers' devices, and Elizabeth Hageman and George Hoffmann on privileges.

[11] In addition to Tilney's monument inside the church, there is also a modern stained-glass window designed by John Hayward at the east end of the north chancel aisles. The Streatham window includes a portrait of Tilney as well as earlier and later residents of the town, among them the Thrales, Dr. Johnson, and Boswell. The likeness of Tilney is entirely imaginary but is based on figures in the painting of Queen Elizabeth being carried on a litter by her courtiers, attributed to Robert Peake the Elder. I am grateful to John Hayward for providing this infor-

Streitberger, he may have written *The Flower* in 1568 as "part of his bid for recognition at court." At the time he was thirty-two and still unmarried. By 1572 he had been elected to the House of Commons. But from perhaps as early as February 1577/8 until his death in 1610, he assumed the duties of Master of the Revels to the queen. After a commission broadened the powers of the office in 1581, Tilney was entitled "to examine, alter, and allow or suppress every play written for public performance" in England. In practice, the Privy Council sometimes functioned on its own to censor the political content of plays, and the archbishop of Canterbury was the chief religious censor. But Tilney was "alternately the instrument and target of policy for all of these special interest groups," including those who objected to the very practice of playing.[12] His power to condemn players of the lower class from his own elite position is suggested in Shakespeare's *Midsummer Night's Dream,* where Philostrate in the quarto texts (whose speeches are given to Egeus in the First Folio) assumes the duties of a Master of the Revels as he advises Theseus against viewing the "tedious and brief" production of *Pyramus and Thisby* prepared by the workingmen of Athens for the duke's wedding night.

Tilney himself did eventually marry, but he waited until he was forty-seven to wed Dame Mary Bray, the widow and formerly the fourth wife of Sir Edward Bray. Lady Bray was both noble and wealthy: her husband had left her the income from his lands in Surrey for use during her life; after her death the lands were to

mation, to Robert Bernard Martin for communicating with Hayward on my behalf, and to Sir Desmond Heap for accompanying me on a visit to St. Leonard's Church.

[12] W. R. Streitberger, *Edmond Tyllney, Master of the Revels and Censor of Plays: A Descriptive Index to His Diplomatic Manual on Europe* (New York: AMS Press, 1986), pp. 4, 5, 9, 10. Tilney was formally appointed Master on July 24, 1579. Although Streitberger prefers to use the old spelling of Tilney's name, which is the form in which he signed himself, I have chosen consistency with modern usage. All editions of *The Flower* print his name as "Tilney" or "Tilnay."

pass through Sir Edward's daughters to his grandson.[13] In determining how a man should choose a wife in *The Flower,* one
humanist spokesman argues against the consideration of wom-
en's status or wealth in order to advise attention to their virtue;
yet this argument commodifies those virtues and the women
who possess them. Master Pedro says that wives' "vertues . . .
ought to be accounted the chiefest dowrie" (305–6). The very
energy with which humanists made these arguments suggests
how compelling the impulse to choose a wife for personal gain
must have been in a society in which marriage was a primary
means of social mobility. The humanist ideology of marriage
during the sixteenth century was opposed to this frequent and
self-aggrandizing practice.[14] Yet though Tilney wrote a text in
support of the ideology, he not only married a woman with status
and wealth but tried repeatedly from the early years of their
marriage to gain possession of the lands in Surrey "in Mary's
right,"[15] since as husband he had legal control of her personal
property. He was unsuccessful in doing so and eventually lost the
income from the lands after Mary died in 1604. As a result his
financial situation was so strained that at his own death Tilney's
large house in Leatherhead had to be sold to cover his debts and
bequests. What these events show is not a contradiction between
Tilney's ideology and his own material practice, but rather how
the commodification of virtue which he articulates in this text is
consistent with a more general appropriation of a wife. Although
humanists tried to oppose blatantly mercenary marriage, their
own arguments against it can justify a form of control over
women's sexual relations which still results in their reification.
Counting a wife's virtues was not entirely unlike counting the
money in her dowry, since in both cases the husband influences
the valuation of the wife.

[13] W. R. Streitberger, "On Edmond Tyllney's Biography," *Review of English
Studies,* n.s. 29 (1978), 24.
[14] Todd, pp. 179–92.
[15] Streitberger, "Tyllney's Biography," p. 24.

From the available evidence it is difficult to determine what Lady Bray's response might have been to Tilney's use of her income from the Surrey lands; she was not a sufficiently important historical subject for her own reactions to be recorded.[16] In legal and economic terms, as Lawrence Stone puts it, "By marriage, the husband and wife became one person in law—and that person was the husband."[17] Unlike the material disappearance of the wife in law, in most economic transactions, and in many historical documents, some texts on marriage did permit women to speak as wives, while many others spoke about wives in the sixteenth and seventeenth centuries, and this discourse constructed wives as subjects even as they were subjected by it to the dominant ideology.[18] William Gouge remarks of his own con-

[16] For a recorded account of the struggle between husband and wife over the latter's lands, see Helen Wilcox's introduction to excerpts from *The Diary of Anne Clifford,* in *Her Own Life: Autobiographical Writings by Seventeenth-Century English Women,* ed. Elspeth Graham, Hilary Hinds, Elaine Hobby, and Helen Wilcox (London: Routledge, 1989), pp. 35–38, and the extracts themselves, pp. 38–53. For the life of a woman who was even more able to reappropriate marriage and property in her own interests, see E. Carleton Williams, *Bess of Hardwick* (London: Longman's, 1959).

[17] Lawrence Stone, *The Family, Sex, and Marriage in England, 1500–1800* (New York: Harper and Row, 1977), p. 195.

[18] For this formulation I am indebted to Louis Althusser's notion of the interpellation of the subject in ideology found in "Ideology and Ideological State Apparatuses," in *Lenin and Philosophy and Other Essays,* trans. Ben Brewster (New York: Monthly Review Press, 1971), pp. 126–86. On ideology, see also Williams, chap. 4, and Michèle Barrett, *Women's Oppression Today: Problems in Marxist Feminist Analysis* (London: Verso, 1980), pp. 29–41 and chap. 3. I use the term *ideology* throughout this introduction in the relatively neutral sense discussed by Williams as "a system of beliefs characteristic of a particular class or group (without implications of 'truth' or 'illusion' but with positive reference to a social situation and interest and its defining or constitutive system of meanings and values)" (p. 69). For the relation between ideology and aesthetic form, I am indebted to Fredric Jameson, who explains in *The Political Unconscious: Narrative as a Socially Symbolic Act* (Ithaca: Cornell University Press, 1981) that "ideology is not something which informs or invests symbolic production; rather the aesthetic act is itself ideological, and the production of aesthetic or narrative form is to be seen as an ideological act in its own right, with the function of inventing imaginary or formal 'solutions' to unresolvable social contradictions" (p. 79).

duct book in 1622 that "when these *Domesticall Duties* were first uttered out of the pulpit, much exception was taken against the application of a wives subjection to the restraining of her from disposing the common goods of the family without, or against her husbands consent." Some people in Gouge's congregation clearly resisted the advice that wives consult their husbands about the disposition of family property, just as they objected to the superiority Gouge granted to a husband of lower social status, one of younger years, or one who was "a drunkard, a glutton, a profane swaggerer, an impious swearer, and blasphemer." They even held "the opinion of many wives, who thinke themselves every way as good as their husbands, and no way inferiour to them."[19] We learn these opinions from Gouge's own comments in his text and from his provision of "objections" to the articles of duty he sets forth there. Conduct books usually attempt to contain such oppositional forces as these, but as enunciations of ideologies the texts are products of the contradictions of their own social conditions. When the texts are not able to contain the exposure of their contradictions, they become neither fully supportive of their dominant ideologies nor entirely subversive; instead they are sufficiently open as texts to be capable of multiple interpretations. If such books do not, therefore, give us seamless ideologies from which to construct pervasive world views in coherent narratives of our own, they may give us some of the best evidence we have of the conflicts within cultures concerning issues of gender, marriage, and power.

Ideologies of Companionate Marriage

The construction of woman as a companion to man has often been based on a passage in the Old Testament, where woman is

[19] William Gouge, *Of Domesticall Duties* (1622; reprint, Amsterdam: Theatrum Orbis Terrarum, 1972), dedicatory epistle, sig. ¶3 and pp. 272–73, 271.

created after God says, "It is not good that the man shulde be him selfe alone: I wil make him an helpe mete for him."[20] Woman's existence then arises from God's perception of man's need, while her construction from Adam's rib ensures that she is always already in relation with him.[21] Many writers from Augustine through Tilney and Milton interpreted Adam and Eve's relation in paradise as a marriage that could provide companionship but was nonetheless hierarchical.[22] In 1632 T. E.'s *Lawes Resolutions of Women's Rights* saw the universal requirement of marriage for women as a form of punishment for Eve's part in the Fall: "See here the reason of that which I touched before, that women have no voyce in Parliament, They make no Lawes, they consent to

[20] Genesis 2:18, in *The Geneva Bible: A Facsimile of the 1560 Edition,* intro. Lloyd E. Berry (Madison: University of Wisconsin Press, 1969), p. 1ᵛ.

[21] Mieke Bal interprets this passage to mean that it is not good for what she calls "the earth-being" to be alone—that is, to be sexually undifferentiated. Bal provides a provocative semiotic reading of the Genesis passage which is worth consulting. Like Paul, interpreters during the sixteenth and seventeenth centuries can be said to have committed what she calls the "retrospective fallacy" of reading Adam's name and gender back into the earliest events of the creation myth, thereby marking the first human being as male. See "Sexuality, Sin, and Sorrow: The Emergence of Female Character (A Reading of *Genesis* 1–3)," in *The Female Body in Western Culture,* ed. Susan Rubin Suleiman (Cambridge: Harvard University Press, 1986), pp. 322, 336. A revised version of the essay appears in Bal's book *Lethal Love: Feminist Literary Readings of Biblical Love Stories* (Bloomington: Indiana University Press, 1987). James Grantham Turner discusses contradictions within and among readings of the same passage from patristic writers through the Renaissance and their implications for interpretations of marriage in *One Flesh: Paradisal Marriage and Sexual Relations in the Age of Milton* (Oxford: Clarendon, 1987).

[22] In observing this relation between companionate marriage and hierarchy, I am following Keith Wrightson in his critique of Lawrence Stone when he says that "it would seem unwise to make too sharp a dichotomy between the 'patriarchal' and the 'companionate' marriage, and to erect these qualities into a typology of successive stages of family development. It may well be that these are less evolutionary stages of familial progress than the poles of an enduring continuum in marital relations in a society that accepted both the primacy of male authority and the ideal of marriage as a practical and emotional partnership." *English Society, 1580–1680* (New Brunswick, N.J.: Rutgers University Press, 1982), p. 104. See also note to ll. 184–86 in Tilney's text.

none, they abrogate none. All of them are understood as either married or to be married and their desires or [are] subject to their husband, I know no remedy though some women can shift it well enough."[23] Since marriage became the primary means by which women in Protestant countries could sustain themselves apart from their parental home, ideologies of marriage became a primary way in which women were constructed as subjects. Unlike Eve, Adam was conceived apart from, and antecedent to, relation with women: his male descendants could trace their lineage back to one who was not of woman born.

Companionate ideologies also derive from the classical as well as the Christian tradition: Foucault discusses them in Xenophon's *Oeconomicus* and in other classical texts.[24] Even Aristotle, who is not remembered for his amicable relations with women, describes marriage as a kind of friendship (*philia*) in books eight and nine of the *Nicomachean Ethics,* one that is based on utility and pleasure, even on virtue "if the parties are good; for each has its own virtue and they will delight in the fact" (8.12.1162a24–27).[25] Friendship may occur between equals or unequals, and "equals

[23] T. E., *The Lawes Resolutions of Women's Rights* (London: J. More, 1632), p. 6.

[24] Michel Foucault, *The History of Sexuality,* trans. Robert Hurley, vol. 2, *The Use of Pleasure* (New York: Vintage Books, 1990), pt. 3, esp. chaps. 2 and 3; also vol. 3, *The Care of the Self* (New York: Vintage Books, 1988), pt. 5. For a brief history of ideologies of companionate marriage which discusses classical and patristic as well as puritan texts, see Edmund Leites, *The Puritan Conscience and Modern Sexuality* (New Haven: Yale University Press, 1986), esp. chap. 4, "Puritan Marriage and the History of Friendship," pp. 75–104.

[25] *The Works of Aristotle,* trans. W. D. Ross, vol. 9, *Ethica nicomachea, Magna moralia, Ethica eudemia* (1915; reprint, London: Oxford University Press, 1963). All references in the text are to this edition. For a longer discussion of Aristotle on friendship, see Elizabeth A. Clark, *Jerome, Chrysostom, and Friends: Essays and Translations* (New York: Edwin Mellen Press, 1979), pp. 37–39. This book includes a more detailed account of patristic writers on friendship than Leites offers and addresses the question of how one can reconcile the negative accounts of women in the works of Jerome and Chrysostom with our knowledge of their enduring friendships with women. I am grateful to Janis Butler Holm for bringing it to my attention. See also Maryanne Cline Horowitz, "Aristotle and Woman," *Journal of the History of Biology* 9, 2 (Fall 1976), 183–213.

must effect the required equalization on the basis of equality in love and in all other respects, while unequals must render what is in proportion to their superiority or inferiority" (8.13.1162b3–4). Marriage is an unequal friendship requiring such "equalization" or a "proportion that equalizes the parties and preserves the friendship" (9.1.1163b33–34). It is likened elsewhere in the *Ethics* to a "reciprocity in accordance with a proportion and not on the basis of precisely equal return" by which "the city holds together" (5.5.1132b31–34). So marital friendship, like relations between the shoemaker and the weaver, may be equalized by the proportional performance of one's duties: "The man rules in accordance with his worth, and in those matters in which a man should rule, but the matters that befit a woman he hands over to her" (8.10.1160b32–35). Aristotle sets up gendered and unequal divisions of labor that can be equalized by proportional performance: women do certain kinds of work in marriage and not other kinds because they are less worthy than men. Again the assumption of woman's inferiority operates in and through the construction, but it does not hamper its description as a companionate relation.

Plutarch, writing in the first century, adapts Aristotle's position that friendship (*philia*) depends on utility, pleasure, and virtue, but his emphasis is less on the inequality of the marital relation than on the ways in which women, as well as men, can exhibit virtue. Plutarch's *Moralia* were translated into English as *The Morals* in 1603, and they had influenced Renaissance humanists many years earlier. Two books in *The Morals* discuss marriage directly: "Precepts of Wedlocke," which Erasmus and Tilney adapted for their own accounts of marriage, and "Of Love," which relates friendship to marital affection. In the dialogue on love, Plutarch rejects the equation of love with erotic relations, since boys may prompt "intemperance and disordinate lasciviousnesse" and women may arouse "a furious passion." Instead, love depends on virtue, and women exhibit virtue through their temperance, chastity, prudence, fidelity, and justice. "Now to

[16]

holde, that being by nature not indisposed unto other vertues, they are untoward for amitie onely and frendship, (which is an imputation laid upon them) is altogether beside all reason." The positive value accorded to women is accompanied by a cautious but affirmative assessment of sexual pleasure within marriage. "As for fleshly pleasure it selfe, the least thing it is of all other: but the mutuall honour, grace, dilection and fidelity that springeth and ariseth from it daily, is highly to be reckoned and accounted of."[26] Erasmus would adapt this very passage in the *Encomium matrimonii*.[27] The love of those who merely live together is an insufficient union; "neither can it possibly make that union which matrimoniall love and mutuall conjunction doeth: for neither doe there arise from any other Loves greater pleasures, nor commodities more continually one from another, ne yet is the benefit and good of any other friendship so honorable or expetible [enviable], as *'When man and wife keepe house with one accord, / And lovingly agree at bed and bord.'* "[28] Marriage in Plutarch is the best and most pleasurable form of love and the most beneficial form of friendship. When Renaissance humanists wanted to create a similar portrait of it, they reached back sixteen centuries to the work of this classical author. Yet much disharmony on the subject was to ensue in the intervening years.

The dispute among patristic writers on the subject of marriage reached its height in the fourth century, when Jovinian argued that marriage could be as holy a state as virginity. Sex, women, and marriage then came under serious attack from this assertion of equality between the two states. Jerome argued in his *Epistle against Jovinian* that virginity was far superior for those who could

---

[26] Plutarch, "On Love," in *The Philosophie, commonlie called, The Morals,* trans. P. Holland (London: A. Hatfield, 1603), p. 1155. For this discussion I am also indebted to D. A. Russell's *Plutarch* (London: Duckworth, 1972), pp. 90–94.

[27] See p. 22 of this introduction for the passage from Erasmus.

[28] Plutarch, "On Love," p. 1156. This quotation is from Homer's *Odyssey* 6. 183–84. For another translation of the passage, see *Moralia,* 16 vols., vol. 9, trans. E. L. Minar, Jr., F. H. Sandbach, and W. C. Helmbold (Cambridge: Harvard University Press, 1961), p. 433.

master their sexual desires; by comparison, marriage was a carnal union with many distractions, although it was still better than fornication. Jerome's catalogue of "wikked wyves" and his description of marriage associated sex and sin with marriage and women: he thereby articulated the misogyny and the disgust in sexuality that lay behind the valorization of virginity.[29] The medieval misogyny that surfaced in response to Jovinian's equality between marriage and virginity seems to have involved not so much the threat of a corresponding equality between husband and wife as the more dangerous threat of a wife's dominance, as if the only alternative to marriages in which men ruled was its opposite: marriages in which women ruled. The hierarchical model and its attendant binary opposition were so fixed in the available discourses that equality as a preferable alternative, or as a way of extending the companionship of marriage, did not often arise; symbolic inversion was the most conceivable alternative.[30] As a woman character who is constructed in opposition to the

[29] See the excerpts from Jerome's *Epistle against Jovinian* and the entire section titled "The Antifeminist Tradition," in *Chaucer: Sources and Backgrounds*, ed. Robert P. Miller (New York: Oxford University Press, 1977), pp. 397–473. Miller sees the connection between ideologies of marriage and of women as so close that in discussing the antifeminist tradition in Chaucerian sources he remarks, "It has been soundly suggested that this tradition should be not labeled 'antifeminist,' but rather 'antimatrimonial,' directed primarily at clerks tempted to search out the 'mixed love' of the world" (p. 402). Although this is a relation important to establish in medieval texts, and although "antimatrimonial" is the more descriptive term in some instances, it is also important to distinguish between places where *women* are being denounced as opposed to where *marriage* is being denounced. If we do not, we contribute to the invisibility of misogyny, which has a much wider field than antimatrimonial texts. R. Howard Bloch characterizes antimarriage literature as a "subgeneric topos" of misogyny "known as the *molestiae nuptiarum*," in "Medieval Misogyny," *Representations* 20 (Fall 1987), 2.

[30] For discussions of symbolic inversion, see Natalie Zemon Davis, "Women on Top," in *The Reversible World*, ed. Barbara A. Babcock (Ithaca: Cornell University Press, 1978), pp. 147–90; and Peter Stallybrass, "The World Turned Upside Down: Inversion, Gender, and the State," in *The Matter of Difference*, ed. Valerie Wayne (Ithaca: Cornell University Press, 1991), pp. 201–20.

writings of Jerome, Theophrastus, and Walter Map, Chaucer's Wife of Bath dramatizes this alternative domination. No literary character shows more clearly the connection between ideologies of marriage and constructions of women, or the destabilizing effect that conjunction can have on interpretation, since Alice becomes at once a confirmation and a refutation of antimatrimonial and misogynist views.

When Augustine continued the argument against Jovinian into the fifth century, he chose instead to assert that marriage could be good. In *De bono conjugali* he identifies its benefits: "The good, therefore, of marriage among all nations and all men is in the cause of generation and in the fidelity of chastity; in the case of the people of God, however, the good is also in the sanctity of the sacrament."[31] These three goods of marriage—*proles, fides, sacramentum*—have remained Catholic doctrine to the present day.[32] Augustine also acknowledges the value of marriage in providing mutual companionship, although he does not stress that benefit: "[Marriage] does not seem to me to be good solely because of the procreation of children, but also because of the natural companionship between the two sexes. Otherwise, we could not speak of marriage in the case of old people, especially if they had either lost their children or had begotten none at all." Even a childless couple, however, is "better in proportion as they begin the earlier to refrain by mutual consent from sexual intercourse,"[33] because sex is inappropriate for any other than procreative purposes. And Augustine was also quick to argue in *De sancta virginitate* that virginity is better than marriage.

James Grantham Turner remarks that Augustine's "application of Genesis to marital relationships is as complex and contradic-

---

[31] Saint Augustine, *Treatises on Marriage and Other Subjects*, ed. Roy J. Deferrari (Washington, D.C.: Catholic University of America Press, 1955), pp. 47–48.

[32] John T. Noonan, Jr., *Contraception: A History of Its Treatment by the Catholic Theologians and Canonists*, enl. ed. (Cambridge: Belknap Press of Harvard University Press, 1986), p. 131.

[33] Augustine, p. 12; also Noonan, p. 128, n. 28.

tory as St. Paul's," especially when one compares his pronounce-
ments in *De bono conjugali* with his account of marriage as an
affectionate, sociable, harmonious relation in *The City of God*. By
refusing to denounce women and marriage while emphasizing
the procreative function of marital sexuality and according a
higher place to holy virginity, Augustine created a consensus that
provided some place, though a radically limited one, for sexuality and for women. Even that consensus was split between
what Turner calls the "narrow-Augustinian" view, which gave
Eve a procreative function without companionship, and the
"broad-Augustinian" view, which described her participation in
a mutual society of love.[34] But the status of marriage that was
established through Augustine's writings effectively concealed
the relation between the denigration of sexuality, the hatred of
women, and the valorization of virginity that the responses to
Jovinian had exposed.

   Thomas Aquinas carried through to the twelfth century some
Aristotelian assumptions about the friendship of marriage, especially in his commentary on the *Ethics,* and he drew from Augustine's *City of God* to describe the sexual delight that Adam and
Eve would have experienced in their rational and unfallen state.
While Aquinas's accounts were adapted in support of erotic delight in marriage by some medieval theologians, his conflicting
statements about the role of sexual pleasure placed a "strain . . .
on the pure procreative theory of intercourse" without entirely
breaking its hold or disrupting the Augustinian consensus that
had been established through it.[35] Although many of these issues concerning marriage were often disputed during the Middle
Ages, the church had so effectively policed its own discourses
through the declaration of Jovinian as a heretic in A.D. 389 that the

---

[34] Turner, pp. 100, 101.

[35] Noonan, p. 292. Also Turner, p. 57; and Eleanor Como McLaughlin, "Equal-
ity of Souls, Inequality of Sexes: Woman in Medieval Theology," in *Religion and
Sexism: Images of Woman in the Jewish and Christian Traditions,* ed. Rosemary
Radford Ruether (New York: Simon and Schuster, 1974), pp. 229.

status of marriage was not seriously challenged again for almost 1,200 years. Yet its consensus was broken once more in the sixteenth century when Erasmus made a stronger case for marriage. In his *Encomium matrimonii* he expresses the wish that those who, like Jerome, frequently exhorted young folk to the single life had instead bestowed the same labor on encouraging them in wedlock (120.11–17);[36] then he takes up that project, challenging the valorization of virginity and reasserting the holiness of marriage: "Let the swarmes of Monkes and Nunnes sette forthe their order never so muche, let theim boaste and bragge their bealies full, of their Ceremonies and church service, wherin they chieflye passe all other: yet is wedlocke (beynge well and trulye kepte) a mooste holye kinde of life" (117.24–118.4).

Here was yet another disruption in Catholic discourses on marriage. One year after its 1518 publication, theologians at Louvain attacked the *Encomium matrimonii;* "in 1533 a vigilant group of theologians raided a Paris bookshop and confiscated" Erasmus's *Colloquies, Moriae encomium, Encomium matrimonii,* and other texts; and in 1559 the entire corpus of Erasmus's writings was put on the *Index of Prohibited Books* in the "highest category of heterodoxy."[37] At its session in November 1563 the Council of Trent declared as anathema anyone who claimed that the married state excelled the state of virginity or celibacy.[38] The Erasmian interpretation of marriage as it was presented in the *Encomium* clearly could not be contained within Catholic doctrine.

This text was objectionable for several reasons. First, Erasmus had naturalized sexual relations within marriage: "For there is nothinge so naturall not onelye unto mankinde, but also unto all

[36] I have used the translation of *Encomium matrimonii* most widely available during the sixteenth century, "An Epistle to perswade a young jentleman to Marriage," printed in Thomas Wilson's *Arte of Rhetorique,* ed. Thomas J. Derrick (New York: Garland, 1982). All references in the text cite this edition by page and line number.

[37] Todd, pp. 206, 209.

[38] *Canons and Decrees of the Council of Trent,* ed. and trans. H. J. Schroeder (St. Louis: B. Herder, 1941), p. 182.

other livinge creatures, as it is for everye one of theim to kepe their owne kinde from decaye, and throughe encrease of issue, to make the whole kinde immortall. The whiche thinge (all menne knowe) can never ben dooen, withoute wedlocke and carnall copulation" (109.8–14). Not only brute beasts but the trees, precious stones, even the firmament and the earth are married in this text. Following Plutarch, Erasmus remarks of sexual pleasure: "Although this pleasure of the body, is the least parte of all those good thynges, that are in wedlocke. But bee it that you passe not upon this pleasure, and thinke it unworthy for man to use it" (126.21–25).[39] Erasmus was anticipated by Aristotle, Plutarch, Augustine, and Aquinas in finding some place for sexual pleasure within marriage, but he was blunt in explaining why most commentators had condemned it: "Wee make that filthye by oure own Imagination, whiche of the owne nature is good and Godlye" (116.3–5).

Erasmus also refused to blame all women for problems of the married state. Regarding failed marriages he says: "All these were the faultes of the persones, and not the faultes of Mariage. For beleve me, none have evill wifes, but suche as are evill men" (129.6–10). In support of this position he offers a long list of good wives and then anticipates the misogynist response: "A good woman (you will saie) is a rare birde, and harde to be founde in all the worlde. Well then sir, imagine your self worthy to have a rare wife, suche as fewe men have" (131.2–5). He continually holds men accountable for their own reactions to women: "Chaste, godly, and lawfull love, never knew what jelousie ment" (129.25–130.1), and "the chifest poyncte standeth in this, what maner of woman you chuse, how you use her, and how you order your self towardes her" (131.8–10). Erasmus turns the misogynist projection of blame around in order to require men's responsible exercise of their own power.

He also finds former commendations of virginity irrelevant to

[39] Plutarch's very similar assessment of sexual pleasure in marriage is quoted on p. 17.

the position of ordinary men: "I thincke that this doctrine of Christe did chieflye belonge unto that time, when it behoved theim chieflye to be voyde of all cares and business of this Worlde" (117.17–19). Hence virginity "hath been much commended, but it was for that . . . tyme, and in a fewe" (136.5–6). The single life is not to be praised in itself, and he who does not marry "because he woulde bee out of trouble, and lyve more free" (102.23–24) is not to be preferred over the man who begets children and follows the law of nature. While virginity is "an heavenlye thing, it is an Aungels life. I aunswer, wedlocke is a manly thinge, suche as in [sic] mete for man" (119.7–9). And to those who argue that Christ was born of a virgin: "Of a Virgine (I graunt) but yet of a maried Virgine" (101.19). Erasmus reversed the correlation between the denigration of sexuality, the hatred of women, and the valorization of virginity by approving sexual pleasure in marriage, by praising women, and by viewing virginity or celibacy as a state to which few persons are called.

The *Encomium* was written as a rhetorical exercise for Erasmus's pupil Baron Mountjoy with the intent of persuading him to marry, and even its author observed that it should be judged as such. Yet Craig Thompson remarks that "we have more than enough writing on the same subject from his pen to assure us that he intended the main points of *Encomium matrimonii* to be taken seriously; nor did he ever repudiate them." He wrote further on marriage in *Institutio christiani matrimonii* and *Vidua christiana* (both 1526); by 1529 his collection of *Colloquia* included eight dialogues on the topic, which Craig Thompson describes as a "marriage group."[40] The interpretations of marriage presented in these texts are not always consistent; indeed, one can find statements in them that directly contradict one another.[41] Hence there was no single

[40] *The Colloquies of Erasmus,* trans. Craig R. Thompson (Chicago: University of Chicago Press, 1965), pp. 100, 86.

[41] For example, in *An Epistle* (*Encomium matrimonii*), p. 129.8–10, Erasmus says, "For beleve me, none have evill wifes, but suche as are evill men," while in *A mery Dialogue* (*Conjugium*) Eulalia remarks that "most commonly our husbandes ar evyll through our owne faute" (sig. B6ᵛ). For a fuller account of Erasmian

Erasmian position on marriage offered during the sixteenth century. But the selections from these texts made by his contemporaries and successors and eventually linked with his name, whether for descriptive, laudatory, or repressive purposes, most often identified him with the positions outlined in the *Encomium*. When William Burton, a puritan minister of Norwich, published his translation of seven colloquies in 1606, he praised Erasmus and observed to his readers that in this book "thou shalt perceive how little cause the Papists have to boast of Erasmus, as a man of their side."[42] Yet by 1606 fewer Catholics were boasting of him at all, whereas before the censorship of his books and the condemnation at Trent, Erasmus's position was even more indeterminate: he could appear as a man of several sides.

The adaptation of this humanist view of marriage by Protestants appears, for example, in Bullinger's *Christen State of Matrimonye,* which was first published in English in 1541. *Conjugium* is a term that humanists often used to identify marriage; it is also one title of the Erasmian colloquy that is behind Tilney's text. A gloss on this word occurs in Bullinger, who says that the Germans call wedlock "Ee, which as it is a very old word, so is it somtyme taken for a law or statute, somtyme for a bonde or covenaunt," whereas "the latinistes call it conjugium, a joyning or yoking together." The word emphasizes the marital union of husband and wife, spiritually as well as physically, and their reciprocal responsibilities. When Bullinger develops his own definition of marriage, he first combines the German and "latinist"

---

interpretations of marriage and the conflicts implicit in them, especially of *Institutio christiani matrimonii,* see Constance Jordan, *Renaissance Feminism: Literary Texts and Political Models* (Ithaca: Cornell University Press, 1990), pp. 56–64.

In quoting from *Conjugium* I use the English translation, *A mery Dialogue, declaringe the propertyes of shrowde shrewes, and honest wyves,* which appears in a facsimile of Kytson's 1557 edition in *Tudor Translations of the Colloquies of Erasmus (1536–1584),* ed. Dickie A. Spurgeon (Delmar, N.Y.: Scholars' Facsimiles and Reprints, 1972), sig. A5.

[42] *Seven Dialogues both pithie and profitable,* trans. William Burton (London: [Valentine Simmes for] Nicholas Ling, 1606), sig. a2.

or humanist meanings, saying marriage is "a coveaunt [*sic*], a couplinge or yokinge together." Then he separates these meanings out: "Wedloke is a laufull knott and unto god an acceptable yokynge together of one man and one woman. . . . Or els set it after this maner folowinge: Wedloke is the yoking together of one man and one woman, whom god hath coupled according to his worde." After combining them in his own definition, Bullinger "sets" these definitions in alternative orders (since the reference to God's "word" accords with the covenant or "lawfull knott"). He also offers three different versions of the intents of marriage. The first list, accompanying his first definition of marriage, includes "that they maye lyve honestly and frendly the one with the other, that they maye avoyde unclennesse, that they maye bring up children in the feare of god, that the one maye helpe and comforte ther tother." Then he offers two more orders of intents to accompany the German and humanist meanings, respectively. The German intents include dwelling "in frendshippe and honestye, one helping and confortynge the tother, eschuynge unclennesse, and bringinge up children in the feare of god." In the humanist formulation "equall partakynge" (a counterpart to friendship) is emphasized by being made part of the definition, and then the purposes are inverted: first the procreation of children, then the avoidance of whoredom, and finally help and comfort.[43]

Kathleen Davies and Margo Todd point out that we can generally infer very little from the ordering of the purposes of marriage in most works on this subject, but more is going on in Bullinger's text.[44] Like the definitions that precede them, these three formu-

---

[43] Heinrich Bullinger, *The Christen State of Matrimonye,* trans. Miles Coverdale (1541; reprint, Amsterdam: Theatrum Orbis Terrarum, 1974), sigs. A6–A7.

[44] Kathleen M. Davies, "Continuity and Change in Literary Advice on Marriage," in *Marriage and Society: Studies in the Social History of Marriage,* ed. R. B. Outhwaite (New York: St. Martin's, 1981), p. 63; and Todd, p. 99. I am in agreement, however, with the general point that Davies and Todd make in these contexts, where they argue against the positions adopted by James T. Johnson in "The Ends of Marriage," *Church History* 38 (1969), 429–36, and William and Malleville Haller, "The Puritan Art of Love," *Huntington Library Quarterly* 5

lations of marital "intents" are associated with Calvinist, Lutheran, and humanist views, respectively. Their joint presence in Bullinger's text suggests his willingness to bring them together rather than keep them apart, offering us textual evidence for a connection between humanist and Protestant ideologies of marriage during the period. His comprehensive approach reveals one reason why his text was published more often than any other on the subject in England during the sixteenth century, and it enables us to identify some differences among the three positions. By including friendship in their definition of marriage, the humanists could give renewed emphasis to companionship without disturbing the priority of the procreative function established for it by Augustine. Both Protestant groups, by contrast, were free to reorder the purposes of marriage apart from doctrinal constraints, so they gave first place to the honest and friendly life of the married couple, thereby extending the list of intents from three to four. Later, help and comfort would be combined with friendship, so the intents were back down to three.

The other "latinist" most associated with humanist views on marriage and women in England during the sixteenth century was Juan Luis Vives. His remarkably popular *Instruction of a Christen Woman* (*De institutione feminae christianae*) was dedicated to Catherine of Aragon; it appeared in Latin in 1523 and in English about 1529.[45] In the section of the text addressed to wives, Vives remarks that Aristotle exhorted men to marriage for the purpose of companionship as well as procreation, and then he offers his own view: "Wedlocke was nat ordeyned so moche for generation, as for certayne company of lyfe, and contynuall felowship." He reckons wedlock "a bande and couplyng of love,

---

(1941–42), 235–72, concerning the supposed puritan emphasis on companionship as compared to that of humanists and Protestants. Bullinger's own text calls those positions into question.

[45] Carlos G. Noreña, *Juan Luis Vives and the Emotions* (Carbondale: Southern Illinois University Press, 1989), p. 33.

[26]

benyvolence, frendshippe, and charite, comprehendynge with in hit all names of goodnes, swetenes, and amyte."[46] Vives also prepared a conduct book for men, *The Office and Duetie of an Husband*, in which he argues that since marriage is not "dominion," men should not threaten their wives and handle them roughly, as they would servants; instead "there ought to be betwene them such society and felowship, as is betwene the father and the sonne."[47] In Tilney's text Vives's one response is to approve the story of the wise Solon, who condemned equally a father who had not brought his son up "in due correction" and the son who was disobedient (833–42). Again the humanist's concern is not whether husbands and fathers have greater power, but how they should use it: Vives's analogy advises kindness and affection in marital relations while implying that wives are as inferior as children.

In *Christian Humanism and the Puritan Social Order*, Margo Todd shows how classical and humanist ideologies of companionate marriage were transmitted to puritans via Erasmus and Vives. As she traces the reformist tendencies in humanist as well as Protestant and puritan household theory and social thought, she argues against the innovative character of puritanism in these areas. Todd also explains how historians could be led to think the puritans were innovative because Catholic and conformist Anglican thought diverged on two separate occasions from the humanist-puritan consensus: at the Council of Trent in the mid-sixteenth century, Catholic doctrine separated itself from humanism; and with the Laudian reaction in the seventeenth century, Anglicans set themselves against puritans. During the years be-

[46] Juan Luis Vives, *The Instruction of a Christen Woman*, facsimile ed. of 1529?, in *Distaves and Dames: Renaissance Treatises for and about Women*, ed. Diane Bornstein (Delmar, N.Y.: Scholars' Facsimiles and Reprints, 1978), sigs. T4ᵛ, U1ᵛ, and T3. My essay on this text appears in *Silent But for the Word: Tudor Women as Patrons, Translators, and Writers of Religious Works*, ed. Margaret P. Hannay (Kent, Ohio: Kent State University Press, 1985), pp. 15–29.

[47] Juan Luis Vives, *The Office and Duetie of an Husband*, trans. Thomas Paynell (London: John Cawood, [1555?]), sigs. K8ᵛ–L1.

[27]

tween these two conservative reactions, specifically from the 1559 announcement by Pope Paul IV that all of Erasmus's works were anathema to the increasing control by Anglicans exercised through Archbishop Laud in the 1620s, the alignment between humanist, Protestant, and puritan writings on marriage and the family is considerable.[48] The split that eventually emerged between puritans and Anglicans and is so much a part of English political history was not a feature of English society from 1560 to 1620 and should not be "read back" into the texts on household theory.

Nor should humanist approaches to marriage be viewed as consistent with Catholic thought after 1560. The puritan William Perkins claims in *Christian Oeconomie* that the church of Rome has long viewed sexual relations in marriage as acts of "filthines" and "uncleannesse of the flesh," adding that through such condemnations of sexuality "some beganne to detest and hate women." Then he relates these historical positions to Trent: "And the Councell of Trent is of the same judgment. For whereas it opposeth mariage and chastitie; it plainely determineth that in mariage there is no chastitie."[49] Todd cites John Dod as complaining that in 1614 the Jesuits "cut [women] off and bar them from all conference touching the word of God, as absurd and far unbeseeming their sex."[50] Although as a puritan Dod objected to the way the hierarchic authority of the Catholic church refused women access to the Scriptures apart from the doctrinal directions of celibate priests, he did not object to Erasmus, whose translation of the New Testament was prepared to make Scripture more accessible although it was declared inadmissible at

[48] Todd, pp. 206–60. For a discussion of John Donne's position on marriage which shows his reactionary position, see Mary Beth Rose, *The Expense of Spirit: Love and Sexuality in English Renaissance Drama* (Ithaca: Cornell University Press, 1988), pp. 98–105.

[49] William Perkins, *Christian Oeconomie,* in *Works,* vol. 3 (Cambridge: Cantrell Legge, 1618), p. 689.

[50] John Dod, *Bathshebaes Instructions to her Sonne Lemuel* (1614), pp. 61–62; cf. pp. 1–3, 64, as cited in Todd, p. 235.

Trent. Both Perkins and Dod asserted the difference between papists and Protestants on issues of sex, women, and marriage, but they saw this division as reasserted in the middle of the sixteenth century, after the rise of humanism and the Catholic reaction against it. The correlation among these three issues in Catholic thought was no more incidental in the sixteenth century than it had been in the fourth—but the conjunction was not originally contested by Protestants. Nor can we transpose the objections into affirmations, for the humanist, Protestant, and puritan approaches were not unambiguously pro-sex, pro-women, or even unilaterally pro-marriage.

Continuity among humanist, Protestant, and puritan approaches is also affirmed by the publishing history of the Erasmian dialogue that is behind *The Flower of Friendship* and Tilney's Spanish source, a text by Pedro di Luxan. Erasmus's dialogue, *Conjugium,* first appeared in the 1523 Latin edition of the *Colloquies* published by Froben in Basel, and it soon became very well known.[51] Henry de Vocht once remarked that "very few colloquia were as popular as the *Conjugium*" in England and on the continent.[52] In 1557 two editions of an English translation were published as *A mery Dialogue, declaringe the propertyes of shrowde shrewes, and honest wyves.*[53] As this title implies, the colloquy presents a conversation in which a good wife, named Eulalia (meaning "sweetly speaking"), advises a shrew, Xanthippe (named for Socrates's infamous wife), on how to conduct herself in marriage: she is to reform her wayward husband by "good humanitie" and "wyse handlynge."[54] The construction of a character

[51] Thompson, p. 114.

[52] Henry de Vocht, *The Earliest English Translations of Erasmus' "Colloquia," 1536–1566* (Louvain: Uystpruyst, 1928), p. xxix.

[53] *STC* 10455 and 10455.5.

[54] Thompson, p. 114, provides these glosses on the names. Eulalia was also the name of "the most celebrated virgin martyr of Spain." A ninth-century French poem, the "Cantilène de Sainte Eulalie," recounts her story; see Alban Butler, *Lives of the Saints,* rev. ed., ed. Herbert Thurston and Donald Attwater (New

like Eulalia presupposed that wives could be good and marital problems might be resolved by advice that could effect a change in the behavior of both spouses. When Xanthippe is reformed through Eulalia's counsel, Erasmus illustrates the humanist assumption that women are rational creatures who can be taught how to improve their conduct, rather than naturally perverse beings or intransigent marital partners. Most of the advice offered to Xanthippe requires that she silence her complaints and find ways to please her wayward husband—including dissembling in the interests of harmony. So Erasmus's formula for marital bliss is hardly revolutionary: it is a mixture of old-fashioned compliance and newfangled feigning. But the focus of this colloquy was on how women could improve their marriages by making the effort to change their own behavior, especially since, as the dialogue itself makes clear, they lacked the alternative of divorce. Its attention to the problems of women in difficult marital situations may go far toward explaining its popularity.

Conjugium was translated into German, adapted by Lutherans, and translated again into English as a Protestant text. In 1524, the year that Erasmus broke with Luther, two German translations were published, and in 1530? two adaptations appeared under the title *Der bosen Weiber Zuchtschül*.[55] This later German version

---

York: P. J. Kenedy and Sons, 1956), vol. 4, pp. 530–31. Erasmus's choice of this name for his exemplary wife looks like a playful inversion of Catholic celebrations of virginity.

[55] *Short-Title Catalogue of Books Printed in the German-Speaking Countries and German Books Printed in Other Countries from 1455 to 1600 Now in the British Museum* (London: Trustees of the British Museum, 1962), p. 907. Charles E. Herford translates the full title of *Der bosen Weiber Zuchtschül*, or this "reformatory for shrews," as "a proper dialogue of two sisters; the first a godly and virtuous widow of Meissen, the other a shrewish, obstinate and evil-tempered woman of the Gebirge," in his *Studies in the Literary Relations of England and Germany in the Sixteenth Century* (1886; reprint, London: Frank Cass, 1966), pp. 66–67. Both Herford and Karl Goedeke identify the author as Wolfgang Resch; Goedeke indicates another issue of the dialogue from Frankfurt in 1565. See his *Grundrisz zur Geschichte der deutschen Dichtung,* vol. 2 (Dresden: LS. Ehlermann, 1886), p. 272.

became the basis for an English translation by Walter Lyn, which appeared in London in 1548? as *The Vertuous Scholehous of Ungracious Women;* after the dialogue appeared a sermon on marriage by Martin Luther and another exhortation to the married couple. The same translation was published in England in 1581 under a new title, *A Watchword for Wilfull Women,* together with the sermons.[56] These Lutheran adaptations offer a more hierarchical view of marriage by characterizing the good woman, Justina, as an exemplary Lutheran, while the shrew not only avoids going to church but complains when her husband, Simplicius, does go. Serapia the shrew is therefore the only guilty party in this dialogue, and the advice she receives is doctrinal as well as behavioral. Justina's husband, Pius, taught her to accept the blessings of the Lord by faith when she had tried to justify herself through works alone; in the dialogue Justina gives Serapia the same lesson. So these adaptations do mark some differences between humanist and Protestant views of marriage: faith is added to the behavioral reform that Erasmus accorded to Xanthippe, while the men in this dialogue are initially more holy than the women, and hierarchy is maintained throughout. At the same time, those differences are articulated within a text that imitates the form and much of the advice of the Erasmian colloquy.

Conjugium was also adapted by puritans. A translation was made by the puritan William Burton for his collection of Erasmian dialogues, which was printed twice in 1606 under two different titles.[57] And the colloquy was also adapted and expanded by the puritan Robert Snawsel as *A Looking Glasse for Maried Folkes,* which appeared in 1610, 1619, and 1631.[58] Snawsel

---

[56] STC 21826.6 and 21826.8. The title of the former is an allusion to the misogynist poem *The Schole House of Women,* first published in 1541. *A Watchword for Wilfull Women* is dedicated to the widow of a London alderman and presents itself as an original edition.

[57] *Seven Dialogues both pithie and profitable* (STC 10457), and *Utile-dulce: or, trueths libertie* (STC 10458).

[58] STC 22886, 22886.5, and 22887. This text is not a straightforward translation from Erasmus, as Andrew McLean suggests in "Another English Translation of Erasmus' *Coniugium:* Snawsel's *Looking Glasse for Maried Folkes* (1610)," *Moreana*

says in his preface that he had considered merely translating Erasmus's text, but he concluded, no doubt like the Lutherans, that women "might attaine to all that which hee counselleth there, and yet be damned"; so he decided to add "thereunto the substance of faith and repentance."[59] He expands the dialogue to five characters and requires a reciprocal submission of both husband and wife, first to God and then to each other. By making their mutual repentance a precondition of marital unity, this puritan alters the Lutheran stress on hierarchy and the association of guilt with the wife alone; but he retains a strong biblical and doctrinal base. The various versions of this colloquy challenge Todd's assertion that there were no significant differences between humanist, Protestant, and puritan treatments of household theory; but her argument for humanist innovation in this area is confirmed by the diffusion of the texts and their imitation of Erasmus's advice. Since they affirm their differences while working within a tradition established by the famous humanist, one can see considerable continuity within these texts without converting the likeness into a claim of identity or sameness that is suggested by Todd's discussion and her use of the word "consensus."[60] Such claims also assume a coherence and stability within the advice offered by conduct books that a close reading of them does not always support.

When Edmund Tilney puts Erasmus and Vives into a text on

---

11 (1974), 55–59. As the editorial inclusions following this article begin to convey, it is an adaptation and expansion of the colloquy from a puritan perspective.

[59] Robert Snawsel, *A Looking Glasse for Maried Folkes,* 1610 (Ann Arbor: University Microfilms, Reel no. 728), sig. A4ᵛ.

[60] For example, Todd does not consider questions of emphasis when she observes that "there is no evidence that protestants in the sixteenth century were saying anything about women and their role in the household which Catholic humanists had not already said" (pp. 115–16). I have offered some evidence of differences in the foregoing discussion, although my divergence from Todd is also, primarily, one of emphasis. She threads her way through the religious thicket of the sixteenth century with great care, and I am obviously following her path.

marriage which he dedicates to his Protestant queen, and when he adapts a pre-Tridentine Spanish Catholic text for a post-Tridentine English Protestant one, he is again affirming a relation between humanist and Protestant ideologies in 1568. Tilney's direct source for *The Flower* was Pedro di Luxan's *Coloquios matrimoniales,* which appeared in at least eleven editions from 1550 to 1589.[61] The long Spanish text is a set of six dialogues. At the end of the first, Luxan acknowledges his use of Erasmus for his second and fifth dialogues "como fundamento, sobre que yo edificasse estos dos coloquios" (as a foundation on which I would build these two colloquies; fol. 39);[62] all of the colloquies show some indebtedness to him.[63] Like the Lutherans and puritans, Luxan does more than merely imitate the elder humanist, "mostrando otras muchas y muy diversas cosas, de que el no se acordo: o no quiso escrivir" (showing many other and very diverse things which he did not remember or did not want to write; fol. 39–39ᵛ). In particular he offers numerous classical and patristic authorities and examples in support of his advice, and it is these for which Tilney is especially indebted to him. Ernest J. Moncada attributes to Luxan thirty-five of the forty-five sources that Tilney cites.[64] The Englishman was less concerned with the theol-

[61] Ernest J. Moncada, "The Spanish Source of Edmund Tilney's 'Flower of Friendshippe,' *Modern Language Review* 65 (1970), 241–47. Ruth Kelso was actually the first to see some connection between Tilney and Luxan; see *Doctrine for the Lady of the Renaissance* (Urbana: University of Illinois Press, 1956), pp. 416, 385. For the editions of Luxan's text, see Marcel Bataillon, *Érasme et l'Espagne: Recherches sur l'histoire spirituelle du XVIᵉ siècle* (Paris: Librairie E. Droz, 1937), p. 691.

[62] *Coloquios matrimoniales del licenciado Pedro de Luxan* (N.p. [Seville]: Dominico de Robertis, 1550). All citations in the text will be to this, the first edition, which is in the British Library. A more recent nonscholarly edition of the text is also available; see Pedro de Luxan, *Coloquios matrimoniales,* Coleccion Cisneros (Madrid: Ediciones Atlas, 1943).

[63] For the identification of some of the colloquies behind Luxan's text and for the summary of Luxan, I have used Bataillon, pp. 691–92, and Moncada, p. 242. The account of Tilney's adaptation of Luxan that follows is my own, but those who helped me with the sixteenth-century Spanish text—Joseph Chadwick and Harold Irving—have made it possible.

[64] Moncada, p. 242.

ogy of Luxan's text than with its assemblage of authorities in traditional humanist manner. He used Luxan almost as a reference text, and then acknowledged his use through placing his "friende . . . Maister *Pedro di luxan*" (54–55) in the conversazione of *The Flower of Friendship*.

Despite its name, Luxan's *Coloquios matrimoniales* creates not so much a "marriage group" as a "family group" addressing concerns of persons from youth to old age and in various positions within the family. It also constructs a narrative recounting relations among these family members over time. The first dialogue presents Eulalia in conversation with a learned woman named Dorothea. It is Dorothea who is the exemplary woman and who is trying to persuade Eulalia to marry, as Erasmus had done for Baron Mountjoy. Through eliminating Xanthippe the shrew, Luxan shifts his emphasis from redeeming a bad wife to advising one in need of more information. By the second dialogue Eulalia is already married and receives advice from Dorothea that draws heavily on *Conjugium*. At the end of the Erasmian colloquy, Eulalia had promised to talk with Xanthippe's husband to advise him on his responsibilities in marriage; Luxan enacts that conversation in his third dialogue between Dorothea and Eulalia's husband, here named Marcelo. The advice occasions peace by the fourth dialogue, at which time Eulalia is pregnant. She and Marcelo are advised by Dorothea on the nursing of infants, the duties of fathers, and the importance of educating children, in line with Erasmus's colloquy *Puerpera,* or *The New Mother*. The fifth dialogue imitates *Pietas puerilis,* or *The Whole Duty of Youth,* through a conversation between Hippolyte, son of Eulalia, and Jules, son of Dorothea, concerning how to be a good son. The sixth presents two old men, Fulgence and Laurance, discussing the faults of old age.

Tilney incorporates material from the first four dialogues into *The Flower of Friendship*. For Julia's discourse on wives he draws entirely from the second dialogue, and for Pedro's on husbands he uses especially the first, the third, and the fourth. The first and fourth provide him with his cross-cultural survey of marriage customs; from the second he takes the notion of herbs nourishing a marriage and applies them to the husband rather than to the wife; the third dialogue gives him examples of men who loved their wives, behavior (or weeds, in Tilney) that threatens marriage, and the duties of a husband; the fourth offers diverse examples including the story of the wise Solon approved of by Vives. Yet Tilney makes important changes in that material. Ernest Moncada observes that he is more concise than the Spanish text; he creates more characters in his dialogue who are appropriate to different points of view; and he omits or alters some of Luxan's passages "which express a religious sentiment."[65]

This last change is in keeping with the secular character of Tilney's text, for his dialogue does not claim alignment with any one religious group. Its statement that virginity is a purer state than marriage (179) is more clearly in keeping with Catholic doctrine after Trent, but Richard Hooker would offer the same opinion in 1597.[66] Its emphasis on marriage as a companionate relationship or a friendship is consistent with some classical, patristic, and humanist sources as well as the Elizabethan homily on marriage, but the 1559 Prayer Book says nothing about marital friendship, and differs from the homily in its ordering of the marital purposes.[67] As a secular text *The Flower* does not take up partisan positions on these issues; one even wonders whether that

[65] Ibid., p. 246.

[66] Hooker characterizes "single life [as] a thing more angelicall and divine," in *Of the Laws of Ecclesiastical Polity: Book V*, vol. 2 of *The Folger Library Edition of the Works of Richard Hooker*, ed. W. Speed Hill (Cambridge: Belknap Press of Harvard University Press, 1977), p. 401.

[67] *Certaine Sermons or Homilies Appointed to be Read in Churches in the Time of Queen Elizabeth I (1547–1571): A Facsimile Reproduction of the Edition of 1623*, ed. Mary Ellen Rickey and Thomas B. Stroup (Florida: Scholars' Facsimiles and Reprints, 1968), p. 239; *The Book of Common Prayer, 1559: The Elizabethan Prayer Book*, ed. John E. Booty (Charlottesville: University Press of Virginia for Folger Shakespeare Library, 1976), pp. 290–91. The Elizabeth homily describes marriage as a "perpetuall friendship, to bring foorth fruite, and to avoide fornication"; the 1559 prayer book says it was ordained first for "the procreation of children," then "for a remedy against sin, and to avoid fornication," and finally for "mutual society, help and comfort," without any definition of marriage that refers explicitly to friendship or companionship.

would have been possible given the inconsistency within treatments of the topic. Instead, Tilney's text presents an ideology of marriage that is grounded in Erasmian humanism but is far more secular than religious. Like Bullinger, Tilney links humanists and Protestants in his view of marriage; like Elizabeth, he avoids partisan statements so as to promote religious and political peace in the realm. So rather than viewing this text as a product of one religious group to the exclusion of others, I believe it is more appropriate to say that *The Flower of Friendship* represents a dominant ideology of marriage in England in the 1560s, 1570s, and 1580s, one that was supported by those in power and related to humanist, Protestant, and puritan positions at the time it was written and read. Nor were its ideas necessarily outmoded by the end of the century. Dod and Cleaver's *Godlie Forme of Householde Government* of 1598—which was the second most reprinted Renaissance text on marriage to appear in English—imports whole passages that appear in Tilney's text into its own, specifically those on possessing the wife's will, on the duties of husbands and wives, and on the wife as looking glass for her husband.[68] Such blatant uses of earlier material suggest that puritans were presenting their interpretations of marriage as consistent with some earlier texts on the subject. They established their differences within the context of continuity.

Conjugium addressed the practical problems of women in marriage in a way that few earlier texts had done, and that is surely one reason why it was adapted for German Lutherans, Spanish humanists, and English puritans. As an ideology it subjected women to the authority of their husbands: Eulalia tells Xanthippe

---

[68] These parallel passages are Tilney, ll. 440–44, and Dod and Cleaver, pp. 168–69; Tilney, ll. 726–40, and Dod and Cleaver, pp. 170–71; Tilney, ll. 1316–20, and Dod and Cleaver, p. 229. The latter text in each case is *A Godlie Forme of Householde Government: For the Ordering of Private Families, according to the direction of Gods Word* (London: F. Kingston to T. Man, 1598) (*STC* 5383). I am grateful to Cristina Malcolmson for first observing some of these parallels. See the explanatory notes to these passages in this edition for a further discussion of their sources.

that "it is the hyghest dignitie that longethe to the wyfe to [be] obsequyous unto her spouse. So hath nature ordeined so god hath apoynted, that the woman shoulde be ruled al by the man." But it also offered wives a subject position from which to speak. To use Göran Therborn's terminology, this ideology of marriage *quali-fied* women for their roles as wives,[69] and the position became so established that it made possible a new dramatic character. Eulalia first appears in an English play in conversation with Xanthippe in the interlude titled *Nice Wanton,* which was performed from 1547 to 1553 and printed at least twice. The interlude was an adaptation of *The Rebelles,* a play written by the Dutch humanist Georgius Macropedius.[70] Another instance of Erasmian material being transferred to the drama through the creation of character occurs in Shakespeare's *Comedy of Errors.* Luciana's ineffectual advice to the shrew Adriana assumes a rigid hierarchy between husbands and wives that is like the Lutheran adaptation of Erasmus's colloquy, while Adriana's version of marital duties assumes a more companionate approach, and the Abbess's warning that Adriana's behavior is alienating her own husband is very close to Eulalia's counsel. In the drama, as in Tilney's text, these characters lose their close connection to theological issues when they are transposed to a secular text, but the positions from which they speak originated in the discourses on marriage that circulated

[69] Erasmus, *A mery Dialogue,* sig. C1. Therborn breaks down the interpellation of the subject as described by Althusser into "the double process of subjection and qualification." The subject of an ideology recognizes through it first, what exists and does not exist; second, what is good, right, just and its opposites; and third, what is possible and impossible. See Göran Therborn, *The Ideology of Power and the Power of Ideology* (London: Verso, 1980), p. 18. Cf. Julia Kristeva's discussion of the wife speaking in the Song of Songs in "A Holy Madness: She and He," in *Tales of Love,* trans. Leon S. Roudiez (New York: Columbia University Press, 1987), pp. 99–100: "Limpid, intense, divided, quick, upright, suffering, hoping, the wife—a woman—is the first common individual who, on account of her love, becomes the first Subject in the modern sense of the term."

[70] *Annals of English Drama, 975–1700,* ed. Alfred Harbage, 2d. ed., rev. S. Schoenbaum (Philadelphia: University of Pennsylvania Press, 1964). The two printings of *Nice Wanton* are *STC* 25016 and 25017.

earlier in the century. Whereas previous ideologies of companionate marriage had presented or implied women's obligations, these sixteenth-century texts actually dramatized women as they confronted their responsibilities. The dialogue form, whether in a colloquy or transposed to the drama, was especially appropriate for exploring a subject that was being revised and contested as it had never been before. Eulalia, Luciana, and the Abbess were not the only result.

Ideologies of Marriage in Tilney's Text

Tilney's project in *The Flower of Friendship* is not to debate the question of marriage versus celibacy as Erasmus had done in the colloquies associated with the "marriage group"; nor is he concerned with the larger problems of family members beyond the husband and wife as Luxan was in enlarging Erasmian concerns into *Coloquios matrimoniales*. Rather, Tilney presents the dominant ideology of marriage by setting it off against other ideologies that were articulated in Renaissance discourses on marriage. He not only assumes that the humanist ideology is being contested; he asserts his approach against the opposition of alternative ideologies. His procedure supports Raymond Williams's claim that "any hegemonic process must be especially alert and responsive to the alternatives and opposition which question or threaten its dominance."[71] Since Tilney uses the dialectic of the dialogue form to articulate these alternatives, and since he is so careful to align them with historically identifiable positions, his text becomes a kind of fictional record of the available ideologies of marriage in 1568.

The means by which he aligns ideologies with particular characters is the same as that used by Erasmus and all of the writers

[71] Williams, p. 113.

who adapted *Conjugium:* names. The humanists are easy to identify in this text, for they are called Erasmus, Vives, Master Pedro di Luxan, and Lady Julia—from Eulalia. Master Pedro is a
spokesman for a husband's duties in marriage on the first day of
the conversazione, and Lady Julia speaks for a wife's duties on the
second day. Tilney himself as first-person narrator is present in
the dialogue at its beginning, when he goes for a walk with
Master Pedro, and at its end, when he is asked by Lady Isabella
and encouraged by the other women present to "penne the whole
discourse" (1430) that has transpired. But there are three other
participants who are not humanists: Master Gualter of Cawne,
Lady Aloisa, and Julia's daughter, the Lady Isabella.

Master Gualter articulates the misogynist ideology that Erasmus had voiced briefly in order to argue against it in *Encomium
matrimonii.* Gualter's most immediate ancestor is Lord Gasper in
Castiglione's *Courtier,* but Tilney's character gets his name from a
long line of literary misogynists: Gaultier, the disciple who is
instructed in Andreas Capellanus's *De amore;* Walter Map, the
author of *The Courtier's Trifles,* a text included in Jankyn's book of
wicked wives in the Wife of Bath's prologue; and Griselda's
rather savage husband, Walter, in *The Clerk's Tale.* When Gualter
tells a story to prove that all women make bad wives, the women
of the text try to drive him out of the arbor, but Gualter is in this
arbor, and this text, so Master Pedro can look good beside him.
In response to Gualter's story Pedro explains: "It is no parte of my
charge to disprayse women, but to speake the best of them, and
to plant the *Flower of Friendship* betweene them, and their husbands" (406–9). Gualter's misogyny ensures Master Pedro the
position of advocacy for women as well as marriage: Pedro objects to the attempt to banish him by explaining, "He increaseth
our sporte, and therefore we can not well want him" (478–79).
The recuperation of misogyny advances the "sporte" of this
text by making it appear that Pedro's position on marriage and
women is the opposite of Gualter's.

The ideology of marriage that Gualter offers is residual in the sense that it "has been effectively formed in the past, but it is still active in the cultural process."[72] Gualter's name aligns him with medieval Catholicism, and by 1568 the Catholic church had reaffirmed its Augustinian consensus at Trent. Misogyny—even as narrowly defined by Renaissance discourses on marriage and women—was still an active ideology during the period, although it was even more prolific during the Middle Ages.[73] The popularity of Joseph Swetnam's *Arraignment of Lewde, Idle, Froward, and Unconstant Women* of 1615 and the responses to it are indications that it was still alive as a discourse and could be vigorously contested. Linda Woodbridge finds over three dozen stage misogynists in Renaissance drama: there was much to be gained by evoking and then containing this response to women.[74] What Pedro gains from the presence of Gualter in Tilney's text is the illusion that he is entirely on women's side.

Gualter's other adversary is the Lady Aloisa, who complains that he is always "pratling against women" (476–77). Yet like Gualter, Aloisa is an opponent of marriage from a medieval perspective. She gets her name from Heloise, who argued in letters to her lover, Pierre Abelard, that marriage was incompatible with love. Heloise became known to English readers

---

[72] Ibid., p. 122.

[73] See Bloch, pp. 1–24. During the Renaissance the term *misogyny* was generally applied to speeches or texts that articulated views highly critical of women, such as the tirades of Le Jaloux in the *Roman de la rose* or the texts in Jankyn's "boke of wikked wives" in the Wife of Bath's prologue. There was even a play called *Misogonous* performed at Cambridge c. 1560–77 (*Annals*, pp. 40–41). The word therefore had more reference to rhetorical display than to personal feelings, and claims of women's inferiority would not necessarily have been described as arising from or evincing misogyny. As the word is used today, we are more ready to make such connections, because we apply it more broadly to feelings and responses of which one might not even be fully conscious. Hence the very use of the word during the Renaissance created the illusion that misogyny might be contained or destroyed because it was confined to specific characters or ways of speaking. In effect this narrow usage functioned as a displacement for the larger range of misogyny in Renaissance culture. I discuss this issue in "Historical Differences: Misogyny and *Othello*," in *The Matter of Difference*, pp. 153–79.

[74] Linda Woodbridge, *Women and the English Renaissance: Literature and the Nature of Womankind, 1540–1620* (Urbana: University of Illinois Press, 1984), pp. 275–99.

through Jean de Meun's translations of the lovers' letters in the *Roman de la rose*. Ami explains in his friendly advice to the Lover that

> the young lady of good understanding, well educated, loving and well loved in return, brought up arguments to convince him not to marry; and she proved to him with texts and reasons that the conditions of marriage are very hard, no matter how wise the wife may be. . . . She asked him to love her but not to claim any right of her except those of grace and freedom, without lordship or mastery, so that he might study, entirely his own man, quite free, without tying himself down, and that she might also devote herself to study, for she was not empty of knowledge.

Ami ends his account by quoting a famous remark from Heloise and adding his own assessment:

> "If the emperor of Rome, to whom all men should be subject, deigned to wish to take me as his wife and make me mistress of the world, I still would rather," she said, "and I call God to witness, be called your whore than be crowned empress." But, by my soul, I do not believe that any such woman ever existed afterward; and I think that her learning put her in such a position that she knew better how to overcome and subdue her nature, with its feminine ways. If Pierre had believed her, he would never have married her.[75]

Yet Abelard may have wished that he had believed Heloise, since after their marriage her relatives castrated him as a punishment. Given the popularity of this account, D. W. Robertson says that Heloise thereby "became famous in literary history, not for her devotion as an abbess, but for her supposed views of marriage."[76] She also appeared in a French manuscript of about 1500 instruct-

---

[75] Guillaume de Lorris and Jean de Meun, *The Romance of the Rose,* trans. Charles Dahlberg (Princeton: Princeton University Press, 1971), pp. 160, 161.

[76] D. W. Robertson, Jr., *Abelard and Heloise* (New York: Dial Press, 1972), p. 153.

ing a character named Gaultier in the art of love.[77] Her function in
Tilney's text is to expose Gualter's misogyny while reinforcing
his medieval opposition to marriage. This aim was best accomplished by shrewish objections, because then the character's manner would alienate men and provide further support for the antimatrimonial position. Some of Aloisa's responses in *The Flower*
can be traced through Luxan's comparable character (who is
confusingly named Eulalia) back to Erasmus's Xanthippe in *Conjugium:* the "bed of nettles, or thornes" (1376–77) that she would
prescribe for an unfaithful husband appears in Luxan as "un hace
de ortigas, y aulagas" (a bed of nettles or gorse; fol. 69ᵛ) and in
Erasmus as "a bundel of nettels: or a burden of thistels."[78] So
although Luxan and Tilney technically eliminate any character
who could be described as a shrew, both authors retain some of
the objections that Erasmus had voiced through that character.[79]

Lady Isabella is also given lines that were associated with the
woman in need of correction in Luxan's text. Eulalia there says,
"Tambien seria cosa muy justa, que el marido obedezca a la
muger" (It would also be a very just thing if the husband obeyed
the wife; fol. 60). Isabella remarks that "as meete is it, that the
husband obey the wife, as the wife the husband" (1132–33); then
she describes comparable abilities between the sexes and asks
why women should be bound when nature made them free
(1135–38). Her attempt to naturalize sexual equality offers an
emergent ideology in the sense that Williams uses that term:
"What we have to observe is in effect a *pre-emergence,* active and
pressing but not yet fully articulated"; "a social experience which
is still *in process,* often indeed not yet recognized as social but
taken to be private, idiosyncratic, and even isolating, but which

[77] Peter Dronke, *Abelard and Heloise in Medieval Testimonies* (Glasgow: University of Glasgow Press, 1976), p. 29.

[78] Erasmus, *A mery Dialogue,* sig. B4.

[79] In my essay "Refashioning the Shrew," *Shakespeare Studies* 17 (1985), 159–87,
I discuss the importance of this character as a challenge to hierarchical views of
marriage in plays by Shakespeare and the Wakefield Master.

in analysis (though rarely otherwise) has its emergent, connecting, and dominant characteristics."[80] Lady Isabella consistently exposes the inequality behind humanist ideologies of marriage in this text: she questions Pedro's notion of parity as consisting in the inequality of the ages of spouses (354ff.); she reminds Julia that a woman cannot love her husband if he delights more in another (1007–9); she objects to Julia's advice that wives ought to obey their husbands (1131ff.); and she challenges humanist counsel that a wife should be her husband's looking glass (1321–22). Hers is the dialogue's most extended case for equality within marriage: she desires parity in the performance of household tasks and claims that if husbands do not obey their wives, "at the least that there be no superioritie betwene them" (1133–34).

The articulation of this emergent ideology from Tilney's Spanish source involves a complex maneuver on his part. When Catherine Belsey discusses the problems of women assuming subject positions in discourse during the Renaissance, she identifies the discursive instability that withheld from them any single position they could identify as theirs. Women in Renaissance texts "speak with equal conviction from incompatible subject positions, displaying a discontinuity of being, an 'inconstancy' which is seen as characteristically feminine"; they had not yet attained the status of the unified, autonomous authors of their choices that the subject of liberal humanism claimed for himself.[81] The emergent ideology that Isabella offers in Tilney's text was still not yet fully articulated within the culture, and its discursive instability is most apparent in the passage from Luxan that Tilney uses for Isabella's extended speech on equality.

Isabella argues that "women have soules as wel as men, they have wit as wel as men, and more apt for procreation of children than men. What reason is it then, that they should be bound,

---

[80] Williams, pp. 126, 132.

[81] Catherine Belsey, *The Subject of Tragedy: Identity and Difference in Renaissance Drama* (London: Methuen, 1985), p. 149.

whom nature hath made free?" (1135–38). The comparable passage in Luxan's text asserts that histories say: "Que la muger tenia anima, como el hombre, moria como el hombre, y era apta para la generacion como el hombre. Y dezian que no tenian sobre ellas ninguna juridicion los hombres: salvo ygualdad: porque dezian que no es razon, que aquellas que la naturaleza hizo libres, que ninguna ley las haga esclavas." (That the woman had a soul like the man, died like the man, and was apt for procreation like the man. And they said that men had no jurisdiction over them: except equality: because they said that it is not right that those whom nature made free be made slaves by any law; fol. 55–55ᵛ.) When Tilney adapts these lines, he substitutes the humanist assertion of women's rational capacity for the proficiency in dying affirmed for them in the Spanish dialogue. To do so, however, he must take the lines not from the oppositional character Eulalia but from the exemplary wife, Dorothea, because she speaks these words in apparent support of her general assertion that a woman should obey a man—"la muger obedeciesse al varon"—not the reverse. Luxan's good wife provides argumentative evidence against the position from which she claims to be speaking: she is unaccountably "inconstant" in asserting some equality between men and women since her general argument in the passage and text is that women should obey men. She also provides the example of the Achaians as a society in which wives commanded their husbands: although she describes their practices as foolishness ("necedad"), in citing them she nonetheless offers more evidence that controverts her own position.

When Tilney appropriates the good woman's remarks for the character of Isabella, he constructs an emergent position from a discursive inconsistency within his source. His method illustrates how an emergent ideology can be articulated from the contradictions within an antecedent discourse, and how the articulation thereby removes some discursive instability by creating a new, more consistent subject position for a character. Isabella's role as a speaking female subject had not been fully developed in previous Renaissance texts, and the egalitarian ideology of marriage that she asserts was not fully articulated by 1568; but Tilney's *Flower* marks the emergence of both from the unstable subject positions in Luxan's text.

The social conditions of the narrative also played a part in producing an emergent ideology at this historical moment, for around the year 1568 Queen Elizabeth offered much of Europe an instance of discursive instability on the subject of marriage. The connection between the queen and Lady Isabella was first observed by Ernest Moncada, who ventured that "it is more than incidentally interesting that the young lady who shows such spirit and argues so often for the woman's rights should be named Isabella, i.e. Elizabeth" in Spanish.[82] Even Elizabeth's presence as a woman on the throne was taken as a cause for instability and objection: in 1558 John Knox described a woman's rule as "repugnant to nature, contumlie to God, a thing most contrarious to his reveled will and approved ordinance, and finallie, it is the subversion of good order, of all equitie and justice."[83] C. S. Lewis remarked that Knox's ill-timed *Blast* against the regiment of women "was embarrassing because in a certain sense nearly everyone (except regnant queens) agreed with Knox."[84] In answering Knox in 1559, John Aylmer explained that although Elizabeth was entitled to be her husband's head in guiding the commonwealth, she would still be subject to him in their marital relation: "I graunte that, so farre as perteineth to the bandes of mariage, and the office of a wife, she muste be a subjecte: but as a Magistrate she maye be her husbands head." Aylmer's position is based on requirements not for all women but for wives, since in his opinion a wife is "the mans subject . . . in that she is his wyfe, not in that she is a woman."[85] The dominant ideology of mar-

---

[82] Moncada, p. 246.

[83] John Knox, *The First Blast of the Trumpet against the Monstrous Regiment of Women, 1558,* ed. Edward Arber (Westminster: Archibald Constable, 1895), p. 11.

[84] C. S. Lewis, *English Literature in the Sixteenth Century Excluding Drama* (London: Oxford University Press, 1954), p. 199.

[85] John Aylmer, *An harborowe for faithfull and trewe subjectes* (1559) (Ann Arbor: University Microfilms, Reel no. 194), sigs. C4ᵛ, D.

riage threatened to withhold from Elizabeth in her marital relations the power accorded to her in civil affairs by inheritance. This inconsistency between descriptions of women's domestic and public power is surely one of many reasons why Elizabeth could not declare herself either for her own marriage or against it—or, to be more precise, why she declared herself in both directions at once.

During the time that Tilney's text was probably being composed (it was entered in the Stationers' Register between July 1567 and July 1568),[86] Elizabeth was considering, and then rejecting, terms for marriage with the Archduke Charles of Austria. In April 1567 the Spanish ambassador, Guzman de Silva, remarked in a letter to Philip II on the delay in a trip to Germany that the earl of Sussex was making to negotiate with the archduke. Then he added: "The hatred that this Queen has of marriage is most strange. They represented a comedy before her last night until nearly one in the morning, which ended in a marriage, and the Queen, as she told me herself, expressed her dislike of the woman's part."[87] Traditional marriage would have required Elizabeth to play a part far inferior to the one she was already playing. Her contemporary William Camden commented on her dilemma in his *Annals of Queen Elizabeth:* "Some were of opinion that she was fully resolved in her Mind, that she might better provide both for the Commonwealth and her own Glory by an Unmarried life than by Marriage. . . . Her Glory also, which whilst she continued unmarried she retained intire to herself and uneclipsed, she feared would by Marriage be transferred to her Husband."[88]

---

[86] *A Transcript of the Registers of the Company of Stationers of London: 1554–1640 A.D.,* ed. Edward Arber, vol. 1 (1875; reprint, New York: Peter Smith, 1950), p. 164ᵛ.

[87] *Calendar of the Letters and State Papers Relating to English Affairs of the Reign of Elizabeth Preserved in, or originally Belonging to, the Archives of Simancas,* ed. Martin A. S. Hume, vol. 1, *Elizabeth, 1558–1567* (1892; reprint, Neudeln, Liechtenstein: Kraus, 1971), p. 633. I am grateful to Carole Levin for providing me with this reference.

[88] William Camden, *The History of the Most Renowned and Victorious Princess*

There was nothing unreasonable about this fear, given the ideology of marriage then current in English society. Mary I even served as an object lesson for Elizabeth in this regard. In her marriage to Philip of Spain, Mary had assumed the conventional wifely role described for her in Vives's *Instruction of a Christen Woman,* and it had proved a political disaster for a regnant queen.

When in 1581 an agreement was prepared for Elizabeth's impending marriage to the duke of Anjou, its conditions concerning civil authority were articulated precisely: "After the Marriage consummated, he shall enjoy the Title and Honour of King, but shall leave the management of Affairs wholly and solely to the Queen. . . . The Queen alone shall bear the Superiority, and no Title shall accrue to the Duke as Tenant by the Custome of England."[89] Having already held political power, the queen was not about to give it up; having achieved a precarious religious harmony among her people by 1567, she decided not to disrupt it by proceeding further with the marriage to the Archduke Charles, which would have required her to permit him to practice his Catholic religion in private. What is notable about Elizabeth's situation is that she could speak as a woman about marriage from a position of genuine power. The subject position created for Isabella by Tilney's text also grants this character the ability to reject marriages that do not assume women's equality with men. Both Elizabeth and Isabella assert their right to refuse marriage when it threatens to limit some exercise of their power. So the subject position from which Queen Elizabeth spoke on occasion, and which was imitated for Lady Isabella's remarks in *The Flower,* also made possible the articulation of an emergent, egalitarian ideology of marriage at this historical moment. That subject position was available not in Luxan's text but in the social conditions of the narrative: in this sense *The Flower of Friendship* is

---

Elizabeth, Late Queen of England, ed. Wallace T. MacCaffrey (Chicago: University of Chicago Press, 1970), pp. 136–37.

[89] Ibid., pp. 132–33.

Tilney's textualization of history, as mediated by the prior textualization of the queen's discourses.

Elizabeth's situation was, as Williams says of emergent positions, "taken to be private, idiosyncratic, and even isolating" at the time, though from our present moment we can analyze her self-representation for the skillful ways in which she appropriated the available discourses.[90] When she consistently opposed the efforts of Parliament and her own people to control her marriage, she did so as no ordinary woman but as England's queen. Her articulation of this ideology therefore depended on a conjunction of gender and monarchic rule. After a parliamentary delegation of 1559 urged her to marry and bring forth children, she replied that it might "seem a point of inconsiderate Folly," given her public care of the kingdom, "to draw upon me also the Cares of Marriage." Then she reminded them that she was already married to "an Husband, namely, the Kingdom of England." Displaying her coronation ring as if it were a wedding ring, she commended those present "that ye have not appointed me an Husband, for that were most unworthy the Majesty of an absolute Princesse, and unbeseeming your Wisedom, which are Subjects born," adding that it would be sufficient for her memory and honor if she were described as a virgin at her death.[91] The "husband" created by this discourse has remarkably little power, either as a mute kingdom or as a collection of petitioning subjects born in subjection to the queen's divine right. Parliament issued another petition for her marriage in 1563, and when they tried to prepare still another on marriage and the succession in 1566, the queen forbade their free discussion and told them through Cecil:

[90] Williams, p. 132. See Leah S. Marcus's essay "Shakespeare's Comic Heroines, Elizabeth I, and the Political Uses of Androgyny," in *Women in the Middle Ages and the Renaissance: Literary and Historical Perspectives,* ed. Mary Beth Rose (New York: Syracuse University Press, 1986), pp. 135–53, and her book *Puzzling Shakespeare: Local Reading and Its Discontents* (Berkeley: University of California Press, 1988), pp. 51–105. See also Louis Adrian Montrose, "The Elizabethan Subject and the Spenserian Text," in *Literary Theory/Renaissance Texts,* ed. Patricia Parker and David Quint (Baltimore: Johns Hopkins University Press, 1986), pp. 303–40.

[91] Camden, pp. 29–30.

"I am your anointed Queen. I will never be by violence constrained to do anything."[92]

Although she remained open to the possibility of marriage during the next two decades, Elizabeth invoked her royal prerogative to decide this issue for herself rather than be directed by her advisors, Cecil in particular. In doing so she was, as Louis Montrose has explained, refusing "to enact the female paradigm desired by those advisors: to become the medium through which power, authority, and legitimacy are passed between generations of men."[93] During the ten years of Elizabeth's reign that had passed up to 1568, as a queen she had been able to sustain her resistance to the ideologies of marriage and of women that were dominant in her society. Her oppositional position is evoked through Isabella's resistance to humanist marriage within Tilney's text: the two figures were sufficiently parallel, and Elizabeth's own connection with the text through its dedication sufficiently apparent, to invite readers to make the connection between them. The aristocratic structure behind the conversazione that requires the choice of a queen to oversee each day of the pastime reinforces this conjunction of female power and monarchic rule.

Given the more positive constructions of women by Renaissance humanists, who often explicitly positioned themselves against misogynist discourse, and given the close connection between humanists such as Erasmus, Vives, or More and English queens, it is not surprising that Tilney should represent women speaking from positions of power in his text. What is surprising and, I will argue, disrupting is that Isabella explicitly applies the implications of these reassessments to the subject of power relations in marriage. In *The Flower* the Lady Isabella is presented as

---

[92] J. E. Neale, *Queen Elizabeth I: A Biography* (1934; reprint, New York: Doubleday, 1957), pp. 121–22, 148–51; quote at p. 150. In a biography published after the present edition had gone to press, Anne Somerset provides considerably more evidence of Elizabeth's objections to marriage. See *Elizabeth I* (London: Fontana, 1992), pp. 94–103, 177–91.

[93] Montrose, p. 310.

the daughter of the Lady Julia (70), hence as a descendant of a humanist woman. Her characterization is appropriate since Elizabeth received her own education at the direction of the Cambridge group of humanists, which included William Grindall and Roger Ascham, themselves members of the second generation of humanists; Catherine Parr also supervised her education after the death of Henry VIII. The fiction of familial relation between Julia and Isabella further supports a connection between humanist and more egalitarian ideologies of marriage, yet that relation can also become an occasion for identifying the differences between those two positions. The interplay between characters in Tilney's text does assume that readers can identify the representatives of its residual, dominant, and emergent ideologies: much of the pleasure of the text comes from associating the characters with their literary and historical antecedents and observing the witty repartee between the various positions they articulate. But before considering the differences between the dominant and emergent ideologies, we need to consider the contradictions within the dominant ideology of marriage as it is presented here, particularly since the humanist position claims to be egalitarian as well as companionate.

It is Master Pedro who first says that "equalitie is principally to be considered in this matrimoniall amitie. . . . For equalnesse herein, maketh friendlynesse" (286–89). In considering a husband's choice of a wife, Pedro addresses equality through three categories: "yeares," or age, "giftes of nature, and fortune" (287–88). Kathleen Davies points out concerning mid-seventeenth-century puritans that "the sacred condition of equality" was interpreted by them "as meaning similarity of social status and age in partners, not as equality of status after marriage";[94] the same is true for this humanist advice. The gifts of fortune that Pedro

---

[94] Davies, p. 65. Tilney's association of friendship with equality goes back to Aquinas and Aristotle. See note to ll. 288–89.

considers include both rank and wealth; he takes these up first by asserting that a man should imitate a game that children play, called "*take to thee thy peere*" (294–95). Then he cites Plutarch, whose text *The Education or Bringinge Up of Children* was printed three times in Sir Thomas Elyot's English translation,[95] as advising, "Marry not a superiour. . . . For in so doing, in steede of kinsfolkes, thou shalt get thee maisters, in whose awe thou must stande" (295–97). Nor should a man marry a woman with more wealth rather than superior social status, for "a riche woman, that marieth a poore man, seldome, or never, shake off the pride from hir shoulders" (297–99). These marriages so invert hierarchy that, as Menander says, "suche a man hath gotten in steed of a wyfe, a husband, and she of him a wyfe, a straunge alteration, a wonderfull metamorphosis" (299–302). This account of the inversion of marital authority shows that hierarchy is already embedded in the definitions of husband and wife.

Then Pedro considers the possibility that a man might choose a woman who is his inferior in rank or wealth. He describes Alexander the Great as exemplary for matching with Barcina, daughter of "a poore gentleman, but of noble parentage, wherein not riches, but nobilitie adorned with vertues prevayled" (313–15). When Julia asks how a woman so far Alexander's inferior could be described as his equal, Pedro replies that Barcina's "great vertues" and her "sufficient parentage" make her "comparable to the great greatnesse of *Alexander*" (328–31). He states the more general principle thus: "A vertuous woman, being wise, and of good linage, wanteth no equalitie on hir parte to counterpeise the greatest ryches, or treasure, that any man can have." Then he notes the importance of choosing the right wife so that a man "may leave hys childe parentage, which being joyned to vertues maketh them perfite" (334–40).

In valuing a woman's virtue more than her rank, Pedro's advice is keeping with some humanist criticism of hereditary nobility.

---

[95] See note to ll. 295–99 of Tilney's text.

Erasmus in particular redefined nobility by berating its tradi-tional association with birth: "There are three kinds of nobility: the first is derived from virtue and good actions; the second comes from acquaintance with the best training; and the third from an array of family portraits and genealogy or wealth."[96] For humanists, then, virtue as opposed to birth was the best determi-nant of status, and Erasmus deplored the emphasis on title in the choice of marital partners.[97] But Tilney's adaptation of this hu-manist valuation of virtue diverts its original disruption of estab-lished class boundaries. Master Pedro attributes economic value to women's virtue when he cites Lycurgus as ordaining "that women shoulde be married without dowries, so that then they had nothing to be prowde off, save onely their vertues, which ought to be accounted the chiefest dowrie" (303–6). Virtue here is likened to wealth as having exchange value, and it replaces wealth as the primary qualification for a wife; it is described later as "the onely ryches to be required in a woman" (329). This commodifi-cation of virtue was a result of the gendered associations it ac-quired in Tilney's discussion. Since a woman's virtue is also connected with her husband's paternity and their children's par-entage, the wife's primary virtue is her chastity: virginity before marriage and fidelity after it. It is women's sexuality that is being reified, exchanged, and controlled through this valorization of their virtue.[98]

Vives had stressed the importance of female chastity in *The Instruction of a Christen Woman:* "Chastyte is the principall vertue

---

[96] Erasmus, *The Education of a Christian Prince (Institutio principis christiani),* trans. L. K. Born (New York: Columbia University Press, 1936), p. 151, as cited in Todd, p. 189.

[97] Todd, pp. 186–88.

[98] Lady Julia also commodifies "shamefastness" in part two when she describes it as "that most excellent gift," as "the chiefest dowrye, the greatest inheritaunce, and the preciou st Jewell that a woman can bring with hir" (1123–26). The similar treatment of a different value, though one that still helps women "to kepe their reputation, to preserve their chastity, to maintein their honor, and to advance their prayse" (1119–21), reinforces the reification of women's *sexual* virtue articulated in part one.

of a woman and countrepeyseth with all the reste: if she have that, no man wyll loke for any other: and if she lacke that, no man wyll regarde other."[99] Tilney's use of the word "vertue" also relates to sexual behavior and extends further to a person's reputation, righteousness, and holiness (379–82), as Vives's sometimes did. Yet Tilney uses the word only three times in reference to men in *The Flower,* as compared to thirteen applications to women; and for women the word always included the requirement of sexual constancy, as it did not for men. Pedro's discussion of equality in marriage first asserts that a man should marry his equal rather than his superior in rank or wealth; then he shows how a woman of inferior wealth can be made equal to a man if she is sexually controlled. A woman's sexual virtue and her adequate lineage make her the peer of a wealthy man.

This "equalization" of a man and a woman on the basis of different criteria reveals that women's status is being determined by a prior consideration of gender difference. In *The Creation of Patriarchy* Gerda Lerner argues that women's subordination antedated slavery and made it possible. When she traces the development of slavery as an idea during the second millennium B.C., she explains its effects on the definition of woman: "Female persons, whose sexual and reproductive services had been reified in earlier marriage exchanges, were toward the end of the period under discussion seen as persons essentially different from males in their relationship to public and private realms. As men's class positions became consolidated and defined by the relationship to property and the means of production, the class position of women became defined by their sexual relationships."[100] When patriarchy was encoded in Mesopotamian law, these gendered definitions of class

[99] Vives, *Instruction,* sig. L4ᵛ.

[100] Gerda Lerner, *The Creation of Patriarchy* (New York: Oxford University Press, 1986), p. 96. In earlier chapters Lerner accepts the research of Claude Meillassoux and Peter Aaby, who argue, in direct opposition to Engels, that the reification of women preceded the origin of private property. "Thus, the first appropriation of private property consists of the appropriation of the labor of women as *reproducers*" (p. 52).

became legally inscribed. In the Hebrew Covenant Code, for example, which was framed during the formation of class society, Lerner encounters a principle very close to that in Tilney's text, "the principle that a man's class status is determined by his economic relations and a woman's by her sexual relations. . . . It is a principle which has remained valid for thousands of years."[101]

This principle which permitted the development of patriarchy received additional support from the humanist ideology of marriage. For Tilney, equality within marriage is constructed primarily from an inequality of sexual control and wealth: those criteria therefore function as the gendered determinants of class. Pedro goes on to claim that "for the equalitie in age, I say, consisteth likewise in the inequalitie of yeares" (341–42), since hierarchy is also preserved if the wife is younger than the husband. The compositor of the fourth edition had trouble with this concept, so he changed "inequalitie" to "equalitie," hence making the equality of age consist in the equality of years. While such a numerical difference is recognizable to compositors and readers alike, the contradictions of gender difference are still so ubiquitous that they have become invisible to the same persons. Tilney's text tries to rationalize this contradiction by asserting its grounding in ethical considerations. Yet there is nothing equal about the distribution of ethical concern here, for much less emphasis is given to the sexual control of men than of women.

Tilney raises the subject regarding men only once, when he says in discussing adultery that "the fayth that the woman oweth to hir husbande, the lyke fidelitie ought the man to repaye unto hys wyfe, and though the civill lawe giveth man the superioritie over his wyfe, that is not to offende, or dispise hir, but in misdoing, lovingly to reforme hir" (523–28).[102] The focus in this pas-

[101] Ibid., pp. 105–6.

[102] The treatments of male chastity in Vives's *Instruction* and in Milton's *Apology for Smectymnuus* also address that subject by comparing religious duty with the "lawes of the worlde," in Vives's case (sig. f2ᵛ), or with what is "commonly . . . thought" in Milton's, *Complete Poems and Major Prose,* ed. Merritt Y. Hughes

sage moves from a wife's fidelity to the comparable obligations of the husband, but then it moves back rapidly to possible infractions by the wife. The text shows how reciprocal sexual control originates in and returns to the control of women's bodies, even as a means of controlling men's. The concept of equality presented by Pedro is therefore contradictory because it is grounded in the antecedent inequality of gender difference. Any equality that women might be said to achieve with men is not a matching of like with like, because for men class does not depend on their being sexually controlled, just as for women it is not solely dependent on their wealth or social status. Tilney's discussion of equality reveals that it is strictly impossible for a woman to be a peer of a man, given the gendered determinants of class.

In discussing her interpretation of legal sources for historical analysis, Gerda Lerner says that when we find laws prohibiting a certain practice, they give us evidence that "(a) the custom existed and (b) it had become problematical in the society."[103] Applied to conduct books, this axiom suggests that the enunciations of an ideology generally arise from an instability within the culture that they are attempting to regulate. All of the argument against mercenary marriage in Tilney's text implies that men had been marrying wives for their money and so needed to be cautioned against doing so: Pedro admits that "wee all seeke the fayrest, the richest, and noblest" (374), and Tilney himself may have chosen a wife for these reasons. Marriage was an important means either of preserving the existing forms of social relations or of changing them during what Lawrence Stone has called "the century of mobility, 1540–1640"; and it was the "commonest method of upward movement for gentlemen."[104] Stone does find "a very high degree of social and economic endogamy" among early

---

(Indianapolis: Odyssey Press, 1957), p. 695. See also Wrightson's discussion of the sexual double standard and disapproval of adultery by either party, pp. 99–100.

[103] Lerner, p. 102.

[104] Lawrence Stone, "Social Mobility in England, 1500–1700," *Past & Present* 33 (1966), 48, 35.

modern marriages, although status "was a quality which might be traded in for money, for example by the marriage of the son and heir of an impoverished nobleman to the heiress of a rich merchant."[105] "Between 1600 and 1659," for instance, "some 4% of all marriages of peers were to the daughters or widows of aldermen."[106] Marriage also produced *more* money at this point in history than in earlier periods: Lillian Robinson points out that "the increasing dominance of a cash economy . . . led to inflation in the dowry market; the size and strategic importance of the dowry increased, and the payment was likelier to be in cash or marketable real estate than in family-held land."[107]

Pedro's advice to *"take to thee thy peere"* encourages the consolidation of rank and wealth among members of the upper classes, thereby countering the trend toward mercenary marriage with an emphasis on virtue that masks a social conservatism: social and economic stability are ensured when a husband maintains his lineage and inheritance through exercising control over his wife's sexuality. Humanist counsel could therefore be used to legitimate the hierarchies of class and gender that sustained the Tudor social order by maintaining the current distribution of status and wealth and men's dominance over women.[108] But the commodification of women's virtue associated with this advice could also function as an agent of social mobility by according women's sexual control the value previously granted to their wealth or social status. The king in *All's Well That Ends Well* can encourage Bertram to

[105] Stone, *Family, Sex, and Marriage*, pp. 60–61.
[106] Stone, "Social Mobility," p. 38.
[107] Lillian S. Robinson, "Woman under Capitalism: The Renaissance Lady," in *Sex, Class, and Culture* (1978; reprint, New York: Methuen, 1986), pp. 157–58.
[108] Frank Whigham supplies further support for the conservative function of this advice when he cites courtesy literature as implying that virtue was implicit in persons of upper rank and that the promotion of one's rank was a corresponding stipulation of virtue, in *Ambition and Privilege: The Social Tropes of Elizabethan Courtesy Theory* (Berkeley: University of California Press, 1984), p. 73. My discussion of the ways in which Tilney's ideology originated as a "gesture of exclusion" (Whigham, p. 5) or an attempt to preserve social stability, yet might also function to justify and increase mobility, owes much to Whigham's work.

marry Helena because she is a virgin and has already performed virtuous deeds. "Virtue and she / Is her own dower," he proclaims in lines that parallel Pedro's reference to Lycurgus; then the king offers to provide Helena with the "honor" of rank and "wealth" (II.iii.143–44) which she needs to become Bertram's peer.[109] The king even argues more generally for personal status on the basis of one's actions, like the more liberal Erasmian position: "From lowest place [when] virtuous things proceed, / The place is dignified by th' doer's deed" (II.iii.125–26), whereas rank without virtue is "a dropsied honor" (II.iii.128). Helena can prompt these fluid definitions of honor because, as a woman, her status is ensured more by her virtue than by rank, and it is in the interest of the state to reward her for having stabilized its power by curing the king. The advice in Tilney's text could therefore be adapted in support of the "inflation of honors" which Elizabeth and James brought about during the century of social mobility. Yet Helena's advancement, like Barcina's, rewards her with status because of her readiness to be sexually controlled, thereby ensuring her role in reproducing more members of her new and elevated class.[110]

[109] William Shakespeare, *All's Well That Ends Well,* in *The Riverside Shakespeare,* ed. G. Blakemore Evans (Boston: Houghton Mifflin, 1974). All references in text and notes to Shakespeare's works are to this edition.

[110] In "Social Mobility" Stone analyzes differential fertility (pp. 40–42). Members of the upper classes had more children than members of the lower classes between 1500 and 1630 owing especially to a later average age and reduced frequency of marriage among the lower classes, a reduced fertility occasioned in lower-class women who served as wet nurses or nursed their own children, and a higher infant mortality rate for children of the poor. "In other words between about 1580 and 1630 the children of peers were producing 50% more children per generation" (p. 42). Dorothy McLaren extends this research in "Marital Fertility and Lactation, 1570–1720," in *Women in English Society, 1500–1800,* ed. Mary Prior (London: Methuen, 1985), pp. 22–53, where she argues that "the use and abuse of human milk was so linked with infant mortality and therefore fertility that it was an important ingredient—perhaps the most important ingredient—in the history of population change in the transition to an industrialized England" (p. 46). McLaren finds too "that rich women of the period had an entirely different reproductive pattern, which was mainly due to their having abandoned maternal breastfeeding" (p. 23).

The gendered determinants of class became all too clear when Henry VIII had the power to execute two of his queens, one of them Elizabeth's mother, on allegations of adultery. As a commoner, Anne Boleyn was especially vulnerable to charges of infidelity because she could not be considered a peer of her husband on any ground but that of her own, often questioned sexual virtue.[111] If the execution of Anne Boleyn was a lesson to her daughter, the execution of Catherine Howard might well have remained one to Edmund Tilney, for in 1542 his own mother was sentenced to life imprisonment and loss of her goods for concealing evidence from the king concerning Catherine's adultery with Francis Dereham. Malyn Chambre Tilney had been a chamberwoman to Queen Catherine, and although she was eventually pardoned for her part as an accessory to the crime, she apparently lost her tenure in a manor in Suffolk. At the time of these events Tilney was about six years old. Edmund's great-aunt Agnes Tilney, who was by then the dowager duchess of Norfolk, was also charged for permitting Catherine's relation with Henry Mannox in her own household. Tilney and his mother were probably taken into the household of the Howards after the scandal was over, since his father, an Usher of the Privy Chamber under Henry VIII, had died in debt the previous year.[112]

The story offers lurid evidence of the consequences of adultery for wives as compared to husbands during the period. The body of a queen without political authority was made to function like a state possession through which, it was hoped, male heirs to the throne would eventually pass, and any possibility of an illegitimate heir would taint the line of inheritance which sustained divine right. Catherine's permitting the sexual invasion of her body was therefore a treasonous act, and Malyn Chambre Tilney's concealment of the evidence was thereby "misprision of

[111] Carolly Erickson, *Mistress Anne* (New York: Summit Books, 1984); see e. g., pp. 61, 102. See also Amussen, pp. 196–217, for differences in the treatment of men and women as the subjects of defamation suits.

[112] Streitberger, "Tyllney's Biography," pp. 13–14.

treason," punishable by the imprisonment of her own body and the confiscation of her property.[113] Once the queen's body natural was contaminated, it had to be destroyed, and no English king went through more marital bodies on the assumption they were state property than Henry VIII.

In his dedication to this text, Tilney asks that Elizabeth receive it like "that Noble *Alexander* of *Macedon*," who esteemed a poem given him by the philosopher "Pirrho"; then he refers to his sovereign as the "noble *Alexandra*" (30–32, 35). Elizabeth's position in seeking a marital partner was comparable to Alexander's in that marrying a peer was difficult for her unless she married another monarch, and in her case members of Parliament and her own people were attempting to control her reproduction by influencing her marriage. Elizabeth refused that control by delaying and eventually avoiding marriage, but one of the personas that she created for herself acknowledges its presence while eluding it. By presenting herself as the Virgin Queen, married only to England, Elizabeth reassured her people that she was justified in exercising supreme power over them because she would exercise the most extreme control over her own sexuality. The restrictions on her body natural thereby ensured the authority of her body politic. My point is not that she did exercise that control, but that she created herself as a female subject entering into an asexual (though not nonerotic) marriage with her own people as a way of securing her class position as monarch while acknowledging her gendered position as a woman. Her solution to the problem raised by the patriarchal principle articulated in Lerner's and Tilney's texts shows how a female monarch could maintain her power by manipulating the relationship between the gendered determinants of class.

[113]Ibid., p. 13. Anne Boleyn was also charged with treason; see Erickson, pp. 254–55. So is Hermione in *The Winter's Tale* (III.ii.14). In the cases of Queen Anne and Hermione, the charges of adultery are combined with accusations that they conspired to kill the king, but one wonders about the relative weight of these charges. Leontes worries more about his paternity than his own life.

3. The only known likeness of Edmund Tilney, from a drawing of the funeral procession of Queen Elizabeth on April 28, 1603. Tilney appears on the far left. Many of the faces in this very long drawing, however, look remarkably alike. Reproduced by permission of the British Library.

The word "virtue" as it is used in this ideology of marriage most often describes a woman whose chastity ensures her appropriation—but not just sexually. In Erasmus's *Conjugium*, Eulalia describes an exemplary wife as one who reconstructs herself in accordance with her husband's identity: "For as a glasse (if it be a true stone) representeth ever the physnamy of hym that loketh in it, so lykewyse it becommeth a wedded woman alway to agre unto the appetite of her husbande, that she be not mery when he murneth nor dysposed to play when he is sad."[114] This advice reappears in Luxan's text and is voiced in Tilney's by the Lady Julia when she is explaining the duties of a wife: "Shee shal enlarge the *Flower of Friendship* betwene hir and hir husband, whose face must be hir daylie looking glasse, wherein she ought to be alwaies prying, to see when he is merie, when sad, when content, and when discontent, wherto she must alwayes frame hir owne countenance" (1315–20). These passages ask that a woman deny her own emotional life and substitute her husband's in its stead. The mirror functions as a window onto the affective life of the man, and the woman is to be always "prying" into that glass so she may impose the feelings she finds there over her own reactions. The advice creates a wife as an acting subject and constructs her husband as the object of her gaze only so that she may mirror his affective life, which process requires an erasure of her own.[115] Hence the good wife is an active agent in what Luce Irigaray has called the "dominant scopic economy" only insofar as her mirroring activity ensures a simultaneous erasure of her own feelings.[116] The most debilitating aspect of this advice is that it

[114]Erasmus, *A mery Dialogue*, sig. A7. Erasmus is adapting a passage in Plutarch quoted in the notes to ll. 1316–20.

[115]Arthur F. Kinney sees in this passage an instance of "a married couple mirroring each other, as one half of Tilney's perfectly balanced work inversely images the other half," in *Humanist Poetics: Thought, Rhetoric, and Fiction in Sixteenth-Century England* (Amherst: University of Massachusetts Press, 1986), p. 154. But there is no reciprocal mirroring advised for husbands in the text; it is only the wife who mirrors her husband, just as Julia's discourse on the second day of the conversazione mirrors Pedro's on the first. For a discussion of how the mirror functions in other conduct literature, see Ann Rosalind Jones, *The Currency of Eros: Women's Love Lyric in Europe, 1540–1620* (Bloomington: Indiana University Press, 1990), pp. 26–27. For information on the sources of the image in Erasmus and Tilney, see note to ll. 1316–20.

[116]Luce Irigaray, "This Sex Which Is Not One," in *This Sex Which Is Not One*, trans. Catherine Porter (Ithaca: Cornell University Press, 1985), p. 26. In *Spec-*

solicits the wife's complicity in denying herself the very subjec-
tivity granted to her by the discourse so that she may become the
object of her husband's desire.

There is then a violence, a defacing implicit in this process, not
only because of the requisite erasure, but because the wife is asked
to cooperate actively toward that end, as the shifting pronouns
that function as subjects in the following passage indicate. For his
part the husband is supposed to participate in the appropriation of
the wife's affective life by becoming a thief of her will and desire:
"The wise man maye not be contented onely with his spouses
virginitie, but by little and little must gently procure that he maye
also steale away hir private will, and appetite, so that of two
bodies there may be made one onelye hart, which she will soone
doe, if love raigne in hir" (440–44). Here marital love is described
as a process in which two bodies become one heart, but the
remaining heart is plainly the husband's. He is the only subject
left in the "union." The wife loses not only her "appetite," or
sexual desire, but her "private will," the volition by which she
establishes herself as a separate person. Tilney is not advising that
the wife be brought to submit her volition to God's will as an act
of humility and faith; instead he counsels a husband to seduce his
wife's will so that it comes to accord entirely with his own. Love
reigns in the marriage when his command becomes her wish; and
the close association here between will and appetite suggests that
the loss of volition accompanies the wife's total sexual submission, so that she finally desires only her husband's "reign" of love,
physically and entirely. "Such pleasure is," as Irigaray says of
related sexual imaginaries, "above all a masochistic prostitution

---

ulum Of The Other Women, trans. Gillian C. Gill (Ithaca: Cornell University Press,
1985), p. 51, Irigaray describes psychoanalysts as constructing women's psyche so
as to provide a man with "his projected, reflected *auto-representations,*" an apt
phrase also for describing Erasmus's and Tilney's constructions of the wife's
duties in their texts. She continues: "If woman had desires other than 'penis-envy,'
this would call into question the unity, the uniqueness, the simplicity of the mirror
charged with sending man's image back to him—albeit inverted." Tilney's later
advice that a man steal his wife's desire seems designed to avert just such an
eventuality.

of her body to a desire that is not her own, and it leaves her in a familiar state of dependency upon a man. Not knowing what she wants, ready for anything, even asking for more, so long as he will 'take' her as his 'object' when he seeks his own pleasure."[117] Tilney's construction of a woman's submission seems designed to suit male fantasies of prowess and power, and it reveals a prime attraction of companionate marriage from a husband's point of view. Since this account represents an important way in which the requirements of companionate marriage could be read during the Renaissance, Lawrence Stone may be correct in his judgment that the ideology prompted an increase in the authority of husbands rather than greater parity between the partners.[118]

The examples of wives who have loved their husbands well support this account of the consequence of marital unions, for Tilney's praise of exemplary wives celebrates their love when it results in death or self-sacrifice (1020–93). The wives of the Mimians enter a prison where their husbands are detained, exchange clothes with them, and allow the men to escape: instead they become the imprisoned subjects and avoid death only because their Lacedemonian captors admire their devotion. Panthea and Porcia both kill themselves when their husbands die. Alcesta kills herself to cure her husband's disease, and he responds by joining her in death. Paulina slits her wrists when she learns that a similar death was required of her husband by Nero; she would have died as well had Nero not bound her wounds. Triara does manage to stay alive when she chooses to accompany her husband into battle, but Julia is so overwrought at the mere sight of Pompey's bloody coat that she dies in premature labor before—as Boccaccio explains but Tilney does not[119]—she can be told that the blood belonged to an animal that her husband was sacrificing.

[117] Irigary, "This Sex Which Is Not One," p. 25.

[118] Stone, *Family, Sex, and Marriage*, p. 202. There is also an important similarity between Tilney's passage and ll. 708–21 of Chaucer's *Clerk's Tale*, which I am grateful to Charlotte C. Morse for observing. See *The Riverside Chaucer*, 3d ed., ed. Larry D. Benson (Boston: Houghton Mifflin, 1987).

[119] See note to ll. 1077–85 of Tilney's text.

Pliny tells the story of a fisher's wife who jumps off a cliff with her husband when she cannot find a cure for his disease. The proof of love conveyed by these stories is catastrophic and tragic: every one of Tilney's loving wives metaphorically jumps off a cliff. These particular female subjects are not only defaced but destroyed by the very love that constitutes them. Their construction as subjects requires their own death, which suggests that the very best wife in this narrative is one who proves her love through her own annihilation.[120]

Only four husbands in the first part of *The Flower* are praised by Master Pedro for loving their wives well: Adam, whose uxoriousness is condemned in many other texts; Darius, who laments the imprisonment of his wife with abundant tears; Tiberius Gracchus, who is told by soothsayers that the order in which he kills the male and female serpents in his bed will affect the order in which he and his wife die; and an anonymous poor man who offers himself up to pirates rather than lose the company of his wife (450–93). None of Tilney's stories about husbands requires their immediate death or painful sacrifice. Even so, Lady Julia comments after the first three accounts of those who loved their wives that "there be . . . fewe such husbandes in these oure dayes, or rather none at all" (469–70). While women were encouraged to abandon their wills through total union with their husbands, the same degree of abandon was not asked of

[120] For a study of the conflict between the self-effacement and beautiful deaths of Stoic heroines and the self-assertion of a woman's own translations, see Mary Ellen Lamb's essay "The Countess of Pembroke and the Art of Dying," in Rose, *Women in the Middle Ages and Renaissance,* pp. 207–26. In "Jewels, Statues, and Corpses: Containment of Female Erotic Power in Shakespeare's Plays," *Shakespeare Studies* 20 (1988), 215–38, Valerie Traub says, "It is by now a commonplace [in feminist criticism] that Shakespeare was preoccupied with the uncontrollability of women's sexuality" (p. 216), and she explores various ways in which masculine anxieties about female erotic power are contained in Shakespeare's plays. A consideration of exemplary women in passages such as Tilney's which appeared so frequently during the Renaissance can remind us that this was far more a cultural than a personal construction.

men: on the contrary, their love required a self-conscious volition, even a seduction, an awareness that by it they might steal
their wives' private wills away.

Some of the advice from Pedro and Julia also encourages wom-
en's love as an act of self-conscious seduction,[121] but that seduction is justified by its being in the greater service of their marital
chastity: "Let hir indevor to increase a perfection of love, and
above all imbrace chastitie" (968–69). Such love did not result in a
comparable appropriation of the husband; instead, it identified
him as the single object of his wife's affection. After the examples
of wives who loved their husbands well, Gualter concedes that
women "love passingly, when ye do love" (1100–1101), just as
they hate extremely when they hate. The misogynist contends
that it would be good "if you coulde bring your maryed women
unto a meane" (1102–3), but Julia objects: "Not so . . . I wil have
no meane in love" (1104–5). In the context of the list of loving
wives, this assertion rejects women's moderate love for their
willing self-sacrifice. Julia advises wives to be chaste and to have
"no meane in love" because they are to channel all of their ardent
affection toward their husbands: they should deny an erotic response to anyone other than him and exalt their devotion to him
alone. Hence the object of advising a husband to steal away his
wife's appetite is to enable him to become the sole object of her
desire. As she becomes his possession, he becomes her obsession.

So the claims that this text makes for equality as a means of
ensuring friendship are contradicted by its own analysis and
advice. The terms by which women are judged men's peers reveal
how unequal the genders are as this text constructs them. The
exercise of women's love requires an erasure of them as willing,
feeling subjects and a self-sacrifice that results in their own destruction. What feelings remain to wives are supposed to dilate
entirely upon their husbands, although no comparable request is

---

[121] See, for example, ll. 1341–83 in Tilney's text and note.

made of the men. It is difficult to see how this relation could be equal or even very amicable in a reciprocal way. Tilney's ideology of companionate marriage does not overthrow hierarchy any more than earlier versions had done, and its greater emphasis on love finally works to ensure women's abasement. Catherine Belsey remarks that marriage viewed as a partnership reinforces patriarchy "to the extent that true love becomes the solvent of inequality, the source of women's pliability and the guarantee of marital concord. . . . Love makes slavery blessed."[122]

Nor does Tilney's text fully convey the "flower" of that friend-ship. There are several figurative ways in which this word func-tions in the title. "Flowers" was a common Renaissance expres-sion for rhetorical tropes, as in Gascoigne's title for his collection of poems, *A Hundreth Sundrie Flowers*.[123] "Fioretti," or little flowers, was a title often given to volumes of selections or ex-tracts from stories in the Middle Ages, as in *The Fioretti of St. Francis*, and in Italian it came to identify something like a good deed that was offered up as an act of sacrifice or mortification.[124] Tilney's text contains many stories, employs rhetorical devices to tell them, and requires the benevolent action of both partners for the happiness of the marriage. And "flower" could also suggest "the best, choicest, most attractive or desirable part or product of anything," as when Sir Thomas Hoby translates Castiglione's task in *The Courtier* as "to picke out the perfectest trade and way, and (as it were) the floure of this Courtiership."[125] Most of these meanings are included when Philip Knight identifies the multiple

---

[122] Belsey, p. 214.

[123] *OED*, sb. 6d.

[124] *Cambridge Italian Dictionary*, ed. Barbara Reynolds, vol. 1, *Italian-English* (Cambridge: Cambridge University Press, 1981), p. 301.

[125] *OED*, sb. 8. Baldassare Castiglione, *The Book of the Courtier*, trans. Sir Thomas Hoby (1561), ed. J. H. Whitfield (New York: E. P. Dutton, 1975), p. 16; also p. 216. This meaning appears more plainly in a word we still use, *flour*, which originally described the finest portion of the meal, whether wheat or some other grain, from which it was separated. See *OED*, "flour," sb. 1a.

"aspects of Renaissance flower poetics: diversity, rich ornateness, brilliance, perfection, and *copia*/anthology."[126] Tilney's title does support Master Pedro's assertion that "no friendship, or amitie, is or ought to be more deere, and surer, than the love of man and wyfe" (143–45).

The word was also used in medieval and Renaissance literature to suggest the *flos foeni,* or flower of the flesh, more specifically "the rose that is the maidenhead," or the genital site of women's sexuality.[127] By synecdoche the word also functioned to refer to an entire woman, especially a virgin, as when Capulet laments over Juliet's supposedly dead body: "There she lies, / Flower as she was, deflowered by him" (IV.v.36–37). In these instances the syndecdoche signals a figurative reduction of a woman to her sexuality, just as "deflowered" identifies the debased, nonvirgin state occasioned by Juliet's having, as Capulet thinks, "lain" with "death." For several fathers in Shakespeare's plays, a deflowered daughter is no better than a dead one. When the king turns to Diana at the end of *All's Well* and says, "If thou beest yet a fresh uncropped flower, / Choose thou thy husband, and I'll pay thy dower" (V.iii.327–28), the very rhyme shows the connection between the commodification of virginity and the form of inheritance prescribed for women by marriage. It is clear, then, that Tilney could be using the word to evoke an interpretation of marriage as an erotic as well as a companionate relation. Since the word "flagrant" (rather than "fragrant"), from the Latin verb *flagrare,* is applied three times to the text itself, in the sense of "ardent, burning, intensely eager or earnest,"[128] Tilney signals the text's associations with both kinds of affection and invites his

---

[126] Philip Knight, *Flower Poetics in Nineteenth-Century France* (Oxford: Clarendon, 1986), p. 13.

[127] D. W. Robertson, "The Doctrine of Charity in Medieval Literary Gardens," in *Essays in Medieval Culture* (Princeton: Princeton University Press, 1980), p. 30; Eric Partridge, *Shakespeare's Bawdy* (New York: E. P. Dutton, 1969), p. 107.

[128] See "Note on the Text," p. 96.

readers to consider the erotic character of marital friendship. More well-informed readers may have connected such affection with the pleasure that Augustine describes in *The City of God* for the union of the unfallen Adam and Eve, who "would have come together in a blaze of holy love" or "flagrabat caritas," but such ideal pleasure was not fully available to fallen men and women.[129]

Despite these invitations to consider the erotic or pleasurable aspects of marital affection, Tilney's text says very little about sexual relations in marriage. In an evasive parenthesis it sets virginity aside "as the purest estate" (179), asserting that marriage too is holy and necessary. It does not address the vexed question of erotic pleasure apart from procreation, nor does it make marriage look like a very exciting encounter between husband and wife. Instead it encumbers that encounter with duties. The erotic meaning of women's "flower" and the sexual pleasures of husband and wife are evoked by this text only to be repressed, just as its use of "friendship" posits an equality between husband and wife that the ensuing discussion contradicts. What the text does offer as the consummation of marriage is duty itself: "for the knowledge of duetie, is the maintenance of friendship" (146–47). This duty requires an obligation to love, but love becomes a means of ensuring women's cooperation in their own appropriation. Although wives are created as subjects by this humanist ideology and are given a degree of influence and power not advocated for them previously, the same ideology also encourages their erasure and destruction by a union in which the wife does not function as a separately desiring subject. Marriage defined in this way does not recognize the erotic choice of both partners, nor is it an equal friendship; instead, it makes possible the continued dominance of men and of the ruling classes by invoking "love" to control women's "flower."

[129] Turner, p. 50.

Introduction

Rupture in the Arbor

While Tilney does not directly address issues of sexuality in marriage, he also does not consider the spiritual implications of the union at any length. His emphasis on conduct focuses on daily practice as other humanists' had done, but he goes further than his predecessors in secularizing the "spiritualized household."[130] Nearly all humanist and puritan accounts of marriage asserted spiritual equality between partners: Erasmus's colloquy *The New Mother,* for example, leaves unresolved the debate about which sex is superior, but both participants in the dialogue agree that salvation is equally available to all human beings.[131] Galatians 3:25–28, which affirms the unity of the faithful and proclaims there is neither Jew nor Greek, bond nor free, male nor female among them, was often cited in support of spiritual equality. Tilney does assert that God is the author of matrimony (184–86 and 1406), and he considers the spouses' duties to God at the end of each section: the husband "must above all thinges have the feare of God before his eyes" (858–59). But Tilney likens spiritual worth to material advantage when he has Lady Julia advise a wife to do the same so that even a "foule deformed woman" will be "so well beloved of hir husband, as if she were the fayrest of bewtie in a countrie" (1408–11). Conversely, as to those women who are devoid of God's favor and grace, "seldome, or never enjoye they the happie estate of matrimony" (1411–14). For Tilney, marriage confers respectability and desirability upon wives, while its absence implies their unregeneracy. In contrast to Eras-

[130] Christopher Hill, *Society and Puritanism in Pre-Revolutionary England,* 2d ed. (New York: Schocken Books, 1967). Hill describes the effects of puritan teachings as bringing about "the spiritualization of the household," a phrase that serves as the title to chap. 13 (pp. 443–81).

[131] Todd, pp. 113–16. See, for example, *The New Mother* in Thompson's translation of *The Colloquies,* p. 269. A portion of the argument in this text is summarized later in this introduction.

[69]

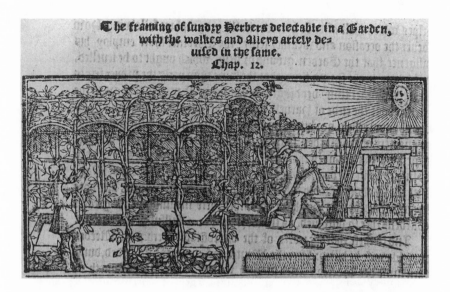

The framing of sundry Herbers delectable in a Garden,
with the walkes and Allers artely de=
uised in the same.
Chap. 12.

4. An English arbor, from Dydymus Mountaine, *The Gardeners Laby-rinth* of 1577. Reproduced by permission of the British Library.

mus's transformation of social boundaries on ethical and religious grounds, Tilney addresses the social value of religious redemption.

It is appropriate, then, that he looks to secular authors evincing primarily social concerns to frame his dialogue. Both Castiglione's *Courtier* and Boccaccio's *Filocopo,* the two texts that Tilney uses for his frame, are symposia, or in Latin *convivia,* topically structured dialogues occurring in formal social gatherings, having conventional seating arrangements and ceremonial openings but permitting relatively informal relations among the participants. Like other such works by Plato, Xenophon, Alberti, Ficino, and Erasmus, *The Courtier* and *Filocopo* address issues of love and occur "inside an enclosing structure, in a room or house or walled garden."[132] The walls of the estate in Urbino, the meadow in *Filocopo* "about the which grew store of yong trees very faire and thicke,"[133] and the arbor in Lady Julia's garden, an Edenic enclosure and "terrestriall paradyse" (119) that is "wreathed about with the sweete Brier, or Eglantine" (114–15), the flower considered the queen's own[134]—all such environments protect their noble participants from the intrusions of the outside world, including its problems, its hierarchies, and the common people who live there. Wayne Rebhorn remarks that "the gaze of participants" within this confined space "should surely be described as centripetal,"[135] and each of these dialogues does reinforce the dignity of its participants through the containment established by this textual geography. Symposia appear to function on egalitarian principles: they exclude those of unequal class and posit women as temporarily equal to men. Women even preside over the activities of these pastimes. The duchess of Urbino and Elizabeth Gonzaga, the Lady Fiametta in Boccaccio, and the Ladies Julia and Aloisa are permitted and encouraged by the male participants to oversee the symposia's events as a temporary inversion of normal social order.

Yet within these dialogues the rule of women appears more in name than in substance. *Filocopo* is a small portion of Boccaccio's romance about the lovers Florio and Biancifiore, called *Filocolo*. The fourth book of *Filocolo* contained a discourse on thirteen questions of love which was translated separately and published in England as *Filocopo* in 1567, just one year before Tilney's text

[132] Wayne A. Rebhorn, *Courtly Performances: Masking and Festivity in Castiglione's "Book of the Courtier"* (Detroit: Wayne State University Press, 1978), pp. 159–68; quote at p. 162.

[133] Giovanni Boccaccio, *A pleasaunt disport of divers Noble Personages . . . entituled Philocopo,* trans. H. G. (1567; reprint, New York: Da Capo Press, 1970), sig. A4ᵛ.

[134] Roy Strong, *The Cult of Elizabeth: Elizabethan Portraiture and Pageantry* (New York: Thames and Hudson, 1977), pp. 68–71. See note to l. 115.

[135] Rebhorn, p. 164.

5. An Italian conversazione occurring within an arbor, from Boccaccio's *Decameron*, Venice, 1498. Reproduced by permission of the British Library.

appeared.[136] When the Lady Fiametta puts on a crown of green laurel prepared for her by King Ascalion, she is empowered to answer each of the questions proposed to her by the other participants, and they have the right of reply. But Fiametta uses her power to undercut the worth of her own sex. For example, in the eighth question she is asked whether a man should choose as his

[136] Three more editions were published in 1571, c. 1575, and 1587 (*STC* 3180–82).

lover a wealthy noblewoman of good lineage or one with neither wealth, class, nor parentage. She justifies her choice of the former on the grounds that "the meanest man (in what belongeth to natural vertues) is of greater and better condition, than the noblest woman of the world."[137] The celebration of spiritual love in *The Courtier* occurs at the site of a sexless marriage, and the discourse is presided over by a noblewoman whose worth is commensurate with her sexual control. When the duchess asks Emilia Pia to begin the pastime, the latter suggests that "every man . . . propound a device not yet heard of"; by this proposal Emilia avoids proposing her own device, and the duchess reasons accordingly that "the other Ladies should be partakers of the same privilege."[138] The effect of this "privilege" accorded to women, as of the prominence of the duchess and her deputy, is the silencing of most other women in the conversazione.

There is a kind of reciprocity between Ascalion and Fiametta, the duchess and Lord Julian, and Tilney's Pedro and Julia which implies that men authorize women's exercise of their power. This reciprocity reflects a concern the authors of symposia usually have for the women in their audience. Boccaccio claimed that he wrote the *Filocolo* at the request of his beloved Fiametta, whom he identified as Maria d'Aquino, the illegitimate child of Robert of Naples. Whether or not such a person existed or requested that he write the romance, Thomas Bergin infers from the story that Boccaccio directed this book to an audience of women, "which is exactly what he will tell us about his motivation in undertaking the *Decameron*."[139] The same holds for *The Flower*: we cannot be certain Queen Elizabeth requested that Tilney write this text, but the inclusion of Lady Isabella's request at the end and its reinforcement by the rest of the women, along with the dedication, suggest that Tilney was directing it to an audience that in-

[137] Boccaccio, sigs. K2^v–K4.
[138] Castiglione, pp. 22, 24.
[139] Thomas Bergin, *Boccaccio* (New York: Viking, 1981), p. 85.

cluded women. *The Courtier* was not so specifically addressed to
women, but they were a part of its audience and became a subject
in the third and fourth books.

The temporary empowerment that these symposia offer to
women functions as a lure to invite their readership, but the
ideologies offered there do not support a claim they might make
to substantive power. Lord Julian in *The Courtier* and Master
Pedro in *The Flower* appear as women's advocates through their
condemnation of the misogynists, and both Gasper and Gualter
are threatened with expulsion from these contained worlds because they do not participate in their evanescent empowerment of
women. Symposia have to perform acts of surveillance over
misogyny because it constitutes a threat to one of their operant
assumptions. But the misogynists perform a generative function
when their potential subversion is contained by the texts, for then
they provide an occasion for women's praise. Lord Gasper remarks: "Nay, the women have rather great cause to thanke me.
For had not I contraried the Lorde Julian and the Lorde Cesar,
they should not have come to the knowledge of so many prayses
as they have given them."[140] Misogyny can generate the praise of
women in texts: *The Courtier* projects its own continuance within
its last lines for exactly this reason, because as long as a "waver-
ing starter"[141] like Gasper continues to insult women in courtly
contexts, gentlemen who know their aristocratic duty will feel
obliged to oppose him.

This recuperation of misogyny can present a show of support
for women that the advice offered by these texts contradicts.
Once women are engaged as readers, they are reminded by members of their own sex of their inferiority, of the requirements that
wives obey their husbands, and of their need to be sexually
controlled. The temporary inversion of hierarchy does not pre-
vent a reassertion, through explicit advice, of the hierarchies of

[140] Castiglione, p. 233.
[141] Ibid., p. 324.

[74]

gender and class that occur outside the enclosed space of the discourse. Where women themselves offer that advice, it gains a kind of credibility that it would not have if presented by men; the women who rule in these dialogues are therefore created as complicitous with the positions of their male authors. Moreover, although Pedro silences the protests of Gualter, his own position is not as egalitarian as he claims. The containment of misogyny and the authority granted to women in the social exchange of the enclosure work to obscure the texts' unequal assumptions about gender and class.

Symposia do sometimes explicitly address the issue of equality among the sexes, but often that moment becomes an occasion for the inequitable assumptions of the texts to be exposed, such as when Fiametta asserts women's inferiority. In *The Courtier,* when Gasper argues that women are more incontinent than men and should be chaste to ensure the legitimacy of lineage, Lord Julian notes his double standard and observes that lineage would be equally assured if men were continent instead. Julian proposes to resolve this inequity by punishing slander such as Gasper's and by defending women—with weapons if necessary.[142] He thereby justifies the very project of women's defense that Castiglione engages in his third book and carries through the fourth. Yet this exposure of the double standard leads not to an extended argument for its equalization in social conduct but only to the generation of this text and others like it. The narrative therefore posits itself and future texts as a resolution of social problems without engaging them at the level of practice. This centripetal argument made within an enclosure reinforces the very boundaries its argument depends on and encourages the production of more narratives providing a false assurance that the social problems considered therein have been resolved.

The Flower is not such an enclosed and self-generating text in its manipulation of gender and class, because it does not achieve a

[142] Ibid., p. 220.

comparable recuperation for the arguments made by Isabella on behalf of women. When she claims that there should be no "superioritie" (1134) between husband and wife, Isabella once again raises the question that Pedro had tried to put aside with his equation between a virtuous woman who was wise and of good lineage and a wealthy man (334–40). Instead of addressing the question of equality through class, wealth, and virtue as a way of making partners into each other's peers *before* marriage, Isabella wants to know why equality does not obtain *within* marriage, specifically why assumptions of gender difference result in wives' inferiority. This question was one that even women's defenders usually avoided: John Aylmer had supported Elizabeth's right to rule on the same grounds that Erasmus had articulated in *The New Mother:* "It's the wife, not the female, who is subject."[143] Isabella challenges the very concept of marital hierarchy by using the humanists' own descriptions of women against them: "I know not, quoth the Lady *Isabella,* what we are bound to do, but as meete is it, that the husband obey the wife, as the wife the husband, or at the least that there be no superioritie betwene them, as the auncient philosophers have defended. For women have soules as wel as men, they have wit as wel as men, and more apt for procreation of children than men. What reason is it then, that they should be bound, whom nature hath made free?" (1131–38). Her question addresses the *reasonable* grounds of sexual and marital inequality and its basis in nature or natural law. Whereas misogynists had denied women souls and rational ability, it was humanists who claimed both for them. Thomas More's statement on reason in men *and* women is perhaps the best known: "*Both* [sexes] have the name of human being whose nature reason differentiates from that of beasts; *both,* I say, are *equally suited* for the knowledge of learning by which reason is cultivated."[144] The

[143] Aylmer, sig. D; *The Colloquies,* trans. Thompson, p. 271.

[144] From More's *Selected Letters,* ed. Elizabeth Frances Rogers, vol. 1, *Selected Works of St. Thomas More* (New Haven: Yale University Press, 1961), p. 105, as

very arguments for the education of women raise the question that Isabella presents. In this text she is exposing the central contradiction of arguments by Renaissance humanists who combined claims for women's spiritual and rational equality with requirements that they be subordinate in marriage.

The "reason" that Isabella receives in reply—from her mother, Julia, and from the paternal figure of Erasmus—is an assertion of male power and metaphysical authority, not a logically coherent or rational justification. Lady Julia responds first to the classical examples adduced by her daughter in support of the egalitarian position by dismissing Isabella's evidence as irrelevant to Christians: "Al those *Barbarian* customes are to be disanulled, and contemned of Christians" (1173–74). Then Erasmus speaks with all the authority of the humanist tradition: "Ye say well, Madam. . . . For in deede both divine, and humaine lawes, in our religion giveth the man absolute aucthoritie, over the woman in all places" (1175–77). This statement is ambiguous because it appears to apply to all men and women, whereas the context of the discussion concerns only husbands and wives. The passage asserts the metaphysical authority of Christian teachings, biblical and doctrinal alike, on these issues, but its ambiguity also exposes the assumption of universal male dominance that is implicit in those metaphysical requirements.

When Tilney has to exhume Erasmus in order to assert a husband's authority in marriage, Isabella's question has pushed this author into articulating the presuppositions of male dominance and female submission that Christian and natural law reinscribe and depend upon. So the text itself articulates the inequities of gender that underlie the apparent equality it claims to offer women. Julia adds in the next passage that "reason" con-

---

cited by Elizabeth McCutcheon in "Margaret More Roper: The Learned Woman of Tudor England," in *Women Writers of the Renaissance and Reformation,* ed. Katharina M. Wilson (Athens: University of Georgia Press, 1987), p. 452; emphasis added by McCutcheon.

firms this right to male sovereignty because the virtues of intelligence, wisdom, strength, solicitude, patience, means, and courage are common in men but rare in women (1178–86). Yet this assertion rests on observation and cultural conditions rather than logic or monolithic categories for its support. Her defense of men calls into question the early portion of Tilney's text that surveys cultural practices of marriage, which used a relative approach to the subject via custom rather than one that perceives and reimposes universal male dominance. Erasmus and Julia do not address Isabella's question concerning the equal capacities of men and women; instead, both parental figures provide more endorsement for the power of men and ideology without justifying the claims of either, so authority appears as self-perpetuating and self-justifying. Their restatements of hierarchical positions regarding marital relations also expose the inequities of gender difference which are encoded in Christian law and cultural practice: they show that the differences between a husband and a wife finally come down to the difference between a man and a woman—the very difference that Isabella, following humanist teachings, claims does not exist in rational capacity or spiritual worth. Some additional differences must account for the inequity asserted by Christian and cultural authority, but the text, and humanism, are silent about them.[145]

[145] Later writers did address this problem, while admitting that the differences were small ones. Hooker grounds his discussion of difference in concern for "proportion," so it is either physical or reflected in physical stature and being: "It was not possible [the married couple] should concurre unlesse there were subalternation between them, which subalternation is naturallie grounded upon inequalitie, because things equall in everie respect are never willinglie directed one by another, woman therefore was even in hir first estat framed by nature not onlie after in time but inferior in excellencie also unto man, howbeit in so due and sweet proportion as being presented before our eyes might be sooner perceyvd then defined" (p. 402). This difference has a "charm," as C. S. Lewis characterizes it, that becomes "the mainspring of erotic love" (*English Literature in the Sixteenth Century*, p. 460), for Hooker adds that "herein doth lie the reason why that kind of love which is the perfectest ground of wedlock is seldome able to yeeld anie reason of it selfe" (p. 402). Gouge tries to explain why wives might think

Tilney himself produces this subversion of his argument through the responses to Isabella's question, and it exposes the central contradiction in the humanist ideology of marriage. This was, of course, the very contradiction that Elizabeth herself confronted as a queen considering marriage, whether from attackers, such as Knox, who described her rule as a "subversion of good order," or from defenders, such as Aylmer, who claimed she could rule but must be subject to a husband.[146] Louis Montrose has pointed out that Elizabeth "represented an affront to those very principles of hierarchy of which she was the guardian."[147] We can infer from this situation that problems of gender were unlikely to be fully contained by the Elizabethan power structure. While Elizabeth's rejection of marriage on the grounds that it was incompatible with her position of power was a subversion of the dominant ideology of marriage, it was not an attempt to disorder the realm; on the contrary, it was an attempt to ensure its continued but precarious harmony. J. E. Neale believed that Elizabeth made the right choice, for "the supreme need of the country was not, as Cecil and others thought, a royal child to settle the vexed and threatening question of the succession, but salvation from civil and religious war."[148] By refusing to continue with the archduke's suit in 1567, Elizabeth was making possible the maintenance of her country's religious tranquillity. Hence her role as a woman ruler required her resistance to the dominant ideology of marriage in order to maintain peace in the social and religious order. What appears to have been her

---

themselves the equals of their husbands: "The reason whereof seemeth to be that small inequalitie which is betwixt the husband and the wife: for of all degrees wherein there is any difference betwixt person and person, there is the least disparitie betwixt man and wife." If the man is the head, the woman is the heart, "which is the most excellent part of the body next the head" (p. 271). Hooker and Gouge work so hard to rationalize the inequities of gender that their attempts to minimize them sound concessive.

[146] Aylmer, sig. C4^v.

[147] Montrose, p. 309.

[148] Neale, *Queen Elizabeth I*, p. 154.

disruptive position from the perspective of gender and marriage
was simultaneously a conservative action to ensure civil stability.
Elizabeth's initial disruption of the patriarchal order as a woman
ruler even dislodges the categories with which we are accustomed to describe political actions.

A similar disruption occurs when we consider Tilney's text,
which presumably asserts the differences between the available
ideologies of marriage in order to recuperate the residual and
emergent views to its dominant ideology. Yet that project does
not succeed because the emergent ideology exposes the contradictions implicit within the dominant one; and in bidding for
support from the current power structure, the text evokes a
figure who contradicts, through her rule and her relation to
marriage, the inequitable assumptions of gender difference on
which the dominant ideology rests. Hence this emergent position
is not contained by the text; rather it opens *The Flower* up,
exposing the text's contradictions and making it capable of multiple interpretations depending on the position(s) a reader chooses
to accept. When Isabella subverts its argument, all the text can do
is reproduce the instabilities concerning marriage that are present
within its own cultural moment. Any text does this to some
extent, of course; and any portion of a text can be taken by
readers as representative of authorial opinion regardless of its
relation to the overall argument. But the effect of the contradictions within the ideologies of marriage in *The Flower of Friendship*
is to show us the conflicting cultural forces that, as an argumentative text and a narrative, it may have attempted to control and
suppress. Isabella's remarks identify a fault line within the text
that corresponds to a conflict within Elizabethan culture concerning the marriage of the queen.

Yet the figure of Isabella not only subverts *The Flower*'s dominant ideology but requests of the fictional Tilney that the two-
day pastime be reproduced as a text. Her action implies approval
of the pastime and, by extension, the text itself. If Queen Eliz-

abeth also approved of this text, she may have been endorsing not only its dominant ideology but also its representation of her own readiness to call that ideology into question. When Elizabeth defended her right to decide the marriage question for herself against Parliament and her people, she did so on the grounds of monarchic power. In 1563 she claimed to find marriage less appropriate for herself than for other women, "for though I can think it best for a private woman, yet do I strive with myself to think it not meet for a Prince."[149] The shift in gender identity evident in this statement—Elizabeth is not a woman but a "Prince"—marks the difference she projects between herself and other women.

Although the queen does not claim in this remark that her denial of marriage is applicable to anyone else, this distinction between herself and her subjects is not sustained in *The Flower of Friendship* because the female figure for Elizabeth there has no royal prerogative and male identity to invoke; instead, Isabella's objections address the concerns of women as a group. Whereas the subject position from which she speaks is a consequence of Elizabeth's royal position in the culture, and Isabella's assertion is made from a position of class privilege and temporary empowerment, Tilney's character argues for women's equality with men only on the grounds of reason. In a sense the queen's resistance to male authority in the culture and Isabella's objection from her temporarily privileged place within the arbor become accessible to all readers through the latter's argument in this text. *The Flower* makes available to women who are not royal or noble the claims for equality with their husbands that both Elizabeth and Isabella were in an especially strong position to make. Even Aloisa and Julia, whose subject positions are less stable than Isabella's, sometimes assert privileges for women that the text makes accessible to its "common" readers. As it exposes the

[149] Neale, *Elizabeth I and Her Parliaments*, p. 127.

contradictions within women's experiences, *The Flower* emerges from its boundaries of class to confront issues of gender that relate to all women.[150]

Since an emergent ideology is one that is not yet fully articulated within a culture, I have up to now avoided associating Isabella's position in this text with any other ideology. The concerns that she voices here are the concerns typically associated with feminism, especially in its emphasis on sexual equality,[151] but those issues serve primarily to disrupt the dominant ideology of this text, not to establish a counterhegemony. Although I think it is accurate to say that later feminists can see the grounds for the resistance to patriarchy articulated in Renaissance texts such as this one, it is also important to acknowledge the limitations on that articulation. It exists in this text primarily as a question, not as a fully developed answer. Lawrence Stone raises the subject of Renaissance feminism specifically with reference to issues of power in companionate marriage: "The companionate marriage

[150] Since Tilney's text, like others on marriage, places a strong emphasis on the choice of marital partners, it is likely that its audience was not confined to members of the nobility, who frequently engaged in arranged marriages and were less free than the lower classes to choose their spouses. Its popularity might suggest that gentle and "base" readers took pleasure in imitating courtly characters (just as Tilney imitates Italian conversazione), and the advice presented here seems designed for a wide range of readers. Catherine Gallagher discusses the frequent alignment of seventeenth-century feminism and the ideology of absolute monarchy in "Embracing the Absolute: The Politics of the Female Subject in Seventeenth-Century England," *Genders* 1 (1988), 24–39.

[151] See Karen Offen, "Defining Feminism: A Comparative Historical Approach," *Signs: A Journal of Women in Culture and Society* 14:1 (1988), 119–57, for an attempt to relate the word and ideology to a range of cultures and historical periods. Offen considers persons feminists when they meet three criteria: (1) recognize the validity of women's own interpretations of their lived experience; (2) exhibit consciousness of, discomfort at, or anger over institutionalized injustice (or inequity) toward women as a group; and (3) advocate the elimination of that injustice by challenging the coercive power, force, or authority that upholds male prerogatives in a particular culture (p. 152). Within its context Isabella's interruption meets these criteria, although its very brevity makes the degree of "challenge" that such a position conveys problematic.

[82]

demanded a reassessment of power relations between the sexes since it depended on a greater sense of equality and sharing. Consequently, the early feminist movements have a place in this story, even if one concludes in the end that they were largely abortive and without much influence in changing public attitudes."[152] For Stone, the companionate marriage was primarily a puritan phenomenon, which explains its conjunction with the early feminists he discusses—Anne Hutchinson, women in the Civil War sects, and late seventeenth-century feminists. Yet, following Margo Todd and Kathleen Davies, I have tried in this introduction to establish the humanist roots for companionate marriage and the continuity between humanist, Protestant, and puritan positions while suggesting that companionship did not lead directly to equality within marriage. One implication of this revision is that we need to address the relation between feminism and companionate marriage in sixteenth- as well as seventeenth-century texts.

Another way of considering this issue is to ask: How did it happen that a position for women's equality with men was articulated in Tilney's text? The foregoing discussion provides at least two answers to this question. The most immediate is that Isabella infers equality between spouses from the spiritual and rational equality humanists attributed to women. In a sense the emergent position she articulates is a logical consequence of the humanist ideology, but it has to be asserted against that ideology because humanists refused that view. Such a statement acknowledges that humanism itself in some sense produced, or at least provided the logical possibility for, the very egalitarian position that it refused, just as Tilney's text produced its own subversion. Although we could argue that similar subversions of the humanist ideology were produced only to be contained, it is difficult to contain an ideological position that is a logical consequence of one's own, especially if that position is developed through the dialectic of the

---

152 Stone, *Family, Sex, and Marriage*, p. 336.

dialogue form. The absence of containment in Tilney's text is a frequent occurrence in texts on this subject, which is one reason why representing their argumentative positions is not a simple procedure. Authors such as Erasmus and Vives often evince an uneasy awareness that the subject of equality in marriage is a problem; even if they only protest too much, their protest is some acknowledgment that the issue does consistently arise for them and in discourses on marriage generally.

Still another answer to the question is that while the queen's historical situation made possible Isabella's articulation of a feminist position, her situation reveals the preemergent and tenuous character of feminism as an ideology during the sixteenth century. Feminism has repeatedly arisen as a reaction against patriarchy, but women's resistance has not always been accompanied by a fully developed ideology in support of their actions. Elizabeth's achievement as a woman ruler was accomplished through a poignant awareness of the contradictions present within her own "position"—and her "position" in this sense constitutes her ideology as a form of considered action. Yet making an association now between Elizabeth and feminism should not imply that such a connection was entirely accessible to her or her contemporaries. We can admire her understanding and manipulation of her own complex historical situation while acknowledging that the emergent character of feminism at that moment—its articulation in the form of questions and objections to others' claims rather than by advancing its own case in an extended manner, its detachment from any fully developed project for social action, and its reflection in the apparently idiosyncratic situation of Elizabeth's rule—prevented her from making the larger associations with feminism that are now available to us.

Writers from Jacob Burckhardt and Foster Watson to Juliet Dusinberre and Constance Jordan have argued for the presence, or even the dominance, of feminism during the Renaissance, but often they assume that any advocacy for women constitutes a feminist position.[153] Linda Woodbridge has offered an important corrective to this approach by distinguishing between "the assumption that feminism is identical with kindness to women" and "the belief in the essential intellectual, emotional, and moral equality of the sexes." Yet I would question Woodbridge's assertion that "the idea of marital equality was foreign, strange, hardly capable of entering the mind" of Renaissance authors, or her extension of this claim "to all relationships between the sexes, not only marriage."[154] In contrast to those who described the puritan position on marriage as fully egalitarian and an advance for women, James Grantham Turner finds the chief source for an egalitarian interpretation of Genesis produced during the period not in the " 'Puritan Art of Love' " but in "the Renaissance tradition of learned wit."[155] Without describing all of women's defenders as feminist, Joan Kelly argues for "a solid, four-hundred-year-old tradition of women thinking about women and sexual politics in European society before the French Revolution," originating in the fifteenth century with Christine de Pizan and the *querelle des femmes*.[156] Although the advocates for women in the English debate were more often men than women (and often

[153]Jacob Burckhardt, *The Civilization of the Renaissance in Italy* (1860); Foster Watson, *Vives and the Renascence Education of Women* (1912); Juliet Dusinberre, *Shakespeare and the Nature of Women* (1975); Constance Jordan, *Renaissance Feminism* (1990). It is, I think, understandable that those with a focus more on Europe than on England arrive at these assertions sooner and make them more emphatically than those who address only the English context. But what is most objectionable about loose applications of the concept of feminism is that such projects can be recuperated to the operations of dominant ideologies in the present, thereby muting the revolutionary potential of feminism both then and now.

[154]Woodbridge, *Women and the English Renaissance*, pp. 3, 131.

[155]Turner, p. 109. The reference is to the Hallers' essay "The Puritan Art of Love."

[156]Joan Kelly, "Early Feminist Theory and the *Querelle des Femmes*, 1400–1789," in *Women, History, and Theory: The Essays of Joan Kelly* (Chicago: University of Chicago Press, 1984), pp. 65–109; quote at p. 66. See also Moira Ferguson, ed., *First Feminists: British Women Writers, 1578–1799* (Bloomington: Indiana University Press, 1985).

men speaking *as* women), and although most of them defended women in ways Kelly, too, does not consider feminist,[157] still the terms of the debate did sometimes include the presentation of feminist views. Tilney's *Flower of Friendship* participates fully in the debate and shows that some defenders of women were opposed not only by misogynists but also by those putting forward more egalitarian views than the defenders themselves advocated. The very arguments that Isabella makes against her opponents in the text also appeared in other works in the controversy.

In 1526, for example, Erasmus's colloquy *The New Mother* presents Fabulla disputing with Eutrapelus over the supposed superiority of men. She observes that men make such claims only "on the authority of men," and asks if they are longer-lived or immune to disease. When Eutrapelus denies they are but observes men "generally excel in strength," Fabulla reminds him that they are themselves "excelled by camels," or brute beasts. When he poses man's prior creation as a justification, Fabulla suggests that "artists usually surpass themselves in their later works."[158] When he reminds her that "God made woman subject to man," she replies: "A ruler's not *better* merely because he's a ruler. And it's the wife, not the female, who is subject."[159] Then she asks a new and interesting question: "Tell me, Eutrapelus, which is weaker, the one who submits to the other or the one to whom submission is made?" Quibbles ensue on passages in Saint Paul until Eutrapelus agrees that membership in Christ is "granted to all human creatures through faith," a concession to the spiritual equality between the sexes. Having achieved the further agreement that God expressed his image in mental gifts

---

[157] Kelly, p. 75.

[158] Heinrich Cornelius Agrippa also makes this argument against priority in *Of the Nobilitie and Excellencie of Womankynde,* trans. David Clapham, 1524 (Ann Arbor: University Microfilms, Reel no. 71), sigs. A5ᵛ–A8ᵛ.

[159] I have left out discussion of Fabulla's cryptic remark that "the subjection of the wife is such that, though each has power over the other, nevertheless the woman is to obey the man not as a superior but a more aggressive person." *The Colloquies,* trans. Thompson, p. 271. So far as I know, this is a unique assertion.

rather than bodily form, Fabulla inquires: "But in these respects what superiority, pray, have men over us? In which sex is there more drunkenness, more brawls, fights, killings, wars, robberies, and adulteries?" Here she is raising the issue of rational equality. When Eutrapelus replies that men go to war for their country, Fabulla notes that many men desert their posts or surrender; then she adds: "Though you make a special point of boasting of your martial valor—there's not a single one of you who, if he once experienced childbirth, would not prefer standing in a battle line ten times over to going through what we must endure so often." Erasmus's female character works within the limits of biblical argument and Christian teachings yet still challenges the claims of male supremacy. Fabulla gets a total concession on the issue of spiritual equality and a grudging one on rational equality, for Eutrapelus sees he is trapped and yields "for the present."[160] That present was a long time ago.

Robert Vaghane or Burdet's[161] "Dyalogue defensyve for women" of 1542 presents a bird debate in which a pye describes human perfection and the soul's gifts "as reason and knowledge," only to hear a falcon prove "that woman hath these powers rehersed above":

Knowledge in lernynge, as in the artes seaven
In naturall Phylosophye, and morall also
To make dysputacyon, of the bodyes of heaven
And of earthly creatures, in theyr places lyinge so
Facultyes and craftes, to invent and fynde out
And chaunces to tell, are they come a longe season
And these to be the effectes, no man doth doubte
Of the intellectyul power, the wyll and the reason.[162]

---

[160] Ibid., pp. 270–72.

[161] See Catherine Henze, "Author and Source of 'A Dyalogue Defensyve for Women,'" *Notes and Queries* 221 (1976), 537–39, where she discusses the likelihood that Burdet is the author and borrowed his list of good women from Thomas Elyot's *Defence of Good Women,* published two years earlier, in 1540.

[162] Robert Vaghane or Robert Burdet, "A dyalogue defensyve for women," 1542 (Ann Arbor: University Microfilms, Reel no. 157), sig. B1.

In more fluid verse Aemilia Lanyer's *Salve Deus Rex Judaeorum* (1611) infers equality of the sexes from its proof that Eve was less guilty of the Fall: "Your fault being greater, why should you disdaine / Our beeing your equals, free from tyranny?"[163] And in 1620 "Hic Mulier" argues in *Haec Vir; or, The Womanish Man* that "we are as freeborn as Men, have as free election and as free spirits; we are compounded of like parts and may with like liberty make benefit of our Creations."[164] One does not have to believe that these authors fully endorsed the views I have cited in order to see that their texts *voiced* the opinion that women were spiritually and rationally equal to men.

Each of the texts reveals the same license granted to the exercise of rational wit in defense of women's equality that Tilney accords Lady Isabella and that Elizabeth herself exhibited. The discursive field associated with such arguments was not the group of texts addressing the religious subject of marriage so much as the Renaissance debate about women.[165] Through Tilney's use of sym-

[163] Aemilia Lanyer, *Salve Deux Rex Judaeorum*, excerpts in *The Paradise of Women: Writings by Englishwomen of the Renaissance*, ed. Betty Travitsky (Westport, Conn.: Greenwood Press, 1981), p. 100. See also Barbara K. Lewalski, "Of God and Good Women: The Poems of Aemilia Lanyer," in Hannay, *Silent But for the Word*, pp. 203–24.

[164] *Haec Vir; or, The Womanish Man: Being an Answer to a Late Book entitled "Hic Mulier,"* Expressed in a brief Dialogue between Haec Vir, the Womanish Man, and Hic Mulier, the Man-Woman, in Katherine Usher Henderson and Barbara F. McManus, *Half Humankind: Contexts and Texts of the Controversy about Women in England, 1540–1640* (Urbana: University of Illinois Press, 1985), p. 284.

[165] Yet these two discursive fields do overlap, as is clear from Joan Larsen Klein's collection, *Daughters, Wives, and Widows: Writings by Men about Women and Marriage in England, 1500–1640* (Urbana: University of Illinois Press, 1992). The best forms of access to literature in the debate about women, apart from the early editions themselves and their copies on microfilm, are Linda Woodbridge's treatment in *Women and the English Renaissance* and Frances Lee Utley's quirky but inclusive bibliography, *The Crooked Rib: An Analytical Index to the Argument about Women in English and Scots Literature to the End of the Year 1568* (1944; reprint, New York: Octagon, 1970). See also Henderson and McManus, *Half Humankind*, which offers selections from the debate, and Jordan, *Renaissance Feminism*, which is especially helpful on continental texts but has some idiosyncratic readings. For a detailed discussion of defenses authored by women, see Elaine V. Beilin, *Redeem-*

posia, his discussion of more general relations between the sexes, and his articulation of an ideology by setting it off against other positions, his dialogue shows how the Renaissance debate intersects and overlaps with discourses on marriage. Some texts in the debate articulate more sustained, memorable, and playful versions of a feminist ideology, though one that is still only emerging in the culture.[166]

Linda Woodbridge is quite right to argue that "the English Renaissance institutionalized, where it did not invent, the restrictive marriage-oriented attitude toward women that feminists have been struggling against ever since,"[167] so the intersection of discourses on marriage and the debate about women does not mean that advocates for marriage were uniform advocates for women, much less feminist advocates. On the contrary, when writers championed marriage, they generally tempered their more positive views of women with a reminder that wives were

ing Eve: Women Writers of the English Renaissance (Princeton: Princeton University Press, 1987), chap. 9. Joel Altman's approach to Tudor literature via its roots in rhetorical debate seems to me especially appropriate for such texts because he resists our modern tendency to require a resolution of issues that are debated. Contemporary critics often try to identify winners and losers in these controversies when, rhetorically, those determinations may be quite beside the point. See Joel Altman, *The Tudor Play of Mind: Rhetorical Inquiry and the Development of Elizabethan Drama* (Berkeley: University of California Press, 1978).

[166] In *The Renaissance Notion of Woman: A Study in the Fortunes of Scholasticism and Medical Science in European Intellectual Life* (Cambridge: Cambridge University Press, 1980), Ian Maclean remarks that the humor in texts in the debate "may indicate the impossibility of discussing in serious terms the proposition of woman's equality, and therefore represents a strategy of discourse which is subversive in intention" (p. 91). Hilda L. Smith compares sixteenth- and seventeenth-century approaches to women in *Reason's Disciples: Seventeenth-Century English Feminists* (Urbana: University of Illinois Press, 1982). She says that early defenders of women tried to demonstrate the excellence of individual women, who were able to "rise above the general limitations of the sex," while seventeenth-century feminists "argued from the axiom that men and women were given equal rational abilities" (p. 7). The latter instance is precisely the axiom from which Lady Isabella argues in Tilney's text.

[167] See Linda T. Fitz [Woodbridge], " 'What Says the Married Woman?': Marriage Theory and Feminism in the English Renaissance," *Mosaic* 13 (1980), 11.

subordinate to their husbands, even if they could not or did not explain why. Being pro-marriage did not, therefore, mean espousing egalitarian views of the sexes. Although the sixteenth century produced a change in the available ideologies of marriage by reasserting and popularizing the companionate approach with its emphasis on the choice of marital partners and the requirement that they love each other, it does not follow that those changes were an unqualified advance for women. Ian Maclean is no more positive than Woodbridge when approaching the subject of marriage from the perspective of the Renaissance: "Marriage is an immovable obstacle to any improvement in the theoretical or real status of woman in law, in theology, in moral and political philosophy. Its influence is even apparent in medicine, whence comes its 'natural' justification."[168] Since ideologies of marriage serve not only to construct women's identities but also to define everyone's name, lineage, inheritance, and property within a social structure, maintaining stable ideologies of marriage is a primary means by which societies resist changes in their allocation of money, property, and power. Hence it is not surprising that marriage has been a particularly intransigent form of restraint for women from the Renaissance to the present day, or that women who have resisted it have, in a useful displacement, been characterized as correspondingly intransigent. So much depends on marriage; so much can change when its hold over women is released. In the absence or weakening of that social relation, the blatant inequities of gender become so visible that they are not easily enforced.

While some Renaissance texts like Tilney's were designed to present the dominant ideology of marriage as an apparent benefit to women, they also convey women's resistance to those claims. Their representation of a conflict permits a critic such as Woodbridge to perceive the "irrepressible spirit of . . . Renaissance Englishwomen" implied by texts in the debate,[169] while Mary

---

[168] Maclean, p. 85.
[169] Fitz [Woodbridge], " 'What Says the Married Woman?' " p. 18.

Beth Rose reads their form against their content to see how the structural claims of social stability can be asserted against a text's more progressive statements.[170] What I hope this introduction will add to our contemporary analysis of these issues is a further understanding of how such historical readings can be produced by locating a text's feminist ideology without asserting its dominance or inevitably reinscribing its containment.[171] Texts on subjects as contested as Tilney's can affect, even afflict, their readers by confronting them with diverse ideologies and contradictory positions which arise from and reinscribe the cultural conflicts of their own historical moments. Readers of such material may innocently assent to many of its assertions without suspecting that the texts also engender and increase personal and political turmoil. If Tilney's text prompted this response in some members of its audience, I do not regret it, any more than I regret the array of belabored arguments provided by other texts in the Renaissance debate about women. It is often by such means that issues concerning gender and power are addressed in cultural contexts, and it is sometimes by such means that change becomes possible.

Whether this particular text prompted a change that improved cultural conditions for women or men is a difficult question to answer. We are still addressing a much larger question that Joan Kelly posed years ago about whether women had a renaissance during this historical period,[172] and it is important that both

[170] Rose, *The Expense of Spirit.* See, for example, her discussion of the *Hic Mulier/Haec-Vir* controversy, pp. 70–77.

[171] Stone's reference to Renaissance feminism as an "abortive" effort in *The Family, Sex, and Marriage*, p. 336, might argue for its containment; but the ways in which history has worked to obscure our knowledge of women's successes may explain our ignorance of the positive effects of feminism without proving that those effects were not experienced by individual women. In short, our intervening textual versions of "history" may have been far more recuperative of the feminist project than the social forces existing during the Renaissance.

[172] Joan Kelly, "Did Women Have a Renaissance?" in *Women, History, and Theory*, pp. 19–50. See the introduction to *Rewriting the Renaissance*, by Margaret W. Ferguson, with Maureen Quilligan and Nancy J. Vickers, for a further

questions remain open rather than definitively closed down. One response provided by this analysis to the claims of Jacob Burck-hardt, Foster Watson, and other more recent exponents of a feminist Renaissance is that the association between feminism and early modern discourses on marriage and women is more complex than most commentators have suggested.[173] While hu-manist, Protestant, and puritan texts did sometimes produce arguments that look feminist, or at least proto-feminist, the egal-itarian positions in those texts were usually situated within a broader deference to metaphysical and patriarchal authority. As the egalitarian implications of the arguments became more appar-ent, the recognizable contradictions could prompt an articulation of the limits of equality occasioned by women's obligations to men, family, and God. The authors of those discourses could therefore, on occasion, represent some aspects of what we can now call feminism as being in opposition to their own ideologies, so that relation is revealed as a conflict rather than an easy ex-tension of the argument. It is conceivable that these discourses opened up, sometimes in spite of themselves, theoretical possibil-ities for women that the change in their material conditions from the Middle Ages in some respects closed down. But it is equally possible that the commodification of women's virtue associated with such texts, the incessant invocations of chastity, and the ways in which injunctions to love one's husband encouraged the

---

discussion of issues raised by Kelly. In *The Currency of Eros,* Ann Rosalind Jones remarks that "if women had a Renaissance, it was a problematic one, fraught with prohibitions arising from the conflicting interests of emergent social groups" (p. 14).

[173] An exception to the approach via simplification occurs in Heather Dubrow, *A Happier Eden: The Politics of Marriage in the Stuart Epithalamium* (Ithaca: Cornell University Press, 1990), where Dubrow argues that "we should embrace rather than resolve the contradictions among the theories of marriage put forth by contemporary historians. These contradictions reflect not the inadequacies of our historiography but the complexities of marriage in Renaissance England: conflict-ing theories of the nature of that institution coexist in contemporary scholarship precisely because they coexisted in that era" (p. 14).

sacrifice of women's appetites, wills, and identities changed how women were culturally defined and exchanged, so the very texts that permitted a fleeting articulation of feminism were also those that defended women in order to make them the personal and sexual possessions of their husbands. This second possibility would affect a very practical containment of women's energy and power, one more likely to occur as capitalism became more established in the culture.

Tilney's *Flower* offers us both of these possibilities at once, possibilities that contend with each other across the ideological fault line of the text. Yet seen from another perspective, the text that produces such options is not so entirely *at* fault, since it is not the class-bound, centripetal, fully coherent arbor and text that we often assume conduct books try to be. It is even possible that its author and patron preferred that *The Flower* explore a range of issues concerning duty and power in marriage without decisively concluding them. What some would describe as the text's failure[174] may have been for them, and remains for us, a preferable alternative. By enabling readers to confront the concerns of gender beyond the boundaries of class and offering multiple interpretations of Renaissance ideologies on women and marriage, as a text, at least, *The Flower of Friendship* is open—flagrantly—after all.

---

[174] I am aware that the possibility posed in the previous sentence and the "failure" posited here have been offered as assumptions of the foregoing argument. They are also conventional assumptions in critical practice—that texts are designed to offer single and noncontradictory interpretations and that their not doing so constitutes an inadequacy. Having explored these assumptions in this introduction, I want now to call them into question, to suggest that multiple readings of texts like this one may occur not only by accident but by design, especially when they are produced by Renaissance humanists, and that, regardless of intention, such occurrences may benefit texts and their readers.

Note on the Text

The Stationers' Register records a payment from Henry Denham for a license to print "a boke intituled *ye flowre of fryndshippe*" between July 22, 1567, and July 22, 1568 (Arber, I, 164b), and Denham remained the printer for its first six editions. The 𝕭𝖑𝖆𝖈𝖐 𝕷𝖊𝖙𝖙𝖊𝖗 text was printed by him and by Abel Jeffs (1587) in octavo with the title appearing on A1, Queen Elizabeth's coat of arms on A1ᵛ (for Denham's editions only), the dedication from A2 through A3, A3ᵛ blank, and the text extending from A4 through E7ᵛ.

Unlike the previous editor (Ralph Glassgow Johnson) or bibliographical commentator (J. G. Tilney-Bassett) on this text, I have used the British Library's copy of the first edition as a copy text. My collation of the twelve consistent copies of the work that are extant confirms the revised *STC*'s ordering of the seven editions, indicates that each is a paginary reprint of the immediately preceding edition, and reveals increasing deterioration more often than correction among them. Only the first edition refers to Flora's delights with the pronoun "hir" rather than "hys" or "his" (50). It correctly uses the biblical "cleaving" (984) to describe the union of husband and wife (Genesis 2:24, Matthew 19:5, Mark 10:7), and it is otherwise consistent where other editions are not (see textual notes to lines 183, 342, 454, 524, 527, 1209–10).

I have retained the copy text's punctuation, capitalization, and spelling

[95]

except for modernizing *i/j, u/v,* and long *s/s,* expanding contractions, and eliminating accents over double-*e* digraphs. I have also divided the text into paragraphs, since its rhetorical shape anticipates those divisions, and their inclusion is helpful for reading. All other emendations, even of accidentals, appear in square brackets. These are few. In eight instances one letter in a word was added or changed (490, 595–96, 643, 845, 1105, 1151, 1203, 1218); in another instance a word (*folde*) dropped from the end of a page was replaced (666). The other substantial emendation appears at line 348, where the first edition records "eyghtene" as the difference between fourteen and thirty, whereas all subsequent editions print the correct number. These variants and other substantive differences are recorded in the textual notes. I have not, however, included variants from a thirteenth copy of the work once owned by Gretion-Maxfield and offered for sale since 1985 by E. M. Lawson and Co., for it is a made-up copy of three signatures from the first edition, the title page and colophon from one of the first three editions, and the remainder from the fourth edition of 1571.

Some further explanation may be needed for the word "flagrant," which appears four times in the first edition (29, 52, 861, 1430). It is changed to "fragrant" by most later editions but is always retained as "flagrant" in its last occurrence. The word is important because in three instances, including the last, it is applied to the text itself, *The Flower of Friendship*. The *OED* traces it from the Latin *flagrare,* "to burn," and gives as synonyms "ardent, burning, intensely eager or earnest"; "resplendent, glorious." It also records a confusion between the Latin verbs *flagrare* and *fragrare* in MSS, thereby affecting its meaning as "fragrant" (def. 6). *Cotgrave's French-English Dictionary* of 1611 defines *flagrant* as "flagrant, ardent, burning, flaming; earnest, fervent," and the word is applied in these senses to flowers and herbs in Dydymus Mountaine's *Gardeners Labyrinth* of 1577 (pp. 24, 157). Since these older meanings contribute to the text's attention to sexual delight in marriage, if only to evoke and then suppress those concerns, I have retained the copy text's reading of the word.

A brief and

pleasant discourse

of duties in Mariage,

called

the Flower of Friendshippe.

Imprinted at London by
Henrie Denham,
dwelling in Pater noster Rowe,
at the Signe of the Starre.
Anno. 1568.
Cum privilegio.

To the Noble and most
Vertuous Princesse, Eli-
zabeth, by the Grace of God,
of Englande, Fraunce, and Ire-
5   lande, Queene, defender of the
Faith. Etc. Be long life, quiet
reigne, and perfite
health.

WHEN I CONsider (most Noble Queene and Sov-
10   ereigne) that within your Majesties sacred breast, wisedome, adourned wyth Noble vertues, is only harbored.
From whence as from a pure Fountaine, doth flowe, the
deedes of a Noble hart, waying therewithall, your Majesties highe dignitie, and the lownesse of my estate, with
15   my simple skill: I stoode as one dismayde, not daring to
adventure, to put thys my base stile to the hearing eyther
of your Majesties reverent eares, or to the judgement of
your skilfull eyes: so well otherwise, with the learned
labors of more excellent authors satisfied. Yet dailye per-
20   ceyving the clemencie of your highnesse most noble
mind, conjoyned with so high an estate of Sovereignetie,
and noting your Princelye curtesie, and as it were a heav-
enly humilitie matched with the great knowledge, graffed
in the roote of your Majesties royall hart. I was by this
25   (though before discouraged) boldened to presume so

farre, as humblye to offer this my simple Present unto your Highnesse, expressing my good will: which of my fruitelesse Garden and barrayne soyle, have founde out this flagrant Flower of Friendship, craving the only

30 *Alexander* accepting of the same no otherwise, than that Noble *Alexander* of *Macedon,* who greatly estemed the poore Poëme,

Antoninus. given him by the Philosopher *Pirrho:* Or *Antoninus* the Emperor, that considering the givers good will, highly regarded a fewe simple Metres offered unto him. Wher-

35 fore (redoubted Sovereigne ô noble *Alexandra*) my hope is, for that in the person of your Majestie, are assembled the rare vertues, not onely of those Princes, but of many others, you will amongst the Noble presentes of more higher estate, receyve these fewe simple lines, as from him

40 that continuallye prayeth for the long and prosperous continuance of your Majesties happye reigne.

Your Majesties most humble
Subject, Edmunde
44 *Tilney.*

A briefe and pleasaunt
discourse of duties in
Mariage.

WHAT TIME that *Flora,* had clothed the earth and braunches, of the new springing trees, with leaves of livelye greene, and (being as it were in the Prime of hir delights) had garnished the pleasant fields a new, with flagrant flowers. Early on a morning when *Phoebus* also had spreade abrode his blisfull rayes and comfortable beames: I with a friende of mine, called Maister *Pedro di luxan,* devised how to enjoye some part of that delitefull season, and in the ende concluded to walke, and range abrode in the fieldes and pleasant groves, where we were not onelye partakers with the sweete recording birds, in the wonderfull workes of the Almightie: but were thereby also occasioned, to glorifie the Creator thereof.

Thus consuming the time, till it was nere noone, and when the Sunne began to waxe somwhat warme, we determined to go from thence, unto a worthie Ladies house therby called the Lady *Julia,* where we might rest us the heat of the day. And as it chaunced, we came in very good time: for even as we entred the Ladies house, they had newly washed, and were readye to sit downe to dinner, where we founde a jollye companie assembled togithers, both Ladies and Gentlemen, amongst the which,

[101]

70 was Madam *Julias* daughter, called the Lady *Isabella* a verie faire Gentlewoman, there was also the Lady *Aloisa* with many other Ladyes, and their lincked Mates, beside M. *Lodovic Vives,* and an olde Gentleman called M. *Erasmus,* of whome after we had taken acquaintance, and used

75 such courtesie as the time and place required, we satt all downe orderly to dinner, where there was such exceeding cheere, such pleasaunt talke, such melodie, and such sweete cheering of the Ladies, that it was a world to see how merie we were.

80 And being thus in our pleasures, the Lady *Julia* devised with the company in what pastimes we should spende the after noone. Some liked well of carding and dicing, some of dauncing, and other some of Chestes, al which were condemned, by the moste part, who alledged that those

85 Pastimes were not aunswerable to the tyme of the yeare, but more meete for Christmas: and therefore suche games were fittest, that might be used abrode in the fields, as bowling, shooting, and such other lyke.

But M. *Pedro* nothing at all lyking of such devises,

90 wherein the Ladies should be left out, said: that he wel remembred how *Boccace* and Countie *Baltizer* with others recounted many proper devises, for exercise, both pleasaunt and profitable, which (quoth he) were used in the courts of Italie, and some much like to them, are practised

95 at this day in the English court, wherein is not only delectation, but pleasure joyned with profite, and exercise of the wit.

With that, all the whole assemblie, both Ladies and Gentlemen, desired him (for that they were unskilfull in

100 those devises) he woulde put some one of them in use, which he best liked of, and they all would be obedient to his determination, at the first he utterly refused it, but in

Maister the ende at their often intreaties, he aunswered that he
Pedro de- would doe his diligence.

105 *viseth the*　So in haste the table was taken awaye, and the compa-
pastime.　nye having washed, the Ladies withdrewe them for a
while into their Chambers, at whose returne we went all
The discrip- into the Garden, a place mervellous delectable, wherein
tion of the was a passing faire Arbour at the entrance whereof, on ech
110 *Arbor.*　side, sprong up two pleasaunt trees, whose greene leaves
much delighted our eyes, and were supported with two
statelye Pillers, curiously painted with divers devises. All
the whole Arbour above over our heades, and on eche side
was powdred with sundrie flowers, and wreathed about
115　with the sweete Brier, or Eglantine, betweene the
braunches whereof, the cheerefull Sunne layde in his
beames, here and there, so that the heate did not molest us,
neyther did the Sunne want to cheere us. What shall I saye,
it might be called a terrestriall paradyse.

120　And when the whole companie were orderly mar-
shalled by M. *Pedro,* on the benches which were trimly set
wyth Camamile and Daysies, he gathered from the top of
the Arbour, three or foure braunches of Roses with their
greene leaves, whereof he wreathed a garlande, and de-
125　maunded of the whole companie, if they woulde consent
to his election, and obey whome soever he did choose for
their Sovereigne, whereto they all aunswered that they
would.

The Ladie　And then turning towardes the Ladye *Julia* sayd, that he
130 *Julia chosen* in the name of them all, for sundrie respects presented
soveraigne.　unto hir that garland, and therewith the soveraigntie over
them for the daye. And when he had set the same upon hir
head, said: that wheras they had willed him to devise their
pastime, he thought it best the companye being so apt for
135　the purpose, they shoulde by course eyther rehearse some
pleasant stories, or debate upon some such matter, as the
Ladie *Julia* their sovereigne should commaund.

And my opinion is (quoth he) forasmuche as everye
thing sheweth nowe a certaine naturall amitie amongst

[103]

140 *Plinie.* themselves, yea the trees (sayeth Plinie) have a naturall instinct of friendship, the sweete flowers, the pleasaunt herbes, declares the same also, that wee intreat somewhat of friendship, and because no friendship, or amitie, is or ought to be more deere, and surer, than the love of man

145 and wyfe, let thys treatise be thereof, wherein I would the duetie of the maried man to be discribed, for the knowledge of duetie, is the maintenance of friendship.

All the companie commended Maister *Pedro,* for this pleasant devise, and the Lady *Julia* standing up, saide: that

150 for so much as the soveraigntie (though not with hir will) was committed unto hir, with consent of them all, and due obedience promised. I like well (quoth shee) of this which Maister *Pedro* hath alreadie devised, touching friendship, and duetie of the maried man: wherefore, by the same

155 authoritie which I have receyved, I commaund you Sir, (and turned hir towards Maister *Pedro*) to performe this charge, which you have devised of the maried man, not

Maister for that I thinke you to be a better husbande, than any of
Pedro is the rest here: but because we being yet wholy ignoraunt,
160 *commaun-* in this kinde of pastimes, you may (as the principall author
ded to de- thereof) instruct us, in the whole circumstance, and
scribe the againe, being so well languaged as you are, we shall have
maried good sporte, to heare you interlard our countrie speeche,
man. wyth some Spanishe trickes.

165 As I doe (quoth Maister *Pedro*) utterly denie to be the author of these pastimes, which have long ago bene else where practised: So might I right well excuse my selfe, both for want of skill, and also of good utteraunce, but for that I have in the name of all the rest, promised obedience

170 unto your [Ladyship]: I will not be the first, that shall disobey.

Wherfore worthie Ladies and Gentlewomen, (quoth he)
Maister if I doubted of your friendly judgement, and benevolence,
Pedro be- I woulde crave it at the beginning, but because your good

175 *ginneth his*
Flower of
Friendship.

The com-
180 *mendation*
of mariage.

Genesis.

185

190

195

200

205

hartes, and noble natures, have bene by proofe, sufficiently tried of me, (letting that passe) I will go briefly to
my charge, (the *Flower of Friendship*) wherein I will first
declare unto you, the vertues of the matrimoniall estate,
which (setting virginitie aside, as the purest estate) is both
holy and most necessary. It is not unknowne unto us
Christians, howe God the Creator of all things, made of
the rib of Adam, his welbeloved Eva, as an helper, whom
Adam called bone, of his bone, and flesh, of his fleshe, so
that the almightie instituted this holy ordinaunce of matrimonie in the blissefull place of Paradise, when man was in
his chiefest perfection:

And therefore, if antiquitie may give any worthinesse,
what is more auncient than this honourable estate, which
God himself the founder of all ordayned and consecrated?
What is more honorable, and praise worthie, than thys
that Christ with hys mother in Canaan did not onely with
his presence make honorable, but also wyth miracles did
sanctifie the same? What is more just, than to render that
to oure posteritie, which we of our predecessors have
before receyved? What thing is more in humaine, than for
man to contemne that as profane which the eternall hath
halowed, and nature hir selfe bewtified? Christ our Lorde
commaundeth, that man shall forsake Father and Mother
and cleave to his welbeloved Spouse, and what is more
holy than love towards parentes, which God in the com-
maundementes, hath rewarded with the longnesse of lyfe,
yet matrimony is preferred before the same. What is then
more necessarie than Matrimonie, which containeth the
felicity of mans life, the *Flower of Friendship,* the preservation of Realmes, the glorie of Princes, and that which is
most of all, it causeth immortalitie.

I might here alledge a number of authorities in the
commendation of mariage, aswell of auncient Doctors
and Fathers, as also worthie Philosophers, and grave

[105]

210

215

220

225

230

235

240

245

learned men: but bicause you doubt not therin, and the state doth sufficiently commende it selfe, I let them passe, and will before I proceede any further, shew you the rites of dyvers Nations, in celebrating this misterie, whereof as some will make you to laugh, so other some are to be noted. As for the christian orders they are not unknowne unto you. Amongst the auncient Romaines (as *Cicero* recordeth) were two kindes of mariages, wherby they had also two sorts of Wyfes, the one more ordinarie, whom they called Matrones, the other were called Houswyfes, which were maried by conjoyning of handes, almost like unto us, these did they esteeme as their Daughters, and had lyke inheritance of their landes, who bare the rule of theire houses, and therefore called Housewyfes: but no accesse of the husband might be permitted unto them, for on the Matrones begat they their children.

The Babilonians maried their Maydes without Dowries in this maner. All their Maydes which were to be maried, were assembled in a place appointed, and placed orderly the fayrest first, then the meaner sort, and last the foulest: The fayrest was given unto him that would give most money to marrie with hir, stil paying according to their bewtie, more or lesse, till they came to the foulest, and to them that woulde marry any of those, was given parte of the money that was taken for the fayrer sort, paying according to the rate, as they exceeded in foulenesse. The lyke maner also, was used amongst the auncient *Venetians,* as sayeth [*Sabellicus.*

An] unhappie custome was it, quoth the Lady *Julia,* and likely that the *Flower of Friendship* was but weakly rooted betweene them of so slender acquaintance, but I praye you tell us, how the indifferent sorte were maried, that were neyther foule, nor fayre, but lovely browne.

Mary, quoth he, for such amongst the *Venetians,* there was no money either given, or taken, but were maried for naught.

[106]

And so perchaunce, quoth a merie gentleman, that stoode by, called Mayster *Gualter* of Cawne, were some of the fairest, as they be sometimes nowe a dayes.

The french men.

250 I have also read, quoth Maister *Pedro,* that in Fraunce, the maydens did choose their husbands in this sorte. The parents called a number of yong men to a banket, whom they thought fittest, and him, to whom the mayde gave first water, by that signe she chose for hir husband. In

The Mau-ritanians.

255 *Mauritania,* as sayeth *Diodorus Siculus,* there was such store of women, that every man might have five wyfes, and no lesse than three, which also after the death of their husbands, within one moneth eyther wyllingly buried themselves with hym, or were perforce executed by the lawe.

In the Isles of Canaria.

260 In the Isles of *Canaria,* there were contrarywise so many men, and so fewe women, that everie wyfe might have seven husbandes, and could not take lesse than five.

But I trust, quoth the Lady *Aloisa,* that those men were not so kinde harted, as to be buried with their wyfes, as the women in that other countrie were with their husbandes.

265

I thinke not, quoth Maister *Pedro,* and I doubt whether those women of *Mauritania* coulde not have beene contented to have taried behinde their husbandes, had there beene no lawe to have compelled them.

270

Tush quoth the Ladie *Julia,* this is farre from your matter. What appartaineth this to the *Flower of Friendship?*

Lady, quoth he, I am not yet come to the purpose. But one word more, and I will to my charge. The *Chaldeans,*

The Chal-deans.

that honored the fyre for their God, had an easie custome.

275 For when they minded to marry, the Priest kindled the fyre in the good mans house, and both the parties touching it, were assured togither, and when any of them mislyked, one of them quenched the fyre, and so were they as free, as ever they were before. In another countrie the

280 Priest of theire Idols enjoyed the first nightes pleasures of

The Scots.

the Bride, as in Scotlande the Lorde of the Soyle, had the

[107]

first fruites, of all the Virgins, within his Lordship.

A number of suche like customes, I could recite, but I may not spend longer time in those trifles, and the Ladie *Julia* desireth to heare of our friendly *Flower,* wherto now I returne, and saye, that equalitie is principally to be considered in this matrimoniall amitie, as well of yeares, as of the giftes of nature, and fortune. For equalnesse herein, maketh friendlynesse.

Pitachus Mityleneus one of the seaven sages of *Greece,* being demaunded of a yong man, whome he should take to wyfe, aunswered, go, and learne of the children, that play togither, and they will informe thee. For they had a game among them, wherin they often repeated, *take to thee thy peere.* Marry not a superiour, saith *Plutarch.* For in so doing, in steede of kinsfolkes, thou shalt get thee maisters, in whose awe thou must stande, and a riche woman, that marieth a poore man, seldome, or never, shake off the pride from hir shoulders. Yea *Menander* sayth, that suche a man hath gotten in steed of a wyfe, a husband, and she of him a wyfe, a straunge alteration, a wonderfull metamorphosis. But *Licurgus* the law maker well considered that, when he ordayned that women shoulde be married without dowries, so that then they had nothing to be prowde off, save onely their vertues, which ought to be accounted the chiefest dowrie. For that which is more excellent, is to be preferred before things of lower valour. Why then for lack of substance, shall a vertuous wife be repelled, or for want of welth, wisedome bee rejected? *Alexander,* the great monarch of the whole world, shewed his noble courage in nothing more, than in that hee rejecting the ryche Barbarian Queenes, vouchsafed to match with *Barcina,* daughter of *Arbaces,* a poore gentleman, but of noble parentage, wherein not riches, but nobilitie adorned with vertues prevayled.

Well, quoth the Ladie *Julia,* I pray you what is he now a

Margin notes:

What equalities is in mariage. (285)

Pitachus Mityleneus (290)

Plutarch. (295)

Menander. (300)

Licurgus. (305)

Alexander (310)

daies, that had not rather marrie a woman ful of money, wanting vertue and grace, than that having vertues, lacketh money. For my parte, it well lyketh me that equalitie, as you say, be observed, seing equalnesse causeth friendlynesse. But I understande not this kinde of equalitie, wherein you seeme to allow the greatest inequalitie that can be. For *Alexander* being Lorde of the whole worlde coulde finde no equall match, in respect of his greatnesse. Much lesse *Barcina* that was so farre his inferiour, both in parentage, and substance.

Not so farre his inferiour, quoth Maister *Pedro,* for the great vertues, which abounded in *Barcina,* and as I sayde before, the onely ryches to be required in a woman, was in all respects comparable to the great greatnesse of *Alexander* the great, neyther did she want sufficient parentage, and though not a conquerour of the worlde, yet well knowne to be proceeded from the conquerours own linage, so that a vertuous woman, being wise, and of good linage, wanteth no equalitie on hir parte to counterpeise the greatest ryches, or treasure, that any man can have. For where vertue aboundeth, all good things doe flowe. And to conclude, I say, that great regarde ought the man to have in his choise, that he may leave hys childe parentage, which being joyned to vertues maketh them perfite.

Now for the equalitie in age, I say, consisteth likewise in the inequalitie of yeares, but not so much as the Philosophers, in times past affirmed. For *Aristotle* by hys reasons, woulde have the man to be twentie yeares elder than hys wyfe, bicause they might leave off procreation at one time. *Hesiodus* the Greeke poet, and *Xenophon* the philosopher, woulde have the woman foureteene, and the man thirtie yeres old, so that there should bee [sixtene] yeres betwene them, bicause in that time, the man should be best able to rule his housholde, and the woman taken from *Licurgus.* evill occasions. *Licurgus* lawe was amongest the *Lacedemo-*

[109]

nians, that the men shoulde not marry, before thirtie, and
seaven yeres of age, and women at eyghtene.

355 What maner of equalitie is this, quoth the Lady *Isabella,*
I woulde never marry, rather than to take such old crustes,
whose wyfes are more occupied in playstering, than in
enjoying any good conversation.

You say truth, quoth Maister *Pedro,* neyther doe I al-
lowe it, yet may I not condemne the auncient philoso-
360 phers. For in those dayes men lived longer, and their
natures were much stronger. Therefore by likelyhood it
was at that time more tollerable. But my opinion is, that
they differ not above foure or five yeres.

What love   After this match made, and equalities considered, next
365 *in mariage*   followeth, to love, and to [like well]: For perfite love
should be.   knitteth loving heartes, in an insoluble knot of amitie.
Love indifferent serveth not, love fayned prospereth not.
Wherefore it must be true, and perfite love, that maketh
the *Flower of Friendship* betweene man and wyfe freshlye to
370 spring. This love must growe by little and little, and that it
maye be durable, must by degrees take roote in the hart.
For hastie love is soone gone. And some have loved in
post hast, that afterwards have repented them at leysure.
Wee all seeke the fayrest, the richest, and noblest. But
375 vertues are laide aside, and nought accounted off, we seeke
to feede our eyes, and not to content oure eares.

Why? quoth Maister *Gualter,* shal a man choose his
wyfe with his eares.

To choose with oure eares, quoth Maister *Pedro,* is to
380 enquire of hir vertues, and vices, by report whereof you
shall understande hir conditions, and qualities, good, and
bad.

As for that, quoth *Gualter,* it booteth not. For the best of
them all have their faults, and if she be vertuous, she will
385 looke to be so honored, that hir husband shall have the
more a do to please hir. And I remember, that a wise man,

I knowe not hys name, being enquired of a friende of hys, with whome he should marry, answered, that he had beene married foure sundrie times, first with a fayre woman, who was so prowde of hir bewtie, that he was faine to please, and content hir, least she should dishonour him, the seconde verie riche, whose substance made hir so stately, that he was forced lyke a slave to obey hir, the thirde was so vertuous, that he was glad to honor, and reverence hir, to keepe hir still in hir vertuous goodnesse, the last was of good linage, which so exalted hir stomake, that shee made him hir bondman. Nowe choose, quoth he, which of these foure thou canst best content thy self.

You have made a fayre reason, quoth the Lady *Aloisa,* I never knewe that you were so deepely learned before, and all the Ladies woulde have driven Maister *Gualter* out of the arbor. But father *Erasmus* sayde that he remembred the lyke thing of *Anaxagoras,* and therefore he was not to be blamed, because he did but repete the woordes of a philosopher.

What then, quoth Maister *Pedro,* it is no parte of my charge to disprayse women, but to speake the best of them, and to plant the *Flower of Friendship* betweene them, and their husbands. Wherfore, let love be rooted deepely in the mans hart towardes the woman. Let hir person be sought, not hir substance, crave hir vertues, not hir riches, then shall there be a joyfull beginning, and a blessed continuance in amitie, by which all things shall prosper, and come to happie ende. Beware of hatred, be circumspect in love, which of them first taketh place, doth abide during lyfe. And love grounded, remayneth for ever, which being once gone, al other goodnesse followeth for companie.

The man must be-ware in Therefore to confirme this love the married man must, as much as he can, alwayes absteyne from brawling, lowring, and grudging, especially when he is newly mar-

[111]

chyding
when he is
newly
425 *maried.*

430

435

ried. For if the wyfe first conceyve hate, she will never receive love againe. The husband then must be merie, and pleasant with his wyfe, to make hir the more in love with him at the beginning, so that if afterwardes they chaunce to fall at square, it shall rise but of a sodaine anger, which will be gone againe as soone, and not of anye olde conceyved malice. There be manye men, that boast much, how they be served, and feared, like Bugges, of their wyfes, but they marvellously deceyve themselves. For much better were it, if they were better beloved, and lesse feared. For whome the wyfe hateth, in feare she serveth, but whome shee loveth, she gladly cherisheth. It is good reason, that all women doe labor to stande in the good grace of their husbandes, but much more ought we men to foresee, that we fall not into the hatred of oure wyfes. For if she once fasten hir eyes on a nother, he shall enjoy hir in dispite of hir husbands beard.

440 *The maried*
man steale
away his
wyfes pri-
vat will.
445

In this long, and troublesome journey of matrimonie, the wise man maye not be contented onely with his spouses virginitie, but by little and little must gently procure that he maye also steale away hir private will, and appetite, so that of two bodies there may be made one onelye hart, which she will soone doe, if love raigne in hir, and without this agreeable concord matrimonie hath but small pleasure, or none at all, and the man, that is not lyked, and looved of his mate, holdeth his lyfe in continuall perill, his goodes in great jeopardie, his good name in suspect, and his whole house in utter perdition.

450 *Such as*
loved well
their wyves

Adam.
455
Darius.

I will recyte two, or three examples, of those that loved their wyfes well, and then I will proceede. The first, that loved hys wyfe, was our father *Adam,* who being set in Paradise, and forbidden on paine of death, one only tree in the Garden, to content, and please *Eva* his wife, did notwithstanding eate of it, and dyed. *Darius* the great king, being overcome by *Alexander,* in all things shewed

himself stoute and invincible, till he understoode that his
wyfe was taken prisoner, who then poured out hys teares
aboundantlye, as lamenting for that he more esteemed

460 then his lyfe, or estimation.

Tiberius   *Valerius Maximus* sayth, that *Tiberius Gracchus* finding
Gracchus. two serpents in his bed, sent for the soothsayers to knowe
what the straunge chaunce ment, and signified, which
aunswered, that if he killed the male serpent, he shoulde

465 die before his wyfe, but if the female were first slaine, his
wyfe shoulde die before him. He bearing entire love towardes his wyfe, gave his owne death to prolong hir lyfe,
and killed presently the male serpent.

There be, quoth the Lady *Julia,* fewe such husbandes in

470 these oure dayes, or rather none at all.

That is the matter, quoth Maister *Gualter,* that your
Ladyship is so afeard to marry, but yet to tell the truth, and
shame the Devill, there be mo suche husbandes, than like
wyfes, if it were well tried.

475 This sawcie foole, quoth Madame *Aloisa,* woulde be
well beaten, and banished our company. For he is still
pratling against women, and interrupteth oure pastime.

No, no, quoth Maister *Pedro,* he increaseth our sporte,
and therefore we can not well want him. But I will shewe

480 you one example more of later yeares, because the Ladie
Julia sayeth that none nowe a dayes doe love their wyfes so
Baptista   well. *Baptista Fulgosa* recounteth of a certaine poore man,
Fulgosa.   and hys wyfe, that were seeking for their sustenance upon
the Sea side. The woman being taken away, by certaine

485 Rovers, hir husbande swam in the sea after hir, desiring
the pirates to take him also, saying, that he had rather be
with his wyfe in captivitie, than lacking hir to live at
libertie, whereat the Pirates marvelling, receyved them
both into their shippes, and declaring the whole adven-

490 ture, presented them to the king of [*Tunis*], who understanding the case gave them great commendation, and not

onely set them at libertie, but also sente them home wyth great rewarde.

This maye suffise to make you understand, that men doe sometimes love their wyfes, and hereby may you also see of what force, the true Matrimoniall love is, wheron let the married man fasten, and grounde all the rest of his doings, and so shall this friendly *Flower,* be planted in a fertile soyle.

And as there bee certayne sweete herbes, that are great nourishers of thys *Flower:* so be their certayne poysoned weedes, that will overgrowe it, and in the ende utterly destroye it, if they be not weeded out by the roote, whereof the first, and chiefest is adulterie. For what god-lynesse can raigne in that house, where harlots beare the rule, whose fruits *Salomon* doth largely describe. For if the husband please the wicked woman, he must of force dis-please hys owne wyfe being godlye, and that injurie a good woman cannot with anye pacience support. At what time the married man determineth to keepe a harlot, even the same houre, doth he set fyre to his honestie, destruc-tion to his house, and losse of all, that ever he hath. An honest woman will suffer a thousand discommodities in hir husband, so that she be assured, that he is contented with hir, and loveth hir only. What greater cruelty can a man shew unto his wife, then to keepe all his railings, brawlings, and chidings for hir, and another to enjoy all his (good) conversation, and pleasures. I doubt which of them hath the greater hart, eyther he in doing, or she in suffring it. Can there be any greater disorder, than for the husbande to be merie abrode, and lowre at home, to take from his wyfe, and give to his harlots, to want for hys children, and to suffise for his bawdes. The fayth that the woman oweth to hir husbande, the lyke fidelitie ought the man to repaye unto hys wyfe, and though the civill lawe giveth man the superioritie over his wyfe, that is not to

495

500 *Weedes that will over-grow the friendly Flower.*

505

Adulterie.

510

515

520

525

[114]

offende, or dispise hir, but in misdoing, lovingly to reforme hir. Therefore the abhorring of adulterie increaseth
amitie betwene man, and wife, and the chiefest way to
530 ground the *Flower of Friendship* in Matrimonie is, first to
roote out the poyson of adulterie.

Gamning.   The seconde weede that is to be extirped is gaming,
which though the woman can wyth more pacience suffer,
than this other: yet for his owne sake, let him forbeare it.
535 For what wisedome is it, that a man at one chaunce of the
Dice, hasardeth as much, as the toyle of hys whole lyfe
hath gotten, and scrapte together, and small commoditie
the gamester reapeth thereby, when he hath best hap, if all
his cardes be told. For suppose he wynne, yet is there
540 suche cursing, such lying, such brawling, chyding, and
swearing, that the Devill laugheth them all to scorne. If he
lose, he fretteth, and fumeth so, that beside the losse of his
thrift, he hazardeth both body, and soule, with cursing,
and blaspheming. Then if he eyther wynne, or lose, ye see
545 these hys gaines and commodities. I condemne not honest
playing for recreation at times convenient for some small
matter, as the persons hability is. But what a monstrous
thing is it, to consume whole dayes, yea, whole daies, and
nights in gaming, swearing, and for swearing. For it hap-
550 neth often, a daylie gamester, a common blasphemer.
Wherefore it were no great hinderance to the common
welth, if such kinde of persons were utterly banished.

Riotous-   The third pestiferous weede is banqueting, and riotous-
nesse and   nesse. For dronkennesse, whiche commonly haunteth the
555 *dronken-*   riotous persons, besides that it wasteth thy thrifte, con-
esse.   sumeth thy friends, and corrupteth thy body, doth also
transforme thee from a reasonable creture to a brute beast.
Socrates.   *Socrates* compareth the wyt, that is overcome wyth wyne,
unto a horse that casteth hys Maister, what greater re-
560 proche can there bee to a man, then to be called a common
dronkard, which is as much to saye, as a man deprived of

[115]

all vertues. I could recite many examples, what discommodities have chaunced to worthie men by this vice, if the time woulde suffer mee.

565 You have yet day ynough, quoth the Lady *Julia.* Wherfore we pray you to shew us some of those examples for oure instruction.

I am content, quoth Maister *Pedro,* and seing you are so willing to heare, I will declare first somewhat of wyne,
570 which by abuse nourisheth dronkennesse, and by use is
Anacharsis the best liquor of all others. *Anacharsis* the Philosopher sayde, that the Vine bare three kindes of grapes, the first of pleasure, the second of dronkennesse, and the thirde of
Noe the sorrow, so that passing the first, which is to drinke it
575 *first inven-* temperately, and delayed, the other two are naught. *Noe*
ter of wine. was the first that invented Wyne, though some attribute the same to *Ycanus,* and some to *Dionysius.* The first that
Filona first delayed wine, was *Filona,* borne in *Candia,* and being so
delayed dronke temperately, it quickeneth the wyt, it increaseth
580 *wine.* the strength, it cheereth the hart, it taketh away cares, it causeth colour in the face, it strengthneth the sinowes, it helpeth the sight, it fortifieth the stomack, it provoketh urine, it taketh away sorrowes, and to conclude with saint
S. Paule to *Paule* writing to *Timothe,* being sicke in his stomack,
585 *Timothe.* counsayleth him to drinke a little wine. But as many discommodities hath it also, if it be abused, as breeding the gowte, causing the dropsie, decaying womens bewtie, and making them barraine, with many other much worse.
Licurgus. *Licurgus* the *Lacedemonian* law maker, commaunded, that
590 no man before. xviii. yeares of age, should drinke anye wine, and from thence to fortie he gave leave to drinke
Noe the verie little, and much delayed, and from fortie upwardes
first dron- somewhat more, and lesse delayed. As *Noe* was the first
kard. inventer of wine: so was he first dronken, who was therefore laught to scorne of his owne sonnes. *Lot* in his
595 *Lot.* [dronkennesse] lay with his owne daughters. *Alexander*

Alexander the great was so spotted with this vice, that alwayes in his dronkennesse, he woulde kyll his deerest friends, and in *Marcus An-* the ende being dronke, was poysoned himselfe. *Marcus*
600 *tonius.* *Antonius* an invincible Romain captaine, being once over-come with wine, gave himselfe to the pleasure of *Cleo-*
Anacleon. *patra,* and was slaine by *Octavius Caesar. Anacleon* the poet was so great a bibber of wine, that he was choked with the huske of a grape. Loe, here you see the unhappie end of
605 those, that passe the golden meane, and cleave to the excesse. If the married man do weede out these three daungerous weedes by the roote, no doubt this *Flower* will prosper passing well, and yeeld yearely dubble increase.

Certaine And, as I sayd before, the better to nourishe, and main-
610 *delicate* taine thys *Flower,* there are certaine delicate herbes that *herbes, the* must of force be cherished, which bee these. First to be *maintainers* advised in speeche, curteous, and gentle in conversation, *of this* trusty, and secret in that, wherein he is trusted, wise in *friendly* gyving counsaile, carefull in providing for his house, dili-
615 *Flower.* gent in looking to that which is his, sufferable of the importunities of his wife, daungerous, and circumspect in matters touching his honesty, and jeolous in the education of his children.

These be excellent herbes, quoth the Lady *Aloisa,* and
620 rarely founde all in one garden. Wherefore we pray you teach us, how we maye plant, and conserve them.

That appertayneth not to my charge, quoth Maister *Pedro,* and if it did, yet want of skil, and shortnesse of time would not permit me. But I will instruct you in their
625 qualities, which being well considered, will provoke the wise man to seeke after them. In doing whereof, as I shall sufficiently discharge my duetie towardes the Ladie *Julia,* concerning hir commaundement. So trust I to deserve great thanks of al these Ladies.

630 I The first delicate herb, that the married man must plant *Advised in* for the preservation of this friendly *Flower,* is to be advised

[117]

speeche. in speeche. For the man that without discretion speaketh more hastily, than wisely, for the most parte falleth into errors, much babling, declareth a foolishe head, and a
635 silent person, is the exampler of wisedome. First expend with thy selfe, what thou wilt speake, and ponder thy meaning well. Then note to whome, where, and when thou speakest. The tongue that runneth before the wyt, commonly breedeth his maisters wo. The philosophers in
640 their scholes, never taught a man to speake, but first
Salomon. learned him, to holde his peace. *Salomon* sayth, that much talke cannot be without offence, and he that can refraine his tongue is wise. Two occasions [*Socrates*] allowed, that should moove one to speake, when he knewe the matter
645 *Xenophon.* verie well, and when necessitie constrayned him. *Xenophon* sayeth, that nature gave us two eares, and but one mouth, to the intent we should heare more, than we ought to speake.

2   The second herb is to be curteous, and gentle in conver-
650 *Courtise in* sation. For ye see that fierce, and hurtfull beasts, as the
conversation lyon, the serpent, with suche lyke be abhorred of us for their cruell curstnesse, when the tractable beastes, as the spaniell, and the greyhound with others, have not onely place in oure houses: but we have sometime more care to
655 nourishe them up, than a christian creature. The married man then must not be rigorous towarde his wife. For there will discorde grow by hir inward hate, and never shall they have joy, or peace, if the woman cannot refraine hir tongue, nor the man suffer. If he want discretion, and she
660 pacience, it will rather appeere the mansion of fooles, than a house of the wise. For at the last, except one of them yeelde up in tyme, they will fall to raging, and so consequently to blowes. Women for the most part, are froward of complextion, and tender of condicion, whereto the
665 wise husbande must have great regarde, and if he once reprehende them sharplye, he must a [hundreth folde] exhort them lovingly. There are manye occasions, that

causeth variance betweene man, and wife, as for their
children, servants, apparell, and other such houshold mat-
670 ters. In which the good married man must showe his
wisedome, eyther in turning it to sporte, and dissembling
the cause, or aunswering not at all. If so be he cannot
suppresse his anger, let him then goe, and disgest it
abroad. For the ende of indignation, is to be ashamed of
675 our selves. And as in a myste a man appeereth greater,
Diogenes. than in a faire day, sayeth *Diogenes:* so appeereth hys vices
more in hys anger, and rage, than when he is pacient.

3 The thirde is to be secrete, and trustie in that, wherin he
To be secret is trusted. One of the vertues most esteemed in times paste
680 was secrecie, whereby the wisedome of a man was per-
fitely discerned. He is discreete, that keepeth well his
Socrates. secretes, sayeth *Socrates.* But he is not wise, that dis-
Cato. covereth them. The good *Cato* repented him but of three
things, that he did during al his life. First, for disclosing a
685 secrete to a woman, the seconde, for sayling by sea, when
he might have gone by land, and the last, for consuming
one whole day, without doing some profitable deede. A
Anaxa- marveilous example of secrecie, was shewed in *Anax-*
goras. *agoras,* who with others conspired to kill a tiraunt, and
690 being betrayed, and by the tiraunt put to most cruell
tormentes, not sufferable, bit off his owne tongue, bicause
he would not discover that, which he promised to keepe
secret. The like is reported of a woman in *Athens,* bicause
she would not bewraye a conspiracie, wherein hir hus-
695 band was a parte.

It is happie, quoth the Ladie *Aloisa,* that some women
have bene secret in times past. For you men say nowe a
dayes, that women can keepe no counsaile.

See I pray you, quoth Maister *Gualter,* how soone this
700 Ladie, had gotten holde of that sentence, which so little
serveth hir purpose. For I trust it was an easie matter for
that woman to kepe silence, when she wanted hir tongue.

Whereto the Ladies would have replied, but Maister

[119]

705 *Pedro* interrupted them, and sayde that he did not condemne, although the most parte were not tongue tyed, and so there be, quoth he, some men that be open ynough. But I would have this married man to embrace secrecie as a vertue, and thinke it is a great shame not to be so secret, as a woman.

710

4

*To be wise
in giving
counsell.*

Socrates.

715

Plato.

The fourth, is to be wise in gyving counsaile, which is not everie mans office, but such as be of good yeares, that have seene, and heard much. Counsellors must be wise, lerned, vertuous, of good judgement, and without affection. *Socrates* counselleth a man, not to aske counsell of him, that is wholy given to the worlde. For his advise will be, but after his owne pleasure. *Plato* saide, that he studied more to give counsayle to his friendes, than to reade philosophie in the schooles. What a mockerie is it then, for harebraind heads, to give counsayle in matters, wherof they never saw, nor heard before.

720

5

*To be care-
full in
providing*

725 *for his
house.*

The fift, is to be carefull in providing for hys house, as to feede, and cloth his family, to instruct his children, and to pay his servants truely. In which things a man maye not, as in other voluntarie matters be negligent, but play the parte of a good husband in remembring it, and providing for it in time. The office of the husbande is to bring in necessaries, of the wife, well to kepe them. The office of the husbande is to go abroad in matters of profite, of the wyfe, to tarry at home, and see all be well there. The office

730 of the husbande is to provide money, of the wife, not wastfully to spend it. The office of the husband is, to deale, and bargaine with all men, of the wyfe, to make or meddle with no man. The office of the husband is, to give, of the wyfe, to keepe. The office of the husbande is to

735 apparell him as he can, of the wyfe, to go as shee ought. The office of the husband is, to be Lorde of all, of the wyfe, to give account of all, and finally I saye, that the office of the husbande is, to maintaine well his lyvely-

740 hood, and the office of the woman is, to governe well the houshold. And as the man maye not denie his wyfe things, that must be graunted of necessitie: so he ought not to graunt hir things of prodigality, and superfluous. For as great disorder is it to graunt the one, as to denie the other.

6
745 *To accompany no defamed persons.*

The sixt is that the married man accompany no difamed persons, and in any case, that he harbour them not. For many men blame their wyfes for yll lyfe, when they themselves are the causers therof for mainteyning such companions, whereby he himselfe doth hardly escape infamie, and these good fellowes do seeke to creepe into
750 greatest friendship with the husband, to the intent they may have better oportunitie with his wyfe. Yet maye he use his tried friend, or neere kinsman familiarly as well in his owne house, as else where, having alwayes regarde to the olde saying, that a man may shew his wyfe, and his
755 sworde to his friend, but not to farre to trust them. For if thereby grow unto him any infamie, let him not blame his wyfe, but his owne negligence.

7
To be sufferable in the importunities of his wyfe.
760

The seventh herbe of marvellous vertue is, to bee sufferable in the ymportunities of hys wyfe, sometimes disembling, and in trifling matters consenting unto hir. For if all things, that women crave, shoulde be graunted, all thing that they finde fault withall, should be amended, and all things that they are agreeved with, should be redressed, *Sampsons* strength, the pacience of *Job,* and the wisedome
765 of *Salomon* were all to litle. For some men, whose misshaps are to be lamented, are matched with such saints, that devise naught else, but howe to vexe, and molest theire

Socrates.

husbands. *Socrates* pittied three sorts of men. The first was, a good man in the handes of a curst shrewe, the
770 seconde a wise man, under the governaunce of a foole, and the last was a liberall man, in subjection to a covetous caytife.

I thanke you for this, quoth Maister *Gualter,* this is the

truest tale, you tolde to daye, and hitherto, you have but flattered these Ladies.

Not so, quoth maister *Pedro.* For I spake nothing heretofore but the truth, neyther speake I this nowe generally against all women. For that were slaunderous unto them. I do but touch some shrewde wyfes.

Tushe, quoth Maister *Gualter,* they be shrewes all, and if you give the simplest of them leave to daye to treade upon your foote, to morrow shee will tread upon thy head.

Be not angrie, I praye you, quoth Maister *Pedro.* For I give no such leave, but I say that for quietnesse sake, and for the increase of amity, the married man must sometime dissemble, and in this case ought to consider, that if his wife be foolish, it little helpeth to aunswere hir, and lesse profiteth to reforme hir, but if she be wise, one worde will suffise. For it is a certaine rule, that if a woman will not be still with one worde of hir husband, she will not be quiet with as manye wordes, as ever the wise men did write, nor with so many stripes, as a man is able to give hir. The wyse husbande therefore I say, and affirme, must, to preserve this pleasaunt *Flower,* deale with his wyfe, rather by subtiltie, than by crueltie.

8
Not to be jeolous.

The eight, is to be circumspect in matters, that concerne his honestie, and not to be jeolous of his wife. The Stoike philosophers saye, that jeolousie is a certaine care of mans minde, least another shoulde possesse the thing, which he alone would enjoye. There is no greater torment, than the vexation of a jeolous minde, which, even as the moth fretteth the cloth, doth consume the hart, that is vexed therewith. Two kinde of persons are commonlye sore sicke in this disease, eyther those that are evill themselves, or they, that in their youth have gone astraye, supposing that as other mens wyfes have done towards them, so will theirs doe towardes others, which is vanitie to thinke, more folye to suspect, and greatest foolishnesse to speake

off. For as some lewde women be dissolute: so like wise
810 women there be, honest, and verie circumspect. If the
wyfe be to be suspected, let the man worke as secretly, and
closely, as he can to reprehend hir, yet all will not peradventure advaile. For, trust me, no wisdome, no craft, no
science, no strength, no subtiltie, yea, no pacience suf-
815 fiseth to enforce a woman, to be true to hir husbande, if
she otherwise determine. Therefore I conclude to be
jeolous, eyther needeth not, or booteth not.

9   The ninth, and laste herbe is to be carefull in the educa-
To be care- tion of his children. For much better were they unborne,
820 *full in edu-* than untaught. *Diogenes* being enquired what were best
cation of his for a man to doe to be in favour of the Gods, and beloved
children. of the people, answered, that to be incredit with the people, and favorde of the Goddes, a man ought to doe three
things, the first to reverence, and honor much the Gods,
825 then to bring up his children in due correction, and last to
be thankefull to his benefactors. What avayleth riches,
possessions, to be fortunate, to have thy wyfe with childe
safely delyvered, and thy childe well nourished, if afterwards by yll trayning, and for want of education, he
830 *Alexander* become vicious? The monarch of *Macedon Philippes* sonne,
being asked why he honored more hys mayster, than his
father, said, that his maister gave him lyfe everlasting, and
his father lyfe but for a time. There came once before the
wise *Solon,* a father with his sonne, one accusing the other,
835 the father complayned of the disobedience of his sonne,
and the sonne accused the father of his ill bringing up,
Solon. which was the cause of his disobedience. *Solon* well considering the case, determined that because the father had
not brought up his sonne in due correction, he should
840 therefore after his death, be deprived of his sepulchre,
which was verie rigorous in those dayes, and the sonne for
his disobedience was disherited.

I assure you, quoth maister *Lodovic,* that same was an

845

excellent judgement of the wise *Solon,* and if it were put in [use] at these dayes, there would be many fathers to lye without graves, and as many sonnes put from their inheritance.

850

The more pittie, quoth mayster *Pedro,* and I thought to have saide more therein. But the sunne is so much declined, that it is more then tyme to unburden these Ladies of this tedious talke, and I feare me, I have alreadie troubled them to long.

855

Not so, quoth the Ladie *Julia.* For sooner shoulde we want the day light, than good will to heare you, though the day were so long againe.

860

You say your pleasure, quoth mayster *Pedro.* But now to knit up this *Flower* of matrimoniall amitie, and friendship, touching the office of the man, I say, that he must above all thinges have the feare of God before his eyes, which with the rest well considered, and put in execution, no doubt he shall enjoy the flagrant savour thereof.

865

Then rose up the Ladie *Julia,* with the whole company giving my friend mayster *Pedro* great thankes, wishing that there were many such husbands, and therewith she tooke the garlande from hir head, and saide turning hir towards maister *Pedro,* that shee would surrender unto him againe the authoritie, which shee of him receyved, with that charge, that he shoulde the next daye bestowe it on some other in that place. For I shall not be in quiet,

870

quoth shee, till I have heard the married woman prescribed in lyke sorte, as you have done the married man, neyther can this *Flower* well prosper, or bee perfite, except the woman also put to hir helping hande.

875

Whereto mayster *Pedro* aunswered, that in the woman was to be required great helpe for the preservation of this friendly *Flower.* Yet will I not, quoth he, take the authoritie from you. But if you list to departe with it to some other, you shall your selfe to morrowe resigne it to

880 whome it pleaseth you, and in the meane time he willed
hir to leave the garland, and hir authoritie in the place,
where she receyved it, which she did, and then went we
out of that most pleasaunt arbour into the garden, where
we tooke our leave, of the Ladies and gentlemen, who
were verie loth to have left our company. But maister
885 *Pedro* had so apointed, that we could not tarry. Therfore
promising to come againe the next day, we went home the
same waye we came in the morning, where the Night-
ingale saluted us with suche sweete melody, that we were
889 at the end of our journey, before we were ware.

6. This section ornament appears in the first
two editions. Reproduced by permission of
the British Library.

The office, or duetie, of
the married woman, for the preservation, and continuance,
of thys Flower of
Friendship.

895

THe next morning, came there two, or three straungers to
mayster *Pedro,* which letted us of our mornings walke, notwithstanding we sent word to the Ladie *Julia,* that in the
after noone, we determined according to oure promise, to
meete hir in the garden. So after our dinner was finished,

900

and the guestes departed, wee prepared readie our horses,
partly for that the weather was somewhat to hote to travaile on foote, and partly for the more speede. But for all our
haste, the companye was assembled before we came, and
merily sat togithers, gyving care to the pleasaunt harmo-

905

nie, and melodie, that was made by the musitians, to
whome after our reverence accordingly done, we drew
neere, and tooke our places in the arbor, where as the eve-
ning before, the Ladie *Julia* had left hir authoritie.

And everie one orderly set, shee tooke the garland of hir

910

soveraigntie, and standing up saide. That the authoritie,
which she had receyved the day before of mayster *Pedro,*
she purposed to give to some other, least in usurping a
continuance therein, shee might doe injurie to the rest of

The Lady   the companye, and so curteously comming to the Ladie

915 *Aloisa*   *Aloisa,* she set the garlande of principalitie upon hir head,
chosen sove- with election confirmed by assent of us all, with the prom-
reigne. ise of due obeysance.

        The Lady *Julia* sate downe soberly in hir place againe,
and the Ladie *Aloisa,* standing up, declared how muche
920   against hir will she tooke that authoritie, and soveraigntie
upon hir: notwithstanding for as much as the Lady *Julia* by
the free consent of the rest, had elected hir, she neyther
would, uncurtesly, nor might she honestly, contemne, or
reject it, by the vertue wherof, quoth she, I wyll that the
925 *The Lady*   Ladie *Julia* doe briefely (for that the day is farre past)
Julia com- discribe unto us, the office and duetie of the married
maunded to woman, in lyke sort as mayster *Pedro* hath done for the
describe the mans behalfe, and therein to shew in what sort she must
maried applie hir selfe, to maintaine this *Flower of Friendship* be-
930 *woman.* tweene hir husband and hir.

        When the Ladie *Julia* heard this, she began a little to
chaunge hir colour, and standing in doubt what she
shoulde doe, much dissehabling hir self, but in the ende
after hir pawse awhile, I rather choose, quoth she, to
935   hazard the judgement of ignorance, by my unskilfull tale,
than to be condemned of disobedience by ungentle resistance. For disobedience is a fault in all persons, but the
The Lady   greatest vice in a woman. And now, in hope of pardon, if
Julia be- my unlearned speeche be not aunswerable to your expec-
940 *ginneth the* tations, of this married wyfe this is my opinion. In divers
married pointes I agree with maister *Pedro,* which are as well neces-
woman, sarie, in the woman, as requisite in the man. For if in
and agreeth suppressing of the three foresaid weedes, the chiefest en-
with mais- imies to the *Flower of Friendship,* the man must be careful,
945 *ter Pedro in* much more ought the woman to travaile, that they doe
divers not spring in hir, and also the great regarde in choyse wyth
points. others: wherein bycause mayster *Pedro* hath alreadie satisfied you, I maye be unburdened of that travaile. For if the
man ought to be circumspect in the electing of his wyfe,

[127]

950

what shall the sielie women doe, being so often deceyved by you men? Therefore must she with great care consider, and be well assured of the mans honest conversation, of his manners, and affections, and specially what love he beareth. For the venom of love blindeth the eyes, and so

955 *Love blin-*
deth the
eyes, and
bewitcheth
the senses of
960 *women.*

bewitcheth the senses of us poore women, that as we can foresee nothing, so are we perswaded that all the vices of the beloved are rare, and excellent vertues, and the thing most sower, to be verie sweete, and delicate: for the advoyding of which, the woman cannot be to inquisitive. I meane not of the mans welth, and substance, but of his vertues, which be the true riches, and remayneth for ever.

Themisto-
cles.

With which thing mooved, *Themistocles* being demaunded whether he had rather marry his daughter, to a riche man vicious, or a poore man vertuous, worthely aunswered,

965

that he would sooner choose a man without money, than money without a man.

Also I dissent not from mayster *Pedro* in his equalitie of match. And after such hir choyse, let hir indevor to in-

The happi-
970 *nesse of*
mariage
consisteth in
a chast wife

crease a perfection of love, and above all imbrace chastitie. For the happinesse of matrimonie, doth consist in a chaste matrone, so that if suche a woman be conjoyned in true, and unfayned love, to hir beloved spouse, no doubt their lyves shall be stable, easie, sweete, joyfull, and happy. But

975

love taken awaye, in steede of most sweete pleasantnesse is placed a bitter, unsaverie, and an intolerable estate. The first thing therefore, which the married woman must labour to intende, the first thing which she must withall hir force, applie hir whole minde unto, and the first thing which she must hartilye put in execution, is to lyke, and

980 *The woman*
must lyke
and love
well hir
husband.

love well. For reason doth binde us, to love them, wyth whome we must eate, and drinke, whome we must only accompany, of whose joyes, and sorrowes, welth, and woe, we must be partakers, for whome also we forsake parents, friendes, and all, cleaving onely to them, for no

[128]

1125

greatest inheritaunce, and the precioust Jewell that a woman can bring with hir.

There is another great mainteyner of this *Flower,* and that is the goodly grace of obedience. For reason it is that we obey our Husbandes. God commaundeth it, and we are bounde so to doe.

Obedience.

1130

I know not, quoth the Lady *Isabella,* what we are bound to do, but as meete is it, that the husband obey the wife, as the wife the husband, or at the least that there be no superioritie betwene them, as the auncient philosophers have defended. For women have soules as wel as men, they have wit as wel as men, and more apt for procreation of children than men. What reason is it then, that they should be bound, whom nature hath made free? Nay, among the *Achaians,* women had such soveraigntie, that whatsoever they commaunded, their Husbandes obeyed. Yea *Plutarch* sayth, that the man swept the house, drest the meate, and did al other necessaries, where the women governing the house, and keping the money, aunswered all matters, and which worse was, they corrected them at their discretion.

1135

The
1140 *Achaians.*

1145

What did shee, quoth Maister *Gualter,* and might she beate him too? Mary lo. Here is the matter, that some of our Dames in this Countrie take so muche upon them. They think belike that they be in *Achaia.* But sure if I had bene amongst those women:

1150

[You] would have done, quoth the Ladie *Isabella,* as they did. For Dogs barke boldely at their owne maisters doore.

Beleve not daughter, quoth the Lady *Julia,* neither those ignorant Philosophers, nor these fonde customes. For contrary also to this, the *Parthians,* and *Thracians* accounted not of their wifes, more than of slaves, so that after they had borne them a dosen children, or more, they sold the mothers at the common markets, or exchaunged them for yonger.

1155 *Parthians,*
and Thra-
cians.

1020 *of such as*
loved well
their hus-
bandes.

1025
A worthie
example of
the Mimian
Ladies.
1030

1035

1040

1045

Panthea.

1050

Porcia.

matter. I coulde recite divers worthie examples as well of Romaine, as Grecian Ladies, that have so intirely affected their lincked mates, that not only have they indangered themselves in great perills for their sakes, but have also wyllingly spent their bloude to die with them.

Plutarch reporteth, howe that the *Lacedemonians,* waging battayle against the *Mimians,* and by conquest getting the upper hande, tooke a number of them captives, which they imprisoned, intending shortly after to put them to a cruell death. The loving wyfes of those men, when they understood, the wofull hap of their unfortunate husbandes, came to the prisons, where they were, and with sorrowfull teares, and plaintes entreated the Jaylors, that they might have recourse to speake with the prisoners, which thing after long, and tedious sute obtayned, they entred in, and after most loving imbracings, and lamentable bewaylings, these wyfes tooke on them their husbands apparell, sending them out in their womanly attyre, with their faces covered, as the guise of the countrie was, who being taken for women, were let passe, and so escaped, leaving their wyfes in prison to die the death, at the appointed tyme, for their sakes. When the daye of execution was come, and the matter fully knowne, the *Lacedemonians* stood in admiration, and gave these faithfull harts high praise, and pardoning both them, and their husbandes, sent them home with great rewardes, to the incouragement of others, to tread the like steps of honest love.

Panthea, when she hard that hir husband was slaine in battayle, ranne forthwith with a mourning hart to the doolefull place, where he lay, whom after she had bewayled hir fill, and had bathed hir selfe in hys bloude, tooke the same unhappie launce, wherewith he was slayne, and gored hir selfe to the hart. The lyke is reported of *Porcia, Brutus* wyfe.

[130]

1055
*If Alcesta
be dead,
good Ladie
revive hir
1060 not againe.*

Martiall also writeth, howe that *Alcesta,* the wyfe of king *Admetes,* understanding by the *Oracle* of *Apollo,* that hir husbandes grievous disease, wherewith he was sore payned, coulde not be cured, but by the bloude of a deare friend, kylled hir selfe, saying that *Admetes* had not a dearer friend, than she was, which thing when the king hard, he finished his lyfe, with the lyke death, supposing it more better to couple themselves togither by one ende, than seperated, in teares to bewaile the lack of so true hearted, and loving spouse.

1065 *Paulina.*

In lyke maner *Paulina* the wyfe of *Seneca,* when shee had intelligence that hir husbande by the commaundement of *Nero* had by cutting off his vaines bled hymselfe to death, did also cut hir owne vaynes, to accompany hir good husbande in the lyke ende, had not *Nero* preventing hir purpose, caused hir vaynes to bee stopped up agayne.

1070

1070 *Triara.*

What shall I speake worthily of *Triara,* the sweete spouse of *Lucius Vitellus,* who so intirely loved hir husbande, that she accompanied him in the warres being a woman, adventuring daungers with a manly courage, ryding alwayes next hir beloved mate, to garde him, and to be partaker of his chaunces, good, or bad.

1075

Julia.

Did not *Julia, Pompeius* wife, expresse the signe of a most loving heart, who when she sawe hir husbandes coate brought into the City all imbrued with gory blood, fell into a sodaine sound, scriching most ruthfully, and bitterly crying: O *Pompei, Pompei,* farewell. And being with childe, brought forth in extreeme pangues hir untimelye fruite, which immediately with the mother, yeelded up the gasping breath, whose deaths were bewayled with many teares.

1080

1085

*A notable
example of
a fishers
wife.*

Plinie the yonger, in an Epistle writeth of a fishers wife, that finding no meanes to cure an intollerable disease of hir husbandes, and sore lamenting his paynes, that dayly increased, perswaded him, that one of them should slay the

[131]

1090

other, and in the ende concluded, that they both ascended to the top of a highe rocke, which hung over the sea, and being both cowpled togither, threwe themselves downe, and were drowned.

1095

I could occupie you, quoth the Lady *Julia,* till to morrow this time, with like stories of worthie women. But these may suffice, to shew the love of the wife to hir husband, and to let you understande also, Mayster *Gualter,* that there hath beene alwayes women as loving, as men.

1100

No doubt Madam, quoth he, ye love passingly, when ye do love, and you hate as extreemely, when you doe hate. Wherefore it were a goodly matter, if you coulde bring your maryed women unto a meane.

No meane
1105 *in love.*

Not so, quoth the Lady *Julia,* I wil have no meane in love. And when the [woman] hath thus grounded the perfite rootes of love, and planted this *Friendly Flower,* in a faythfull hart, she must be as curious as Maister *Pedros* good husbande in preserving it against all tempestuous stormes, and from all venimous weedes. The greatest

1110 *Shamfast-*
nesse.

helpe whereto is shamefastnesse, which is of such power, and vertue, that it sufficeth alone to defende it against all weathers. And if so be that there were but one onely

The shame-
lesse crea-
1115 *ture is*
voyde of all
vertues.

vertue in a woman, it might well be shamefastnesse. For as in a creature voyd of shame, there is nothing founde worthie of commendation: so in the woman indued with that vertue, is not any thing worthy of reprehension, and there is the roote of godlines, where springeth the branch of shamefastnes, which is the only defence that nature hath given to women, to kepe their reputation, to preserve

1120

their chastity, to maintein their honor, and to advance their prayse. How farre therefore are ye men overseene, when you onely inquire of their bewtye, substance, and parentage, leaving vertue beside, and that most excellent gift of shamefastnesse, which is the chiefest dowrye, the

[132]

985   shorter time, then during lyfe. And albeit they be cancred
of nature, yll in conversation, worse in condition, base of
lynage, deformed of personage, and unadvised in worde,
and deede: yet being our chosen husbands, we may not,
nor can we forgo them, or chaunge with our neighbours,

990   *The Par-*   as did sometime the *Parthians,* but seeke gently to redresse
thians ex-   them, indevor to please them, and labour to love them, to
chaunged   whome we have wholy given oure bodies, oure goodes,
wives with   our lyves, and libertie. But it often falleth out, that discord
their neigh-   groweth betweene man and wife by the ignoraunce of one
995   *bours.*   the others nature, and for this cause we are bound to
learne, and observe them, and let not the woman to hastily
perswade hir selfe, in ymagining that hir husbande lyketh,
and loveth hir intirely, and sheweth hir a good countenance. For in that moment, when he shall perceyve that

1000   she loveth him not hartily, even then will he abhorre hir
utterly. For as to season unsaverie meates, pleasant sawces
be prepared: so to give a good release to the foode of

True love   marriage, it muste bee tempered with true love. For love
the sause of   giveth to harde things an easinesse, to tedious thinges a
1005   *mariage.*   pleasantnesse, a beginning with facilitie, and ending in
felicitie.

Then spake the Lady *Isabella,* and saide, that it was not
possible for a woman to loove that husbande, the which
delighted more in an other.

1010   It is sure, quoth the Ladie *Julia,* a harde matter for a
vertuous wife to live with a vicious husbande. For an
honest woman to love a dissolute man, or a wise spouse to
accept a foolishe mate. Yet notwithstanding, howe much
more the husbande be evill, and out of order, so much

1015   more is it the womans prayse, if shee love him. And you
men, as untractable as you be, yet is it not possible, if your
wyfes doe lovingly imbrace you, though you cannot in-
force your evill inclinations to repaye love for love

Examples   agayne, yet can ye not well hate them, which is no small

[129]

1160

1170

1175

1185

Fye upon that law, quoth the Lady *Isabella*. But what say you to the custome which *Dionysius Alicarnasseus,* wryteth of the *Numidians,* and *Lydians,* where the women commaunded within doores, and the men without.

Yea marie quoth the Ladye *Aloisa,* that was a just law, where the commaunding was equall.

Not so, quoth the Lady *Julia*. For though it were better than the other two: yet not tollerable amongest us, neyther was the soveraignetie so equallye devided, as you thinke. For if the woman keepe alwaies hir house, as dutye is, the man standeth ever at hir commaundement. For as long as she is within, though he commaund hir without, this lawe byndeth hir not to obey. Wherfore in my opinion al those *Barbarian* customes are to be disanulled, and contemned of Christians.

Ye say well, Madam, quoth M. *Erasmus*. For in deede both divine, and humaine lawes, in our religion giveth the man absolute aucthoritie, over the woman in all places.

And, quoth the Lady *Julia,* as I sayde before, reason doth confirme the same, the man being as he is, most apt for the soveraignetie being in governement, not onely skill, and experience to be required, but also capacity to comprehende, wisdome to understand, strength to execute, solicitude to prosecute, pacience to suffer, meanes to sustayne, and above all a great courage to accomplishe, all which are commonly in a man, but in a woman verye rare: Then what blame deserve those men, that doe permit their wyves to rule all, and suffer themselves to be commaunded for company.

A hard adventure, quoth Maister *Gualter,* hapneth to that man, which is matched with a maisterly shrew. For she being once past shame, not onely blabbeth out all, that she knoweth, but thundereth oute that also, which hir mad head conceyveth, or hir fantasticall braine dreameth of, and yet will she mainteine, that she is never angry, or speaketh without great cause.

[134]

There be, quoth the Ladye *Julia,* some such women, but
The woman I doe utterly condemne them. For this maryed woman,
must be whom I have taken upon me to discribe, must of dutie be
obedient to unto hir husband in all things obedient, and therefore if
1200 *hir husband* he, sometimes moved, do chaunce to chide hir, she must
forbeare. In doing whereof he shal neither eate the more at
his dinner, nor shee have the lesse appetite to hir supper.
The wise [woman] must consider, that hir husband chy-
deth, eyther without reason, or hath good cause. If reason
1205 move him, then of dutie she is bound to obey, if otherwise, it is hir part to dissemble the matter. For in nothing
can a wyfe shewe a greater wisedome, than in dissembling
with an importunate husbande. Hir honestie, hir good
nature, and hir prayse is shewed in nothing more, than in
1210 tolerating of an undiscrete man, and to conclude, as the
woman ought not to commaund the man, but to be alwaies obedient: so ought he not to suffer himself to be
commaunded of his wife.

Seneca in his tragedies of this matter sheweth a notable
1215 *A notable* example. In the warres of *Mithridates,* and the *Romaines,* all
example. the soldiours in Rome were commaunded to be in re-
dinesse, to attend upon *Silla* the Consul. This edict being
[published], the officers came to an old knightes house, to
will him to prepare himselfe. But his wife withstood
1220 them, and sayd, that he was not at home, and that he
should not go. For quoth she, though perchaunce he were
able, yet being an olde Souldiour, and exempted from the
warres, I will not gyve him leave. Whereat the officers
being astonied, enformed the Senate thereof, who foorth-
1225 with banished the olde knight, for suffering himselfe to be
commaunded by his wyfe, and hir they kept in prison
during his exile for presumption.

The maryed woman, must be also verye carefull, and
The good circumspect of hir good name. For a good name is the
1230 *name of a* flower of estimation, and the pearle of credit, which is so
woman is delicate a thing in a woman, that she must not onely be

verie deli-
cate.

good, but likewise must apeere so. For you men are naturally so malicious, that you will judge aswell of that you
suspect, as of that which you se.

1235 *The good*
married
woman
must be res-
ident in hir
1240 *owne*
house.

The chiefest way for a woman to preserve and maintaine this good fame, is to be resident in hir owne house.
For an honest woman in sobernes, keping well hir house,
gayneth thereby great reputation, and if she be evill, it
driveth away many evil occasions, and stoppeth the
mouthes of the people. In keping at home, all thinges shall
be better governed, hir husbandes hart better cheered, all
evil suspicions depelled, angers advoided, expences di-
minished, and the great excesse of apparell not required,
wherein we are commonly so curious, that otherwise

1245

Women are
great
wasters in
apparell.

1250

being naturally great savers, onely therein are we as great
wasters, which thing is advoyded by the wyves honest
keping at home. I cannot but marvaile, how a woman of
estimation can delite in gadding abrode, to be a gossipper,
having at home hir husband to conferre with, hir children
to instruct, hir family to looke unto, hir kindred to please,
and the evil tongues to appease.

Seneca saith that his aunt for sixtene yeares space, whiles
hir husbande was in *Egipt,* never went out of hir owne
house. *Faunus* king of the *Aborigines,* had a wife named

1255 *Fauna.*

Fauna, who after she was maried, would never looke upon
any man saving hir husband, in doing whereof, she gate
such reputation, that after hir death she was honoured for
a Goddesse. *Licurgus* commaunded that no woman, at
anye tyme should go out of hir house, saving at certeine

1260

festivall dayes appoynted. For the maried woman, saith
he, hath nothing else to doe, but eyther in the temple to
pray to the Gods, or at home to instruct hir children.

My meaning is not in reciting these examples, to have
the maried wife continually lockt up, as a cloystred

1265

Nonne, or Ancres, but to consider hereby, what respect
she must have in going abroade, and what a vertue it is to

Lucretia.

1270

The woman
1275 *must avoyd*
suspicious
companies.

The Nu-
1280 *midians.*

1285

1290

The mar-
1295 *ried woman*
must be
skilfull in
huswyfery.
The woman
1300 *must not be*
ydell.

kepe well hir house. *Lucretia* the famous Romaine Ladye, obteyned not so great prayse in excelling others in bewtie, and parentage, as shee did in being founde at home a spinning, and carding with hir maydens, whereas the other Romaine Matrones, were roming abrode in feasting, and banqueting, when their husbands came from the warres to visite them.

As the wife must be thus ware in going abroade: so must she be as carefull what is done at home, on hir part not to sit ydlely, nor to permit any one suspitiously to come unto hir, speciallye hir husband being not at home. *Plutarch* telleth of a custome among the *Numidians,* that their husbandes being abroade, the wives kept always their doores shut, and there was a lawe inviolable, that who so ever knockt at such a doore, so shut, should therefore lose his hand.

To be briefe, not onely in chastitie of bodie, but in honestie of behaviour, and talke, doth the womans honour, and good name consist, and is also mainteyned. These bee on the womans behalfe, the greatest nourishers, of this matrimoniall *Flower,* wherewith being adorned, she shall please God, content hir husbande, and get honour of all persons, without which, all trim attyre, all outwarde paintings, and garnishings are nothing. For what avayleth it a man to have his wife of excellent bewtie, great possessions, good parentage, and wel friended, if therwithal she be shameles, proude, curst, and disolute.

Also for the perfiting of this maried woman, certeyne outward qualities are to be required, as to looke well to hir huswifery, and not onely to see that all be done, but that all be well done, to the contentacion of hir husbande, even in thinges of least importaunce, and to occupie hir selfe accordingly, not to sit always ydle, but to spend hir time in some profitable exercise, as with hir needle, and rocke, or suche otherlike, which in times past, have beene in great

[137]

reputation amongest the greatest Ladies, so that *Salomon*

Salomon. commending a good woman, saith that she sought wooll, and flax, and wrought by the counsayle of hir handes.

1305 *Cookerie*. It is also a great want in a woman, if she be unskilfull in dressing of meate. For it is the chiefest point of a houswife to cherish hir husband, who, being sicke, will have the best appetite to the meate of his wyves dressing, and if shee then cherishe him well, hee will love hir the better

1310 ever after.

Strato-
macha. *Stratomacha* the wife of king *Deiotarus,* whensoever he fell sicke, was his cooke, his phisition, and his chirurgion, which worthie qualities so esteemed of suche a noble Queene, why should not the married woman labour to

1315 have them, seing that therby, shee shal enlarge the *Flower of Friendship* betwene hir and hir husband, whose face

The face of
the hus-
band, the
1320 *looking*
glasse of the
wyfe. must be hir daylie looking glasse, wherein she ought to be alwaies prying, to see when he is merie, when sad, when content, and when discontent, wherto she must alwayes frame hir owne countenance.

Why, quoth the Ladie *Isabell,* what if he bee mad, or dronke, must we then shew the like countenance[?]

If you perceive him in such case, quoth the Ladie *Julia,* speake hym faire, and flatter him, till you get him to bed[,]

1325 and there reprehende hym lovingly, with kissing and imbrasing, that he maye perceyve it to come of pure love, more than of malice, for better were it to convert him lovingly in gentlenesse, than to controle him frowardly in shrewdnesse.

1330 It is most true, quoth M. *Pedro.* For in this point, we are not much unlyke to wilde and savage beasts, as the lyon,

Men must
be reformed
by gentle-
1335 *nesse*. or the unicorne, which by force can not be tamed, but by humilitie, and gentle meanes, so that who will reclayme us, must advoide all contrarying, and vexation of minde, wherof I could tell you a pretie story, that of late yeares happened to a gentlewoman, that by suche gentle wyles reclaymed hir husband, being farre gone, but I shoulde injurie the Ladie *Julia,* to entermedle so farre in hir charge.

Not so, quoth she, but you shall greatly pleasure mee therein, wherfore I pray you let us heare it.

There was, quoth he, a gentleman of good calling, that greatly delighted in hunting, who on a day, neere to a little village encountered wyth a poore wydowes daughter, a simple wench, but somwhat snowte fayre, whose gaye eyes, had so intrapped thys jolye hunter, that under the colour thereof, he oftentimes resorted unto hir, and laye divers nightes out of his owne house. When his wyfe, being both fayre, wise, and vertuous, understoode thereof, as well by his demeanour, as by other conjectures, lyke a wise woman she dissembled the matter, and kept it secrete to hir selfe, not altering eyther countenance, or conditions towardes hym, but on a time, when she was assured, that he was gone another waye, hied hir to the house, where she learned of the yong woman the whole circumstaunce, fayning hir selfe to be his sister, and when she had viewed the chambers, and bedding, wherein he laye, which was verie homely, she returned home againe, and trust up a good bed, well furnished, and hangings, with other necessaries, which as secretly, as she coulde, convaide thither, desiring both the olde woman, and hir daughter to be good to hir brother, and see that he wanted nothing. The next day, came this gentleman home, and according to his custome, went a hunting to his old haunt, where he seing this new furniture, marveiled much thereat, and inquired what the matter ment. The old mother aunswered, that a sister of his had bene there, and wylling them to cherishe him well, gave them besides certaine money. The gentleman understanding then how the world went, and knowing it to bee hys wyfes doing,

Mayster Pedro telleth a pretie tale howe a woman reclaymed hir husband.

1340

1345

1350

1355

1360

1365

[139]

1370 returned fourthwith home, and demaunded of hir the truth, and what shee ment thereby, who denyed it not. The cause why, quoth she, I sent such furniture thither, was, bicause I understanding howe daintilye you were accustomed to lie at home, doubted you might by suche

1375 harde entertainement have gotten some harme.

He should, quoth the Ladie *Aloisa,* have had a bed of nettles, or thornes, had it bene to mee. For sure I would not have bene the cherisher of my husband in his un-thriftinesse.

1380 And so should you have made him worse, quoth may-ster *Pedro.* But it happened muche better to this gentle-woman. For he being overcome by hir vertue, lived con-tent with hir ever after.

This storie, quoth the Ladye *Julia,* hath well holpen me

1385 forwarde, for the which I thanke mayster *Pedro,* and now to continue my purpose, I say, that verie circumspect, and warie must the woman be in reprehending of hir husband in suche great matters. For in things of small importance, the best wil be for hir to dissemble, noting diligently the

1390 tyme, the place, and the maner in doing. The best tyme is, when anger, and malincholy raigneth not, and in any case, let no person be in place, to heare hir. For it is a wise mans griefe, to beare the open reproofe of his wife. The best place, is, as I sayde, when they are both in bed, a place

1395 appointed for reconcilementes, and renuing of love, and friendship, let your words not be spitefull, but loving, kinde, gentle, merie, and pleasaunt. For though the woman everie where, ought to be merie with hir mate: yet muste shee chiefely in bed, thereby to shewe what love she

1400 beareth him, where she maye lawfully poure out into his bosome all the thoughts, and secrets of hir loving hart.

But now to conclude, and knit up the married womans office in mainteyning and conserving this *Flower of Friend-ship* in holye matrimonie, she must being of hir selfe

1405 *The maried* weake, and unable besides hir owne diligence, put hir
woman whole trust in the first, and principall author thereof,
must put hir whome if she serve faythfullye, will no doubt, make thys
trust in *Flower* to spring up in hir aboundantly. For daylie we
God. maye see a foule deformed woman, that truely feareth,
1410 and serveth God, so well beloved of hir husband, as if she
were the fayrest of bewtie in a countrie, and women voyde
of Gods favour, and grace, what qualities soever they have
besides, seldome, or never enjoye they the happie estate of
matrimony, nor shall they ever attaine to the sweete, and
1415 perfite smell of thys moste delectable *Flower* of spousall
amity, and friendship.

I think verely, quoth maister *Pedro,* if either *Medea,* or
Circe coulde have obtayned this *Flower,* as cunning in-
chaunters as they were, to have tempered theyr charmes
1420 withall, *Circe* had not so soone lost hir *Ulysses,* nor *Medea*
forgone hir welbeloved *Jason.*

Herewith the whole assembly rising up, gave the Ladye
Julia hir deserved prayse, and thankes, and the Ladie *Al-*
oisa laying aside hir soveraigntie, went all out into the
1425 Garden, where wee roming about the pleasant allyes, dis-
coursed a newe of that which had beene sayde, both by the
Lady *Julia,* and of maister *Pedro,* which was very well
boren away. But the Ladie *Isabella,* who in this seconde
debating fell to my lot, at our departing required me for
1430 hir sake, to penne the whole discourse of this flagrant
Flower. For quoth she, your quiet silence both these dayes,
assureth mee, that you have well considered thereof, and
therewith the rest of the ladies joyned with hir, at whose
importunate request, with the helpe of my friend Maister
1435 *Pedro,* and others, I have adventured to publishe this Discourse.

FINIS.

[141]

Imprinted at London
by Henry Denham,
dwelling in Pater-
noſter Rovve, at
the ſigne of the
Starre.

Anno Domini
1 5 6 8.

Cum Priuilegio.

7. Colophon from the first edition, with McKerrow's printer's device
no. 150. Reproduced by permission of the British Library.

Textual Notes

The only variants in copies of the same edition occur between those of A, where one forme shows three corrections from Yale to the British Library copy. These appear in the notes at 572, 647, and 655. There are no corrected formes among copies of D and F.

A   H. Denham, 1568. British Library; Yale.
B   H. Denham, 1568. Huntington Library.
C   H. Denham, 1568. Bodleian Library: Malone copy.
D   H. Denham, 1571. Bodleian Library: Seldon, Douce, and Tanner copies.
E   H. Denham, 1573. St. John's College, Cambridge.
F   H. Denham, 1577. Bodleian Library: Wood copy; Pierpont Morgan
          Library; Yale.
G   A. Jeffs, 1587. Folger Shakespeare Library.

29	flagrant] fragrant B, C, D, E, F, G
35	*Alexandra*] *Alexander* B, C, D
50	hir] hys B, F; his C, D, E, G
52	flagrant] fragrant B, C, D, E, F, G
68	jollye] joyfull B, C, D, E, F, G
86	games] game B, C, D, E, F, G
88	bowling, shooting] shooting, bowling E, F, G
148	this] his C, D, E, F, G
158	than] that D
170	Ladyship] *expansion for* L *in all texts*

175	his] this C, D, E, F, G
margin	
183	his bone] my bones B, C, D, E, F, G
183	his fleshe] his flesh B; my flesh C, D, E, F, G
184	this holy] this holye B, C, D; hys holye F; his holy E, G
205	Realmes] Reames B
224	accesse] excesse D
225	begat] began D; begatte E
237–38	*Sabellicus. An*] *Sabellicus,* an *all texts*
340	them] men, D, E, F, G
342	inequalitie] equalitie D, E, F, G
348	sixtene] B, E; sixteene C, D, F, G; eyghtene A
365	like well] B, C, E, F, G; lyke well D; likewell A
366	insoluble] in insoluble D
410	Let hir] Let the D, E, F, G
454	content] consent D, E, F, G
459	that he] that which he B, C, D, E; that which hee F, G
464	if he] if ye B; if hee F
490	*Tunis*] *Lunis all texts, but Luxan refers to the* Rey de Tunez *when he tells the same story at sig.* cx^v
493	rewarde.] *Paragraph follows in all texts*
494	suffise] satisfie D, E, F, G
501	so be their] so be there B; so there be C, D, E; so there bee F, G
506	largely] greatly D, E, F, G
519	doing] doing it C, D, E, F, G
524	fidelitie] infidelitie C, D
527	dispise] dispraise D, E, F, G
534	other] others B, C, D, E, F, G
566	to shew] the shewe B; shewe C, D, E, F, G
572	Vine] wine A (Yale)
581	sinowes] sinewes C, D, E, F, G
591	drinke] drinke a C, D, E, F, G
595–6	dronkennesse] drokennesse A, drunkennesse B, C, D, E, F, G
615	sufferable of] sufferable in C, D, E, F, G
621	them.] *Paragraph follows in* B, C, D, E, F, G
643	*Socrates*] *Socrares* A
647	than] then A (Yale), B
655	than] then A (Yale)
666	hundreth folde] hundreth A, B
673	disgest] digest E, F, G
694	she would] we should C; she woulde E, F

732–33	make or meddle] meddle or make C, D, F, G; medle or make E
761	thing] things C, D, E, F, G
812–13	will not peradventure] peradventure will not C, D, E, G; peradventure wyll not F
816	I] to B, C, D, E, F, G
845	use] ure *all texts*
850	then] than C, D, E, F, G
861	flagrant] fragrant C, D, E, F, G
887	waye] way C, E, F, G; daye D
936	than] then E, F, G
964	or a] or to a D, E, F, G
965	than] that D, F
984	cleaving] A, G; leaving B, D; leaning C, E; cleavyng F
	All texts use cleave *at l.* 199.
1022	have they] they have F, G
1033	with] to E, F, G
1048	hard] harde F; heard G
1061	hard] heard C, D, F, G
1069	preventing] prevented E, F, G
1105	woman] B, C, D, E, F, G; women A
1125	precioust] precious B, C, D, E, F, G
1137	than] then F, G
1151	You] you *all texts*
1203	woman] B, C, D, E, F, G; women A
1209	than] then F, G
1209–10	in tolerating] in tollerating D, E; in intollerating F, G
1218	published] B, C, D, E, G; pulished A; publyshed F
1220	he was] it was F
1268	obteyned] obtayned C; obtayning D, E, F; obtaining G
1322	?] . *all texts*
1324	bed,] D, E, F, G; bed. A, B, C
1358	and hangings] with hangings F, G
1377	to] for G
1394	in bed] a bed E; a bedde F, G
1405	besides hir] besides of hir C, D, E; besydes of hyr F, G
1430	flagrant] flagrāt *all texts*

Explanatory Notes

The citation "Johnson" in these notes marks an indebtedness to Ralph Glassgow Johnson's 1960 edition of *The Flower of Friendship*. His annotations are not directly adapted or quoted here, but they offered the present editor helpful directions for research.

29 *flagrant* Ardent, burning, intensely eager or earnest. See note on the text, p. 96, and introduction, pp. 67–68. Cf. Vives's *Office and Duetie of an Husband:* "And our heartes being thus touched wyth matrimonial love, and with the holy and celestial fier we shal by litle and lytle, be so kindled therwith, that it shall conceyve and bring forth great flames" (sig. Cc 5).

30–32 *Alexander of Macedon . . . the Philosopher Pirrho.* "Pyrrho, the founder of the Skeptical or Pyrrhonian school of philosophy, was a native of Elis in Peloponnesus. . . . [He] wrote no works, except a poem addressed to Alexander, which was rewarded by the latter in a royal manner" (Smith, *Classical Dictionary,* p. 777; Johnson, p. 150. Also known as Pyrrhon).

32–33 *Antonius the Emperor* Antonius Pius, Roman emperor, A.D. 137–161, and the adoptive father of Marcus Aurelius (*Oxford Classical Dictionary,* pp. 75–76).

35 *ô noble Alexandra* The Commons' petition of 1563 requesting that Elizabeth marry and resolve problems of the succession described the strife that would ensue if she died without an heir. It also recalled the empire of Alexander the Great and England's Wars of the Roses as precedents to be avoided (Neale, *Queen Elizabeth I,* p. 122).

48 *Flora* The Roman goddess of flowers.

52 *Phoebus*   Apollo, god of light and of the sun.

54–55 *Maister Pedro di luxan*   Tilney's fictional companion is the author of the primary source for his text, *Coloquios matrimoniales* (see introduction, pp. 33–35).

64 *Julia*   From Eulalia, the good woman in Erasmus's colloquy *Conjugium* (see introduction, pp. 29–32).

70 *Isabella*   Tilney's fictional counterpart to Queen Elizabeth. The parallels between this character and the queen are discussed in the introduction.

71 *Aloisa*   I.e., Heloise, the medieval woman, later an abbess, who argued in letters to her lover, Abelard, that love was incompatible with marriage (see introduction, pp. 40–42).

73 *Lodovic Vives*   Juan Luis Vives (1492–1540), whose name in its classical form was Lodovicus. He wrote, among other works, *The Instruction of a Christen Woman* and *The Office and Duetie of an Husband,* which are discussed pp. 26–27.

73–74 *Erasmus*   Desiderius Erasmus (1466?–1536), the Dutch humanist whose colloquy *Conjugium* is behind Tilney's text and its Spanish source (see pp. 29–32).

83 *Chestes*   Probably chess, which is mentioned in book two of More's *Utopia* as similar to the Utopians' games in which one number plunders another or the vices battle against the virtues (pp. 34–35).

91 *Boccace*   Boccaccio's *Filocopo,* a discourse of thirteen questions on love, comes from the fourth book of his romance about the lovers Florio and Biancifiore, called *Filocolo* (discussed at pp. 70–73 and following).

91 *Countie Baltizer*   I.e., Baldassare Castiglione, whose *Cortegiano* was translated by Sir Thomas Hoby and published as *The Book of the Courtier* in 1561 (see pp. 70–73 and following).

92–97 *proper devises . . . of the wit.*   T. F. Crane discusses other literary references to the practice of dialogues and "questions" of love among the English in *Italian Social Customs of the Sixteenth Century* (pp. 545–54).

115 *Eglantine*   Sweetbrier or honeysuckle. "Everyone in the court circle and beyond it knew of the Queen's use of eglantine as especially her flower. She *was* the eglantine." Although Roy Strong, in *The Cult of Elizabeth,* pp. 70–71, says this connection was established by the 1590s, he adds that it "probably goes back still further," instancing a medal struck in the mid-seventies.

119 *terrestriall paradyse*   For the association between marriage and paradise, see note to ll. 184–86. *The Romance of the Rose* (de Lorris and de Meun, p. 39) adapts this relation but makes the garden a site of secular and sensual love: the narrator there remarks, "Believe me, I thought that I was truly in the earthly paradise."

122–32 *he gathered from the top . . . and therewith the soveraigntie over them for the daye.*   Cf. *Filocopo:* "Ascalion [the appointed king] then rose hym up, and gathered certayne twygges of a greene Laurell, the shade whereof dyd overspread the freshe Fountaine, and thereof made a rich Coronet, the which he brought in

[147]

presence of them all." Then he chooses Fiametta as queen and crowns her with the coronet (sig. B1).

140–41 *yea the trees (sayeth Plinie) have a naturall instinct of friendship.* Erasmus remarks in *An Epistle to perswade a young jentleman to Mariage (Encomium matrimonii):* "I will not speake nowe of Trees, wherin (as Plinie mooste certainelye writeth) there is found Mariage with some manifeste difference of bothe kyndes, that excepte the housbande Tree do leane with his boughes even as thoughe he shoulde desire copulation upon the womenne Trees growynge rounde about him: they woulde elles altogether waxe barraine" (Wilson, 109:19–110:2; Johnson, pp. 152–53).

143–45 *because no friendshipe, or amitie, is or ought to be more deere, and surer, than the love of man and wyfe.* Cf. Vives, *Office and Duetie:* "howe much more diligently ought [the choice of friends] to be done in the choyse of a wife, the principal of al amitie and frendshippe, whose name among al other in benevolence and love is most dearest" (sig. D1). And "Matrunonye [*sic*] is the supreme and most excellent part of all amitie" (sig. K8). The Elizabethan homily on matrimony declared it a "perpetuall friendship, to bring foorth fruite, and to avoide fornication" (*Certaine Sermons or Homilies*, p. 239).

164 *some Spanishe trickes* A reference to Pedro di Luxan's Spanish origin.

165–67 *As I doe (quoth Maister Pedro) utterly denie to be the author of these pastimes, which have long ago bene else where practised.* The denial is appropriate to Luxan since in *Coloquios matrimoniales* he enlarges upon characters and subjects already taken up by Erasmus. It also suits Tilney's adaptation of Italian pastimes as depicted by Boccaccio and Castiglione.

179 *(setting virginitie aside, as the purest estate).* While Tilney's exception is consistent with the Catholic position as reasserted at Trent in 1563, it is also affirmed by Richard Hooker, whose 1597 discussion of marriage in book five of *The Laws of Ecclesiastical Polity* characterizes "single life [as] a thing more angelicall and divine" (p. 401). Other Protestant commentators valued marriage as equal to virginity, and the puritan William Perkins even asserts its superiority by claiming in *Christian Oeconomie:* "Mariage of it selfe is a thing indifferent, and the kingdome of God stands no more in it, then in meates and drinkes; and yet it is a state in it selfe, farre more excellent, then the condition of single life" (p. 671).

182–83 *as an helper . . . of his fleshe.* Eve's position as Adam's companion is often inferred from her creation from his rib. In *The Christen State of Matrimonye* Bullinger explains the relation in a formula that was endlessly repeated and probably did not originate with him: "The woman was taken from and out of the syde of man and not from the erth lest any man shulde thinke that he had gotten his wyfe out of the myre: but to considre that the wife is the husbandes flesh and bone and therfore to love her: yet was she not made of the head. For the husband is the heade and master of the wyfe. Nether was she made of the fete (as though thou mightest spurne her a waye from the and nothinge regarde her) but even out of thy syde as one that is set next unto man to be his helpe and companyon" (sig. A4^v).

184–86 *the almightie instituted this holy ordinaunce . . . in his chiefest perfection.* The assertion that marriage was ordained in paradise before the Fall occurs as early as Augustine's *City of God* 14.22. Erasmus claims in *An Epistle* (*Encomium matrimonii*) that the sacrament of marriage should be the most revered because it was instituted of God in paradise "for the felowshippe of felicitie . . . when man was in most perfite state" (Wilson, 100: 16–19. See also Vives's *Instruction,* sig. U1; Bullinger, sig. A4; 1559 *Book of Common Prayer,* p. 290; for contemporary critical discussions, see studies by Dubrow and Turner).

191–92 *Christ with hys mother in Canaan . . . make honorable.* John 2:1–2.

197–99 *Christ our Lorde commaundeth . . . cleave to his welbeloved Spouse.* Genesis 2:24; Matthew 19:5–6; Mark 10:7.

200–201 *love towards parentes . . . longnesse of lyfe.* Exodus 20:12; Ephesians 6:1–3.

204–6 *the preservation of Realmes . . . immortalitie.* Cf. Erasmus in *An Epistle* (*Encomium matrimonii*): "Take awaie mariage, and howe many shall remain after a hundreth yeres, of so many realmes, countrees, kyngdomes, citees, and all other assemblies that be of men, throughout the whole world?" (Wilson, 133:22–134:1; Johnson, pp. 157–58).

212–82 *the rites of dyvers Nations . . . within his Lordship.* This review of marital customs is drawn from three portions of *Coloquios matrimoniales*. The account of the Romans through the French ending at l. 253 and the sentence at ll. 279–82 are from Luxan's first dialogue, fols. 34^v–38^v; the remarks on Mauritania and the Canary Islands come from the fourth dialogue, fols. 135^v–137; and the Chaldeans are discussed later in that dialogue at fol. 151^v.

216–25 *Amongst the auncient Romaines . . . their children.* Cicero makes this distinction in his *Topica* 3.14: "If Fabia's husband has bequeathed her a sum of money on condition that she be *mater familias,* and she has not come under his *manus,* nothing is due her. For 'wife' is a genus, and of this genus there are two species; one *matres familias,* that is, those who have come under *manus;* the second, those who are regarded only as wives (*uxores*). Since Fabia belonged to the second class, it is clear that no legacy was made to her" (pp. 391–93). H. M. Hubbell's note to the passage reads: "In the primitive Roman form of marriage the woman passed from the power of her father into that of her husband and became a member of his agnatic family; such a wife was called *mater familias* and said to be *in manu.* Besides this there grew up very early another form of marriage by which the woman remained *in patria potestate* and did not change her family" (p. 392). Tilney's "Houswyfes" correspond to the *mater familias* who has *manus.* The distinction as Cicero and Tilney make it confers power and wealth upon the wife who does not have sexual relations with her husband. This arrangement is an inversion of Lynda Boose's account of the psychosocial dynamics of the family in Freudian and Lacanian theory: in what Boose describes as the "all-determining game of who's-got-the-phallus," these Roman "Housewyves" or "Daughters" clearly have it and *manus* through the absence of any sexual interaction with their husbands ("The Father's House and the Daughter in It," p. 21).

220–21   *maried by conjoyning of handes, almost like unto us.* "The form of . . . spousals might be anything from a simple promise to the complete ceremonial for public spousals. . . . At least the bride and groom might exchange a handclasp and a kiss, both of which had from ancient times been associated with the marriage contract" (Powell, *English Domestic Relations*, p. 17).

226–35   *The Babilonians . . . in foulenesse.* This custom among the Babylonians is described at greater length by Herodotus in his *History* (vol. 6 of Great Books of the Western World, p. 44; Johnson, p. 159).

237   *Sabellicus* Marcantonio Coccio (1436–1506), the first important Venetian historian of the humanist school, who compiled an official history of Venice (Barnes, *A History of Historical Writing*, pp. 102–3; Johnson, p. 160).

244–48   *maried for naught . . . nowe a dayes.* Gaulter puns on "naught" as "of no worth or value" (*OED* B. adj., 1) and "naught" as "morally bad, wicked, naughty" (adj., 2), implying that women were married not for money but for sex.

247   *Gualter of Cawne* This name associates the misogynist with Walter Map, the author of *The Courtier's Trifles;* Gautier, the disciple instructed in Andreas Capellanus's *De Amore;* and the husband named Walter in Chaucer's *Clerk's Tale.* Renaissance plays based upon the latter story include husbands named Gautier in Phillip's *Play of Patient Grissil* (1565?) and Gwalter in Dekker, Chettle, and Haughton's *Patient Grissil* (1600). Given the frequent comparisons of Catherine of Aragon with Griselda and Henry VIII with Walter (to be examined by Charlotte C. Morse in her forthcoming variorum edition of *The Clerk's Tale*), *The Flower's* Gualter may also evoke the residual figure of Queen Elizabeth's own father. "Cawne" is probably a phonetic spelling for Cannes in southern France (Johnson, p. 161), a region so associated with courtly love that it could produce a reactionary like Gualter (see also introduction, pp. 39–40).

251   *banket* Banquet.

253–61   *In Mauritania . . . lesse than five.* This version of marriage in Mauritania and in the Canary Islands shows how different sex ratios between women and men can affect marital customs and relations between the sexes. For a modern account of the implications of such ratios which claims that women are valued during periods of high sex ratios, when there are fewer women than men, and devalued during periods of low sex ratios, see Marcia Guttentag and Paul F. Secord, *Too Many Women?*, esp. chap. 3, "Love and Misogyny in Medieval Europe," pp. 53–77. Such a correlation reveals how fully women are commodified by marital exchange, for their value fluctuates according to the economic principles of supply and demand appropriate to merchandise. I am grateful to Kathy Ferguson for bringing this reference to my attention.

254 *Mauritania* The people of this northwest African country were largely Moors whose religion was (and still is) Islam.

254 *Diodorus Siculus* A contemporary of Julius Caesar and Augustus who wrote a world history in forty books from the earliest times to Caesar's Gallic War (*Oxford Classical Dictionary*, p. 347). Amyot, the French translator of Plutarch's *Lives*, also translated seven books of his history (*Shakespeare's Plutarch*, ed. Brooke, vol. 1, p. x).

259 *Isles of Canaria* The Canary Islands, off the northwestern coast of Africa, which take their name from the large dogs (*canes*) which Pliny found on the largest island. The islands have been in the possession of Spain since 1461 (Sugden, *Topographical Dictionary*, p. 95).

273 *The Chaldeans* Chaldea in the narrow sense was a province of Babylonia, and in the wider sense the term applied to all of Babylonia and even the Babylonian Empire (Smith, *Classical Dictionary*, p. 219). Since the eastern astrologers and fortune-tellers who flocked to Rome in the early days of the Roman Empire were called Chaldeans, the people were primarily associated by Renaissance writers with soothsayers (Sugden, pp. 108–9).

276 *good mans* The male head of a household; a husband.

281–82 *as in Scotlande . . . within his Lordship.* The custom of *droit du seigneur* is mentioned by Engels in *The Origin of the Family, Private Property, and the State*, p. 170, and Gerda Lerner, *The Creation of Patriarchy*, p. 88. Tilney ends his account of marital customs with a strong example of patriarchal power exercised over women in marriage. He goes out of his way to do so, returning to a portion of Luxan's text that he used for earlier customs (see note to ll. 212–82) and inverting the order of Luxan's examples to end with a Scottish instance, which was closer to home.

288 *giftes of nature, and fortune.* "The distinction between gifts of Fortune and gifts of Nature (both powers being more or less personally conceived) was familiar in mediaeval literature. . . . In general the endowments of the body and the soul are attributed to nature, and the advantages of outer circumstance—honor, rank, prosperity—to Fortune. But the distinction was not consistently maintained, and physical beauty, for example, was sometimes counted among the gifts of Fortune" (F. N. Robinson, ed., *The Works of Geoffrey Chaucer*, 2d ed., p. 728, n. 295).

288–89 *For equalnesse herein, maketh friendlynesse.* This formulation begins with Aristotle in the *Nicomachean Ethics* 8.5.1157b: "For friendship is said to be equality." It does not specifically apply to marriage, however, for according to Aristotle that is a form of unequal friendship (see introduction, pp. 15–16). Cicero's *De amicitia* makes similar statements about friendship, e.g.: "But it is of the utmost importance in friendship that superior and inferior should stand on an equality" (19.69.179). But Cicero does not relate equality to marriage. Aquinas is the first to do so explicitly: he argues in *Summa contra gentiles* 124, regarding

[151]

polygamy: "Besides. Equality is a condition of friendship. Hence if a woman may not have several husbands, because this removes the certainty of offspring; were it lawful for a man to have several wives, the friendship of a wife for her husband would not be freely bestowed, but servile as it were. . . . Further. In perfect friendship it is impossible to be friends with many, according to the Philosopher (8 *Ethic.* vi.). Hence if the wife has but one husband, while the husband has several wives, the friendship will not be equal on either side. . . . Therefore it is not right for one man to have several wives" (pp. 118–19). As in Tilney, the concept of equality in marriage in Aquinas is narrowly, although differently, defined, so that it does not equalize power relations in marriage or challenge the hierarchical assumptions so pervasive about them (see introduction, pp. 50–54).

290–95 *Pitachus Mytileneus one of the seaven sages of Greece. . . . take to thee thy peere.* See Vives's *Instruction of a Christen Woman:* "Also let hym remembre the doynge of Pitachus, the wyse man of Mytilena, whiche whan a yonge man that had chose of ii. wyves, the one of great substance and kynne, the other egall unto his selfe of ryches and byrth, asked hym counsaile, whether were better to marye: the wise man bad hym go to children playenge. Nowe had the children a playe wherin they were wonte to synge and repete often these wordes: Take to the thy pere: wherby they ment that most wysedome was for every man to do so" (bk. 1, chap. 16, sig. R4ᵛ).

295–99 *Marry not a superiour, saith Plutarch . . . hir shoulders.* In Sir Thomas Elyot's translation of *De educatione puerorum*, called *The Education or Bringinge Up of Children* [1532?], Plutarch says: "Above all thynges take hede, that they, whiche be utterly enclyned to lechery, and be incorrigible, may have wives and be maried. For that is the most sure bridell of youth. And provyde for them wyves, that neyther be to ryche, neither of to hygh bloud or stocke. For it is a proverbe replenyshed with wysedome: Seke the a wyfe pareile unto the. For they that take wyves moche better than them selves, they forgete that they have made them selfe not husbandes, but bonde men" (sig. F3ᵛ–F4; Johnson, pp. 167–68). A similar passage occurs in Luxan, bk. 1, fol. 18ᵛ. Aristotle also advises against marrying a wife who is wealthier than her husband in *Nicomachean Ethics* 8.10.1161a 1–2. Dod and Cleaver defy tradition in *A Godlie Forme of Household Government* by their willingness to grant superiority to a wife of high birth: "But yet when it hapneth, that a man marrieth a woman of so high a birth, he ought (not forgetting that he is her husband) more to honour and esteeme of her, then of his equall, or of one of meaner parentage: and not only to account her his companion in love, and in his life, (but in divers actions of publike apparance) hold her his superiour" (pp. 148–49).

299–302 *Yea Menander . . . a wonderfull metamorphosis.* Menander's fragment titled "Who gives the Groom away?" explains: "Whenever one who is poor and who elects to marry receives the dower along with the bride, he does not take her, but gives himself away" (pp. 500–501; Johnson, p. 168).

302–6 *But Licurgus the law maker . . . the chiefest dowrie.* The passage appears in Plutarch's "Laconicke Apophthegmes": "Another asked of him [Lycurgus], wherefore he had ordeined that daughters should be married without a dowrie or portion given with them? Because (quoth he) for default of marriage-money none of them might stay long ere they were wedded, nor be hearkened after for their goods; but that every man regarding onely the maners and conditions of a yoong damosell, might make choise of her whom he meaneth to espouse, for her vertue onely; which is the reason also that he banished out of *Sparta* all manner of painting, trimming, and artificiall embelishments to procure a superficiall beauty and complexion" (*The Morals,* p. 464). Also recounted of "Solon" in Plutarch's *Lives,* vol. 1, p. 162: "Furthermore, he tooke awaye all joynters and dowries in other mariages, and willed that the wives should bring their husbands but three gownes only, with some other litle moveables of small value, and without any other thing as it were: utterly forbidding that they should buye their husbands, or that they should make marchaundise of mariages, as of other trades to gaine, but would that man and woman should marye together for issue, for pleasure, and for love, but in no case for money" (Johnson, pp. 168–69). Neither of these formulations commodifies women's virtue in the way that Tilney does through the statement that wives' "vertues . . . ought to be accounted the chiefest dowrie."

307 *valour* "Worth or importance due to personal qualities or to rank" (*OED,* 1a). But note how close this meaning is to a second one: "Worth or worthiness in respect of manly qualities or attributes" (1b), thereby associating what is valuable with what is masculine.

310–15 *Alexander . . . with vertues prevayled.* The account in Plutarch's "Life of Alexander" emphasizes the emperor's restraint toward the maids or wives of the enemy and does not mention Barsina's poverty: "Alexander thinking it more princely for a kinge, as I suppose to conquer him selfe, then to overcome his enemies: did neither touche them nor any other, maide or wife, before he maried them, Barsine onely excepted, who being left Memnons widow (generall of kinge Darius by sea) was taken by the citie of Damas. She being excellently well learned in the Greeke tongue, and of good enterteinment (being the daughter of Artabazus, who came of a kinges daughter) Alexander was bolde with her by Parmenioes procurement, (as Aristobulus writeth) who intised him to embrace the companie of so excellent a woman, and passing faire besides" (*Lives,* vol. 3, p. 346).

316–19 *what is he now a daies . . . lacketh money.* Cf. Thomas Paynell's dedicatory epistle to Vives's *Office and Duetie of an Husband:* "For in thys our time, a time (I saye) mooste lamentable, menne choose not their wives for their honestie and

[153]

vertue, but for their intisinge beautie: not for theyr civile and womanly manners, but for theyr possessions and ryches: not to procreate and brynge forth children to the prayse and lawde of God, but for carnall lust and pleasure: not to be well and vertuously occupied at home, but ydely and wantonly to spende the tyme abroade: not to be godly, but wordlye [*sic*]: not to be humble and meke, but to be prowde and hawte: not to regard theyr husbandes honestie, houshold, and profyte, but theyr owne lustes and solace" (sig. A2ᵛ).

343–46 *For Aristotle . . . at one time.* In *Politics* 7.16.1335a, Aristotle says: "Since the time of generation is commonly limited within the age of seventy years in the case of a man, and of fifty in the case of a woman, the commencement of the union should conform to these periods. . . . Women should marry when they are about eighteen years of age, and men at seven and thirty; then they are in the prime of life, and the decline in the powers of both will coincide" (Horowitz, "Aristotle and Woman," p. 198; Johnson, p. 169). Cf. Vives's *Office and Duetie:* "*Hesiodus, Plato,* and *Aristotle,* wyl that the man be thre and thyrtye yeares of age, and the woman eyghtene or ever they doe mary" (sig. I3).

346–51 *Hesiodus the Greeke poet, and Xenophon . . . evill occasions.* See Hesiod's *Works and Days:* "In due season bring a wife into your house, when you are neither many years short of thirty nor many beyond it: this is your seasonable marriage. As for the woman, she should have four years of ripeness and be married in the fifth. Marry a virgin, so that you may teach her good ways" (ll. 695–99 in *Works,* pp. 57–58). M. L. West's note to the second sentence interprets "ripeness" as a woman's having began menstruation (p. 78). In Xenophon's *Treatise of house holde,* Isomachus remarks that his wife "can order well inoughe" the household, and Socrates inquires: "Dyd ye your selfe bring your wyfe to this: or els hadde her father and her mother brought her up, sufficiently to order an house afore she came to you?" Isomachus responds: "Howe coude she have ben so, whan she was but fiftene yere olde, whan I maryed her? and afore she hadde ben so negligently brought up, that she hadde but very lyttel sene, very littell harde, and very lytel spoken of the world" (p. 21; Johnson, p. 170).

351–53 *Licurgus lawe . . . at eyghtene.* Recounted of Lycurgus in Plutarch's "Laconicke Apophthegmes": "Having also prefixed and set downe a certeine time, within the which aswell maidens as yoong men might marrie; one would needs know of him why he limited forth such a definite terme? unto whom he answered: Because their children might be strong and lustie, as being begotten and conceived of such persons as be already come to their full growth" (*The Morals,* p. 464).

355 *old crustes* Old men.

356 *playstering* Applying curative plasters to the wounds of their aged husbands.

362–63 *But my opinion is . . . foure or five yeres.* In More's *Utopia:* "A woman is not married before eighteen, nor a man before twenty-two" (p. 58; Johnson, p. 171).

[154]

367 *Love indifferent serveth not, love fayned prospereth not.* A verbal echo of similar sentiments in 1 Corinthians 13:4–7.

372–73 *For hastie love is soone gone. And some have loved in post hast, that afterwards have repented them at leysure.* Tilley, *Dictionary of Proverbs,* H196: Marry in Haste and repent at leisure.

374 *the fayrest, the richest, and noblest.* These qualities are discussed in this order by Vives in *The Instruction of a Christen Woman* in the quotation that appears in note to ll. 386–98 (Johnson, pp. 172–73).

377–82 *shal a man choose his wyfe with his eares. . . . qualities, good, and bad.* An adaptation from Erasmus's *Mery Dialogue:* "Eula. . . . for a woman shold not only take her husbande by the eyes but by the eares. Now it is more tyme to redresse fautes then to fynd fautes. xanti. What woman ever toke her gusband [*sic*] by the eares. Eulali. She taketh her husbande by the eyes that loketh on nothyng, but on the beautye and pulcritude of the body. She taketh him by the eares, that harkeneth diligently what the common voice sayth by him" (sig. B7ᵛ). Erasmus was expanding on advice applied to husbands by Plutarch in no. 22 of "Precepts of wedlocke": "And in trueth we ought not to goe about for to contract marriage by the eie or the fingers, as some doe who count with their fingers how much money, or what goods a wife bringeth with her, never casting and making computation of her demeanour and conditions, whether she be so well qualified, as that they may have a good life with her" (*The Morals,* p. 319; no. 24 in *Moralia,* vol. 2, trans. Babbitt).

386–98 *And I remember, that a wise man . . . content thy self.* This story is standard misogynist fare when it concerns wives who are rich or poor, fair or ugly. It appears in Theophrastus's *Golden Book on Marriage* (excerpted in Miller, *Chaucer,* pp. 412–13); then in *The Romance of the Rose,* ll. 8561–8607, pp. 157–58 (excerpted in Miller, p. 456); in the Wife of Bath's Prologue, ll. 247–75; and also in Shakespeare's *Othello,* II.i.127–35, where Iago applies it to women who are fair and foul, wise and foolish. In Jonson's *Epicoene, or The Silent Woman,* II.i.120–40, Truewit extends the categories to consider those who are fair, young, and vigorous; foul and crooked; rich; noble; fruitful; learned; and precise. In *The Instruction of a Christen Woman,* Vives adapts the approach to husbands rather than to wives: "O folysshe friends and maydes also, that set more by them that be fayre or ryche or of noble byrth than them that be good: and caste your selfe in to perpetuall care. For if thou be maryed to a fayre one, he wyll be proude of his person: And if thou marye to a ryche one, his substance maketh hym stately: And if thou be maried to one of great byrth, his kynred exalteth his stomacke" (sigs. R4ᵛ–S). Luxan discusses wives who are beautiful, rich, virtuous, and of good lineage, describing the third or virtuous wife as she "a la qual aviade adorar" (whom one had to adore; bk. 1, fol. 17). Tilney follows Luxan's approach but reduces the ambiguity regarding the third wife, so Gualter's speech

[155]

asserts her worth but uses a construction so generally negative about women that the virtuous one is easily overlooked in the process.

400–402   *and all the Ladies woulde have driven Maister Gualter out of the arbor.*   Cf. *The Courtier:* "Then a great part of the women there, for that the Dutchesse had beckoned to them so to doe, arose upon their feete, and ran all laughing toward the Lord Gasper, as they would have buffeted him, and done as the wood women did to Orpheus, saying continually: Now shall you see whether we passe to be ill spoken off or no" (pp. 181–82). The wood women tore Orpheus to pieces.

403   *Anaxagoras*   The story is attributed to the Greek philosopher Anaxagoras in Luxan's *Coloquios matrimoniales,* fols. 16ᵛ–17. Erasmus's association of the story with a recognized authority seemingly exonerates Gualter, as though misogyny is justified as long as it comes from a philosopher.

423–28   *The husband then must be merie . . . olde conceyved malice.*   Cf. Plutarch's "Precepts of wedlocke," no. 3: "It behooveth therefore new-married folke, to take heed especially in the beginning, that they avoide all occasions of dissention and offence giving; considering this with themselves, and seeing daily that the pieces of woodden vessels which are newly joined and glued together, at the first are soone disjoined, and go asunder againe upon the least occasion in the world, but after that in continuance of time the joint is strongly settled and soundly confirmed, a man shall hardly part and separate one piece from another with fire or yron edged toole" (*The Morals,* p. 316; no. 3 in *Moralia,* vol. 2, trans. Babbitt; Johnson, p. 173).

429   *Bugges*   An object of terror, usually imaginary; a bugbear, hobgoblin, or bogey.

442–44   *he maye also steale away hir private will . . . if love raigne in hir.*   Tilney's passage reappears more emphatically in Dod and Cleaver's *Godlie Forme of Householde Goverment:* "The husband ought not to bee satisfied that he hath robd his wife of her virginitie, but in that he hath possession and use of her will: for it sufficeth not that they be married, but that they be well married, and live christianly together, and very well contented. And therfore the husband that is not beloved of his wife, holdeth his goods in danger, his house in suspition, his credit in ballance, and also sometimes his life in perill, because it is easie to beleeve that she desireth not long life unto her husband, with whom she passeth a time so tedious and irksome" (pp. 168–69). I am grateful to Cristina Malcomson for observing this connection.

455–60   *Darius the great king . . . or estimation.*   From Plutarch's "Life of Alexander": "Then Darius beating of his head, and weeping bitterly, cried out alowd: Oh goddes! what wretched happe have the Persians! that have not onely had the wife and sister of their king taken prisoners even in his life time, but now that she is dead also in travell of childe, she hath bene deprived of princely buriall!" (*Lives,* vol. 3, p. 355; Johnson, p. 175).

Explanatory Notes

461–68   *Valerius Maximus sayth, . . . the male serpent.* From Plutarch's "Life of Tiberius and Caius Gracchi" (*Lives,* vol. 4, p. 133; Johnson, p. 176).

471–72   *your Ladyship is so afeard to marry.* The Lady Julia is a widow.

472–73   *to tell the truth, and shame the Devill.* Tilley, T566: "Speak the Truth and shame the devil."

478–79   *he increaseth our sporte, and therefore we can not well want him.* Gualter is necessary to the dialogue because his dispraise of women prompts their defense, and his criticism of marriage prompts its praise (see introduction, pp. 74–75).

482–93   *Baptista Fulgosa . . . wyth great rewarde.* The story is from *De conjugali charitate: de neapolitani regni quodam accola* 4.6, from Baptista Campofulgosus (Fregoso), *Exemplorum, Hoc est, Dictorum factorumque memorabilium, ex certae fidei ueteribus et recentioribus historiarum probatis autribus* 9, cited in Scott, *Elizabethan Translations,* p. 21, and Koeppel, *Italienischen Novelle,* p. 19.

485   *Rovers* Sea robbers or pirates.

504   *adulterie* Vives identifies adultery as the first and most grievous sin of wedlock in *The Office and Duetie of an Husband,* sig. Z5. Bullinger condemns whoredom in chaps. 13 and 14 of *The Christen State of Matrimonye.*

506   *whose fruits Salomon doth largely describe.* A reference to the passages on harlots in Proverbs 2:16–19; 5:3–12, 20; 6:24–26; 7:5–27; 11:22; 22:14; 23:27–28, 33; 29:3; 30:20 (Johnson, p. 181).

520–25   *Can there be any greater disorder . . . repaye unto hys wyfe.* In Luxan's text, bk. 3, fols. 84–84ᵛ.

521   *lowre* I.e., lour. To frown, scowl, look angry or sullen. Also to be depressed or mournful.

525–26   *though the civill lawe giveth man the superioritie over his wyfe.* Lawrence Stone, in *The Family, Sex, and Marriage,* says that through marriage a husband "acquired absolute control of all his wife's personal property, which he could sell at will" (p. 195). A husband also had full rights to his wife's real estate, although she might try to claim her own rights of disposition through terms in the marriage contract. Gouge records the objections of seventeenth-century women to his claim that they were obliged to have their husbands' consent before disposing of the common goods of the family in a passage in the dedicatory epistle to *Of Domesticall Dueties,* quoted at p. 13.

532   *gaming* Gambling.

537   *commoditie* Advantage, benefit, profit.

549   *for swearing* I.e., forswearing, swearing falsely or profanely.

568–605   *I am content . . . to the excesse.* Tilney's digression on wine comes from an even longer digression on the topic in Luxan, bk. 3, fols. 86ᵛ–90ᵛ, and all of Tilney's examples are mentioned in the Spanish text.

571   *Anacharsis* "A Scythian prince of royal blood who in the sixth century B.C. travelled extensively in Greece and elsewhere and gained a high reputation for

wisdom." Herodotus and Diogenes Laertius "credit him with many pithy sayings" (*Oxford Classical Dictionary*, p. 57). Some of these aphorisms appear in Plutarch's *Morals*.

575 *Noe* Genesis 9:20: "Noah also began to be an housband man and planted a vineyarde."

577 *Ycanus* Tilney's adaptation of Luxan's "Ycano," who is identified in the Spanish text as the father of Penelope, otherwise known as Icarius. Moncada remarks that "Luxan probably mistook Penelope's father for his namesake, the Athenian Icarius and father of Erigone whom Dionysius had taught to cultivate the vine" ("Spanish Source," p. 243, n. 1).

577 *Dionysius* The Greek name of Bacchus, god of wine.

578 *delayed* Diluting or watering the wine. From Luxan's "aguar el vino," bk. 3, fol. 87ᵛ.

578 *Candia* A city of the north coast of Crete, also called Iráklion or Heraklion, which was occupied by the Venetians from the thirteenth to the seventeenth centuries. Most Elizabethans associated the whole island of Crete with Candia or Candy (Sugden, p. 96), but Tilney's reference to the place comes directly from Luxan, bk. 3, fol. 87.

583–85 *saint Paule writing to Timothe . . . a little wine.* See 1 Timothy 5:23: "Drinke no longer water, but use a litle wine for thy stomakes sake, and thine often infirmities."

589–93 *Licurgus the Lacedemonian . . . lesse delayed.* Montaigne reports a similar opinion of Plato in "Of Drunkennesse": "*Plato* forbiddeth children to drink any wine, before they be eighteene yeeres of age, and to be druncke before they come to forty. But to such as have once attained the age of fortie, he is content to pardon them, if they chaunce to delight themselves with it" (*Essayes,* p. 201; Johnson, p. 185). Plato's prohibition may have been influenced by Spartan policies put into effect by Lycurgus.

593–95 *Noe . . . of his owne sonnes.* Genesis 9:21–27 recounts this story but identifies only one son, Ham, as seeing his father drunk and naked (Johnson, p. 189).

595–96 *Lot in his [dronkennesse] . . . his owne daughters.* Genesis 19:30–38 portrays Lot's daughters as initiating incest so that they might "preserve sede of [their] father" (Johnson, pp. 186–87).

596–99 *Alexander . . . poysoned himselfe.* Plutarch's "Life of Alexander" comments on Alexander's reputation for drinking and then questions it. "Furthermore, he was lesse geven to wine, then men would have judged. For he was thought to be a`greater bibber than he was, bycause he sate longe at the bourde, rather to talke then drinke" (*Lives*, vol. 3, p. 347). Yet Plutarch's story about Alexander's death explains that he had gone to the lodgings of Medius, one of his captains, "and dranke there all that night and the next day, so that he got an agew by it. But that came not (as some write) by drinking uppe Hercules cuppe all at a drawght;

neither for the sodaine paine he felt betweene his showlders, as if he had beene thrust into the backe with a speare. For all these were thought to be written by some, for lyes and fables, bicause they would have made the ende of this great tragedie lamentable and pitifull. But Aristobulus writeth, that he had such an extreame fever and thirst withall, that he dranke wine, and after that fel a raving, and at the length dyed the thirtie day of the month of June" (*Lives,* vol. 3, pp. 395–96).

599–602   *Marcus Antonius . . . Octavius Caesar.*   As with Noah, Lot, and Alexander, the text here tries to make wine more important in the seduction and death of Mark Antony than most sources would have it. Plutarch's life of Antony shows him more overcome by the sensual charms of Cleopatra than by wine itself, though his account does present the wounded Antony as calling for wine when he is nearly dead, "either bicause he was a thirst, or else for that he thought thereby to hasten his death" (*Lives,* vol. 4, p. 353).

602–4   *Anacleon the poet . . . of a grape.*   "Anacreon (b.c. 570 B.C.), lyric poet, son of Scythinus, born at Teos. . . . His death, at an advanced age, was said to be due to a grape-pip sticking in his throat" (*Oxford Classical Dictionary,* p. 57).

609–847   *the better to nourishe, and maintaine thys Flower, there are certaine delicate herbes . . . from their inheritance.*   In his second dialogue Luxan lists five herbs that the wife may use to nourish a marriage. Tilney adapts this metaphor of herbs for duties of the husband instead of the wife, repeating nine of the ten duties of the husband that Luxan sets forth in his third dialogue. The duty in Luxan that Tilney drops is the last, or tenth one: "Lo decimo muy cierto con todos los que tratare" (the tenth very firm with everyone with whom he has dealings; bk. 3, fol. 91ᵛ.). Vives's *Office and Duetie* uses a similar metaphor to discuss the function of marriage: "And therefore herbes and rootes are used to be geven unto some as meat and to other some as a medicine so is matrimonye, the whiche at the beginning was invented of god for the procreation of children, and is now unto the luxurious and incontinente person, as a remedy of so great an evil" (sigs. C6ᵛ–C7). Hence marriage is nourishment for procreation and medicine for incontinence.

614–15   *diligent in looking to that which is his.*   Although this phrase appears as the sixth herb in this list, at ll. 744–45 the sixth duty of the husband is to "accompany no diffamed persons." Luxan is the source of this discrepancy, for a similar difference appears between the sixth duty of the husband as Luxan presents it in his initial list at fol. 91ᵛ and later in his discussion of that duty at fol. 101.

634–35   *a silent person, is the exampler of wisedome.*   Tilley, W799: "Few words show men wise."

638–39   *The tongue that runneth before the wyt, commonly breedeth his maisters wo.*   Tilley, T412: "Your tongue runs before your wit."

641–43   *Salomon sayth . . . his tongue is wise.*   Proverbs 10:19: "In manie wordes there can not want iniquitie: but he that refraineth his lippes, is wise."

[159]

645–48 *Xenophon sayeth . . . we ought to speake.* In "Of Hearing" Plutarch remarks: "And it is commonly said, that nature herselfe hath given to each us but one tongue and two eares, because we ought to heare more than we speake" (*The Morals,* p. 53; Johnson, p. 192).

649–50 *conversation* Relations with others; general behavior.

650–52 *fierce, and hurtful beasts . . . their cruell curstnesse.* In Erasmus's *Mery Dialogue* the good woman, Eulalia, compares husbands to elephants, lions, wild bulls, tigers, and horses which must be tamed and handled with "other knackes to breake their wyldnes, wyth all" (sig. A6). The association is prompted by advice in Plutarch's "Precepts of wedlocke," no. 40: "They that have the government of elephants, never put on white raiment when they come about them, no more do they weare red clothes who approch neere unto bulles; for that these beasts before named are afraid of such colours especially, and grow fierce and wood therewith. It is said moreover, that tygers when they heare the sound of drummes or tabours about them, become enraged, and in a furious madnesse all to teare themselves. Seeing it is so therefore, that there be some men who can not abide, but are highly displeased to see their wives in their scarlet and purple robes; and others againe, who can not away with the sound of cymbals or tabours; what harme is it, if their wives wil forebeare both the one and the other, for feare of provoking and offending their husbands, and live with them without unquiet brawles and janglings in all repose and patience?" (*The Morals,* p. 323; no. 45 in *Moralia,* vol. 2, trans. Babbitt). Later in *The Flower* Master Pedro repeats the association of husbands with "wilde and savage beasts, as the lyon, or the unicorne, which by force can not be tamed" (see note to ll. 1330–34).

652 *curstnesse* Malignancy, perverse crossness, shrewishness.

655–59 *The married man . . . nor the man suffer.* Cf. Vives, *Office and Duetie:* "The husbandes reprehention muste be short, for yf it shoulde continue, hatred would ensue, the whiche would coule matrimoniall love, kyndle disdayne, and chaunge the swetenesse of theyr conversation into byterness" (sig. Aa3–Aa3ᵛ).

663–64 *froward of complextion, and tender of condicion* Perverse and refractory in demeanor and weak in constitution. The passage describes an opposition between wives' deportment and interaction with their husbands, on the one hand, and women's essential or internal nature, on the other. So the assumption that women are weak creates a contradiction between semblance and nature that constructs women as contradictory beings who consistently misrepresent themselves and mislead others.

673 *disgest* Expell, discharge.

675–77 *And as in a myste . . . when he is pacient.* Plutarch uses this simile in "How to bridle anger": "For like as any bodies seeme bigger through a mist; even so every thing appeereth greater than it is, through anger" (*The Morals,* p. 127). Montaigne repeats it in "Of Anger and Choller": "It is passion that speaketh and not we. Athwart it, faults seeme much greater unto us, as bodies doe athwart a foggie mist" (*Essayes*, p. 410; Johnson, pp. 192–93).

678–79   *to be secrete, and trustie in that, wherin he is trusted.*   This phrase includes keeping the secrets of one's wife and keeping the secrets of others from her. The example of Cato reinforces the proverbial assumption that women cannot keep their husbands' secrets, an issue that Aloisa addresses in her reply at ll. 696–98.

683–87   *The good Cato . . . some profitable deede.*   From Plutarch's "Life of Marcus Cato": "This was also his sayinge, that the soule of a lover, lived in an others body: and that in all his life time he repented him of three thinges. The first was, if that he ever tolde secret to any woman: the seconde, that ever he went by water, when he might have gone by lande: the thirde, that he had bene Idle a whole day, and had done nothing" (*Lives*, vol. 2, p. 192; Johnson, pp. 193–94).

687–93   *A marveilous example . . . to keepe secret.*   Cicero and Plutarch recount this story of Zeno rather than Anaxagoras. See, e.g., Plutarch's "Against Colotes the Epicurean": "*Zenon* [i.e., Zeno] also a scholar of *Parmenides* undertooke to kill the tyrant *Demylus,* and having no good successe therein, but missing of his purpose, maintained the doctrine of *Parmenides* to be pure and fine golde tried in the fire from all base mettal, shewing by the effect, that a magnanimous man is to feare nothing, but turpitude and dishonour and that they be children and women, or else effeminate and heartlesse men like women, who are affraid of dolor and paine: for having bitten off his tongue with his owne teeth, he spit it in the tyrants face" (*The Morals*, p. 1128; Johnson, pp. 194–95). Perhaps Parmenides should have done the same before he uttered this doctrine.

698   *women can keepe no counsaile.*   Tilley, S196: "Trust no secret with a woman."

702   *wanted*   Lacked. Gualter implies that the only silent woman is one who lacks a tongue. The "Tale of the Dumb Wife" which filled out the leaves of Antony Kytson's 1557 edition of Erasmus's *Mery Dialogue* offers a narrative version of this opinion. The tale ends with the speech: "Sir I am a devyl of hel, but I am one of them that have least power there. Al be yet I have power to make a woman to speke, but and yf a woman begin ones to speake, I nor al the devyls in hel that have the mooste power be not able to make a woman to be styll, nor to cause her to leve her speakyng" (sig. C4).

711   *good yeares*   Mature age.

726–40   *The office of the husbande . . . the houshold.*   As Marcel Bataillon observes in *Érasme et l'Espagne*, p. 692, Luxan's source for these offices is Antony Guevara's 1524 "Letter to Mosen Puche," which was published in English in *The Familiar Epistles of Sir Antony of Guevara* in 1574 (p. 505). Guevara lists twelve offices of the husband and wife; Luxan includes all of them (fols. 99ᵛ–100). Tilney presents only eight, eliminating some offices that are close repetitions of others. In *A Godlie Forme of Householde Government,* Dod and Cleaver repeat ten of the original twelve offices (pp. 170–71). Some of these passages are discussed briefly by Davies, "Continuity and Change," p. 67; Armstrong and Tennenhouse, *Ideology of Conduct,* pp. 8–9; and Amussen, *Ordered Society,* pp. 43–44. Many of the offices require that men be outer-directed and giving, while women are to be inner-directed and withholding.

726–27 *The office of the husbande is to bring in necessaries, of the wife, well to kepe them.* Tilley, M548: "Men get wealth and women keep it."

732–33 *to make or meddle.* Tilley, M852: "I will neither meddle nor make."

744–45 *diffamed* I.e., defamed, dishonored, attacked in reputation.

754–55 *the olde saying, that a man . . . to trust them.* Tilley, W381: "The wife and the sword may be showed but not lent."

759 *ymportunities* Persistent solicitations, annoying or perverse requests.

764–65 *Sampsons strength . . . wisedome of Salomon.* Samson was beguiled by Delilah into revealing that his hair was the source of his strength. Delilah cut it while he slept, and the Philistines captured, blinded, and enslaved him. Job's wife advised him to "blaspheme God, and dye" (2:9) as a solution to his suffering. King Solomon is traditionally regarded as the author of the Book of Proverbs, which includes the advice: "It is better to dwell in the wildernes, then with a contentious and an angrie woman" (21:19; also 25:24). All three biblical figures are used here to advocate men's resistance to women's solicitations.

769 *a curst shrewe* Socrates's pity presumably derives from his troubles with his own infamously shrewish wife, Xanthippe.

772 *caytife* Caitiff: "a base, mean, despicable 'wretch,' a villain" (*OED,* sb. 3).

774–75 *hitherto, you have but flattered these Ladies.* The same charge is made about Lord Octavian's praises of women in *The Courtier,* p. 260.

778 *For that were slaunderous.* Complaints about women were sometimes associated with slander in Renaissance literature. I have discussed this relation in "Historical Differences: Misogyny and *Othello,*" pp. 161–62.

779 *shrewde* Shrewish. But note the connection between the earlier use of the word to denote objectionable behavior and its later associations with intelligence and cunning. Both meanings had some currency in the sixteenth century (see *OED,* s.v. "shrewd," a. 1, 12, and 13).

780 *they be shrewes all.* This is one of Gualter's most clearly misogynist remarks because it condemns all women by reducing them to one negative type.

780–82 *if you give the simplest . . . upon thy head.* Tilley, I49: "Give an Inch and he will take an ell."

789–92 *if a woman will not be still . . . to give hir.* The association here between words and "stripes," or lashings, beatings, is proverbial (Tilley, W763, W816, W824, W840) and appears, for example, in John Heywood's *Dialogue of Proverbs* II.vii.2253–56: "*The diuell with his dam, hath more rest in hell, / Than I haue here with the, but well wyfe well. / Well well ([quoth] she) many wels, many buckets, / Ye ([quoth] he) and many woords, many buffets.*"

794–95 *rather by subtiltie, than by crueltie.* This advice to husbands is similar to the advice to wives that appears at ll. 1323–90.

801–2 *even as the moth fretteth the cloth.* "There is no clothe so fine but moathes will eate it, no yron so harde but rust will fret it, no wood so sounde but wormes will putrifie it, no mettall so course but fire will purifie it, nor no Maid so free but love will bring her into thraldome and bondage" (from Pettie, *A Petite Pallace of Pettie His Pleasure*, p. 188; Johnson, p. 207).

812–13 *peradventure advaile* Perchance avail.

819–20 *For much better were they unborne, than untaught.* Tilley, U1: "Better (a child is better) unborn than untaught."

830–33 *The monarch of Macedon Philippes sonne . . . for a time.* From Plutarch's "Life of Alexander": "Alexander did reverence Aristotle at the first, as his father, and so he tearmed him: bicause from his natural father he had life, but from him, the knowledge to live" (*Lives*, vol. 3, p. 333).

833–47 *There came once before the wise Solon . . . from their inheritance.* The story is told in Luxan in book four at fols. 153ᵛ–154, and the affirming judgment as a reply comes from Marcelo, Eulalia's husband.

840–41 *sepulchre . . . rigorous.* Deprivation of a burial place was a severe punishment at that time.

842 *disherited* Disinherited.

843–47 *I assure you, quoth maister Lodovic . . . from their inheritance.* "Maister Lodovic" is a reference to Lodovico (or Juan Luis) Vives, whose endorsement of this story reflects the Spanish humanist's attention to children's education and educational reform as set forth in *De ratione studii puerilis* (1523), *De disciplinis* (1531), *De ratione dicendi* (1534), *De conscribendis epistolis* (1534), and other texts (see also introduction, pp. 26–27).

861 *flagrant savour* See note to l. 29. Here the word may suggest an intensity of taste or evoke the "essential virtue or property" (*OED*, sb. 3c) of marriage. Since "savour" also meant "smell, perfume, aroma" at this time (sb. 2), the change to "fragrant" made by the third edition is understandable.

873 *put to* Add, lend. The image recalls the handclasp of the marriage ceremony (see note to ll. 220–21).

885 *apointed* Decreed, ordained, planned the events of the pastime.

889 *ware* Aware.

896 *letted* Prevented, obstructed.

908 *authoritie* I.e., her garland, as symbol of her authority.

917 *obeysance* Obedience.

931–32 *she began a little to chaunge hir colour.* In *Filocopo*, Fiametta blushes when she is crowned queen by Ascalion (sig. B1v). Fiametta is embarrassed at having to assume authority and declares her unworthiness in a show of modesty. In a similarly self-effacing act, Lady Julia has stepped down from her authoritative role and delegated the place of queen to Aloisa, only to be required by her to present the duties of a wife.

933 *dissehabling hir self.* Rendering herself incapable of action; incapacitating herself through her own doubt.

950 *sielie* Helpless or defenseless, weak, simple, or unsophisticated. The more derogatory meanings of "silly" as foolish or senseless were available in the sixteenth century, but were not as commonly implied by the word.

962–66 *Themistocles being demaunded . . . than money without a man.* This story is recounted in the same way by Vives in *The Instruction of a Christen Woman*, bk. 1, chap. 16, sigs. R4–R4ᵛ. It originally appeared in Plutarch's "Life of Themistocles," in *Lives*, vol. 1, p. 220. The same choice between potential husbands is made by a daughter rather than her father in Henry Medwall's humanist play *Fulgens and Lucres* (c. 1500). See Catherine Belsey's discussion of the play in *The Subject of Tragedy*, pp. 194–96.

983–84 *for whome also we forsake parents, friendes, and all, cleaving onely to them.* The language of this passage evokes Genesis 2:24, Matthew 19:5, and Mark 10:7.

985–89 *albeit they be cancred of nature . . . or chaunge with our neighbours.* This account of the faults of husbands in a context reminding wives that there is no way to avoid them (because divorce is impossible) is similar to several remarks in Erasmus's *Mery Dialogue*. For other passages in that text describing the unpleasant qualities of husbands, see note to ll. 650–52.

1020–24 *I coulde recite divers worthie examples . . . to die with them.* Examples of good wives appear in Boccaccio's *Concerning Famous Women*, where entire chapters are devoted to individual women; in Vives's *Instruction of a Christen Woman*, bk. 2, chap. 4, sigs. X4ᵛ–Y2; very briefly in Erasmus's *Encomium matrimonii*, p. 130; with some commentary in Elyot's *Defence of Good Women*, pp. 21–23, and Agrippa's *Nobilitie and Excellencie of Womankynde*, sigs. D7–G3; and at length in Luxan's *Coloquious matrimoniales*, bk. 2, fols. 52–55. Although Tilney certainly used Luxan, he did not do so exclusively; Julia, wife of Pompey, appears, for example, in Boccaccio and Vives, but not in the Spanish source. For purposes of comparison I have included possible sources in the notes that follow. Although Tilney did not make use of Christine de Pizan's *Book of the City of Ladies*, many of these women's stories are also found there, often with important variations produced by Christine's different representations of their lives.

1025–47 *Plutarch reporteth, howe that the Lacedemonians . . . steps of honest love.* Plutarch tells a similar story with a different ending under the subtitle "The Tuscane Women" in "The vertuous deeds of women" (*The Morals*, p. 488; Johnson, p. 212). The story also appears in Boccaccio's *Concerning Famous Women*, chap. 29, "The Wives of the Minyans"; in Vives's *Instruction*, bk. 2, chap. 4, sig. X4ᵛ; and in Luxan, bk. 2, fols. 52–52ᵛ.

1048–53 *Panthea, when she hard . . . gored hir selfe to the hart.* This story is told at greater length in Xenophon's *Cyropaedia*, vol. 2, bk. 7.3.3–16 (Johnson, p. 213).

Xenophon says that Panthea blamed herself for the death of her husband, Abradatas, because she urged him into battle to show himself as a worthy friend of Cyrus. Versions appear in Vives's *Instruction*, bk. 2, chap. 4, sig. Y1ᵡ; in Elyot's *Defence of Good Women*, pp. 21–22; and in Luxan, bk. 2, fol. 53.

1053–54 *The lyke is reported of Porcia, Brutus wyfe.* Recounted in Plutarch's "Life of Marcus Brutus": "And for Porcia, Brutus wife: Nicolaus the Philosopher, and Valerius Maximus doe wryte, that she determining to kill her selfe (her parents and frendes carefullie looking to her to kepe her from it) tooke hotte burning coles, and cast them into her mouth, and kept her mouth so close, that she choked her selfe" (*Lives*, vol. 4, p. 478). Also recounted in Boccaccio's *Concerning Famous Women*, chap. 80; Vives's *Instruction*, bk. 2, chap. 4, sig. Y1ᵛ; Elyot's *Defence of Good Women*, p. 22; and in Luxan, bk. 2, fols. 53–53ᵛ. Tilney does not mention her death by swallowing burning coals, which Shakespeare alludes to in *Julius Caesar* IV.iii.156.

1055–64 *Martiall also writeth, howe that Alcesta . . . and loving spouse.* Alcestis's death is briefly referred to in Martial's *Epigrams*, bk. 4, no. 75 (Johnson, pp. 213–14) and in Vives's *Instruction*, bk. 1, chap. 4, sigs. X4ᵛ–Y1. Luxan (bk. 2, fols. 53ᵛ–54) and Tilney alter the story as it appears in Plato's *Symposium* and Euripedes's *Alcestis* so that Admetes chooses to die with his wife rather than rejoicing in her revival by Hercules. *The Flower*'s marginal note refers to the more common ending.

1065–70 *In lyke maner Paulina the wyfe of Seneca . . . stopped up agayne.* The story appears in Boccaccio's *Concerning Famous Women*, chap. 92; Vives's *Instruction*, bk. 2, chap. 4, sig. Y; Elyot's *Defence of Good Women*, pp. 22–23; and in Luxan, bk. 2, fol. 54–54ᵛ.

1071–76 *What shall I speake worthily of Triara . . . his chaunces, good, or bad.* Recounted in Boccaccio's *Concerning Famous Women*, chap. 94; and in Luxan, bk. 2, fol. 54ᵛ.

1077–85 *Did not Julia, Pompeius wife . . . bewayled with many teares.* This good wife is not mentioned in Luxan, but her story appears in Vives's *Instruction of a Christen Women*, bk. 2, chap. 4, sig. Y1ᵛ, and in Plutarch's "Life of Pompey," *Lives*, vol. 3, pp. 298–99. The account in Boccaccio's *Concerning Famous Women*, chap. 79, unlike the sources just cited and Tilney, makes her appear ridiculous when she sees the blood on her husband's clothes and assumes it is his own.

1080 *sound* Swoon.

1086–93 *Plinie the yonger, in an Epistle writeth of a fishers wife . . . and were drowned.* Pliny's story in *Letters and Panegyricus*, vol. 1, bk. 6. 24, p. 455, recounts that the couple jumped from a house overlooking Lake Como rather than from a rock, and it provides information that might lead to a more complex interpretation of the story than Tilney's Julia gives. "The husband had long been suffering from ulcers in the private parts, and his wife insisted on seeing them, promising that no one would give him a more candid opinion whether the disease was curable.

She saw that there was no hope and urged him to take his life; she went with him, even led him to his death herself, and forced him to follow her example by roping herself to him and jumping into the lake" (Johnson, p. 216). Is this murder?

1100–1103 *No doubt Madam, quoth he . . . bring your maryed woman unto a meane.* Gualter's response is similar to the misogynist's reaction in *The Courtier* to the story of another loving wife, Argentine. "The Lord Gasper saide: it may be that this woman was over loving, because women in every thing cleave alwaies to the extremitie, which is ill. And see for that she was over loving she did ill to her selfe, to her husband, and to her children, in whom she turned into bitternesse the pleasure of that dangerous and desired libertie of his" (p. 211). The observation was also proverbial, as in Tilley, W651: "A Woman either loves or hates to extremes."

1110–21 *shamefastnesse, which is of such power, and vertue. . . . to advance their prayse.* The *OED* explains regarding "shamefast" (a) that "the etymological sense appears to be 'restrained by shame'" and gives as meanings "bashful, modest. In a good or neutral sense: Modest or virtuous in behaviour and character. In a depreciatory sense: Shy, awkward in the company of others, 'sheepish.'" The word was nearly always evoked positively in Renaissance conduct literature addressed to women, perhaps because the negative implications became positive as applied to them. Vives expounds it in relation to chastity in *The Instruction of a Christen Woman*, bk. 1, chap. 11, sigs. L4ᵛ–M1: "Of shamfastnes cometh demurenes and mesurablenes: that whether she thynke ought or say or do, nothyng shalbe outragious either in passions of mynd nor wordes nor dedes nor presumptuous nor nyce, wanton, pierte nor bostyng nor ambitious: and as for honours she wyll neither thynke her selfe worthy nor desire them but rather flee them: and if they chance unto her, she wyll be ashamed of them as of a thynge nat deserved nor be for nothing high mynded, neither for beautie nor proprenes nor kynred nor ryches beynge sure that they shal sone perishe and that pride shal have ever lastyng payne." Vives also discusses the virtue in *The Office and Duetie of an Husband*, sig. U8ᵛ. It is mentioned briefly in *The Courtier* at p. 194 and in *Filocopo*, sigs. H3 and H4; see also Spenser's *Faerie Queene* 2.9.43 and 5.5.25. This "only defence that nature hath given to women" (ll. 1118–19) is an awareness of their guilt *as* women inducing such shame in them that they become modest or shy in behavior. To advise this virtue in women is therefore to offer as their salvation a value that depends upon and reasserts their presumed inadequacies.

1131–38 *I know not, quoth the Lady Isabella, what we are bound to do. . . . whom nature hath made free?* For a discussion of Tilney's adaptation of this discussion of obedience from his source, see pp. 42–45 of the introduction. For the ideology associated with Isabella's remark, see pp. 75–84.

1135 *For women have soules as wel as men.* The debate about whether or not women had souls began at the Council of Macon in A.D. 585, and by the end of the sixteenth century the verdict had come down in their favor (see Powell, *English Domestic Relations, 1487–1653*, p. 150; Johnson, p. 219).

1136 *wit* Reason, intellect, mental faculties.

1139–45 *among the Achaians, women had such soveraigntie. . . . they corrected them at their discretion.* The Achaeans were identified by Homer as the Greeks who fought at Troy. Tilney's account appears in Luxan, bk. 2, fols. 56–57. Although I have not found this discussion in Plutarch, Herodotus explains in his *History*, vol. 1, 146, p. 34, that the "purest Ionians" of Athens brought no wives with them when they came to Achaea "but married Carian girls, whose fathers they had slain. Hence these women made a law, which they bound themselves by an oath to observe, and which they handed down to their daughters after them, 'that none should ever sit at meat with her husband, or call him by his name': because the invaders slew their fathers, their husbands, and their sons, and then forced them to become their wives" (Johnson, p. 220).

1146–47 *might she beate him too?* For an excellent discussion of this threat and the topoi it generated, see Natalie Zemon Davis, "Women on Top." T. E.'s *Lawes Resolutions of Women's Rights* of 1632 asserts that it was legal for a husband to beat his wife. "Justice Booke 12. H. 8. fo. 4 affirmeth plainly, that if a man beat an out-law, a traitor, a Pagan, his villein, or his wife it is dispunishable, because by the Law Common these persons can have no action: God send Gentle-women better sport, or better companie" (p. 128; Johnson, pp. 222–23). When this issue was disputed at Oxford University in 1608, William Heale wrote an outraged response: "But nowe this bad cause [the condemnation of women] hath gotten better patrones: especially when in the Universitie, in the open Act, in publike disputation their names are called in question, their capacitie thought unfit for learning, themselves adjudged worthie of blowes. To let passe the rest; what more strange and prodigious paradoxe? What opinion more unnatural and uncivill then this of theirs, *That it is lawfull for a husband to beat his wife?*" (*An Apologie for Women*, p. 3).

1147–49 *some of our Dames in this Countrie. . . . think belike that they be in Achaia.* This remark may recall the description of England from a continental perspective, "England is the paradise of women, the hell of horses, and the purgatory of servants," which appears in Tilley as E147.

1149 *Achaia* Although Achaea was originally a small district in the north of the Peloponnesus of Greece, after the Roman conquest the term was applied to the entire Peloponnesus and the greater part of Greece. Renaissance writers usually associated the word with this larger area (Sugden, p. 2).

1152 *For Dogs barke boldely at their owne maisters doore.* Tilley, D465: "Every Dog is stout at his own door (is a lion at home)."

1154 *fonde* Foolish.

1155–59   *the Parthians, and Thracians accounted not of their wifes . . . exchaunged them for
yonger.*   This example is offered by Dorothea in Luxan, bk. 2, fols. 56ᵛ–57ᵛ (see
also Moncada, p. 245).

1160–63   *Fye upon that law, quoth the Lady Isabella. . . . and the men without.*   The
example of the Numidians and the Lydians is adduced by Dorothea in Luxan,
bk. 2, fol. 57 (see also Moncada, p. 245).

1166–72   *Not so, quoth the Lady Julia. . . . this lawe byndeth hir not to obey.*   Julia's
objection considers one implication of the public-private split between husband
and wife, exploding the separate-but-equal argument from a conservative position.

1175–88   *Ye say well, Madam, quoth M. Erasmus. . . . and suffer themselves to be
commaunded for company.*   See introduction, pp. 77–78. Tilney's representation
of Erasmus as requiring women's unqualified submission is not totally inaccu-
rate, but it does obscure the complex and even contradictory positions Erasmus
articulated and presented through his characters. Here Erasmus differed considerably from Vives, who was more consistently heavy-handed on the subject of
marital supremacy. "Therefore the husbande without anye exception is maister
over al the house, and hathe as touching his familie, moore authoritie then a
kynge in hys kyngdom." *Office and Duetie of an Husbande,* sig. T8ᵛ. Yet even here
the assertion is made of husbands and wives, not men and women.

1185–86   *but in a woman verye rare.*   Julia's position is in keeping with the numerous
writers, such as Boccaccio and Spenser, who praised courageous and strong
women as remarkable exceptions to the norm. The implicit criticism of *most*
women conveyed by this approach becomes more apparent in *The Flower,* since
Julia is shown to oppose Isabella's arguments for equality.

1189–95   *A hard adventure, quoth Maister Gualter. . . . or speaketh without great cause.*
Gualter's reassertion of the threat of the shrew is appropriate to the misogynist.
Yet he describes her mastery primarily in terms of garrulity. The association
between language and power is consistently reaffirmed through characteriza-
tions of women as shrews, since their use of words is interpreted as an illegitimate and insurgent activity.

1189   *adventure*   A chance occurrence; a happening without design. When combined with "hard," the word implies that men who marry shrews are the victims
of bad luck rather than poor judgment.

1201–2   *In doing whereof he shal neither eate the more at his dinner, nor shee have the lesse
appetite to hir supper.*   That is, the husband who reprimands his wife is not taking
more than his fair share of the marital meal, and his larger part should not affect
her appetite for her own portion. Nor, by implication, is the wife justified in
participating less or withholding sex in response to her husband's reproofs.

1214–15   *Seneca in his tragedies of this matter sheweth a notable example.*   As an example
of a wife who tolerates an indiscreet man, Tilney may be referring to Seneca's
tragedy of *Octavia,* wife of Nero (Johnson, pp. 229–30).

1215–27 *In the warres of Mithridates, and the Romaines. . . . for presumption.* This story appears in Luxan, bk. 2, fol. 60. Although it is told in *The Flower* as an instance of a wife commanding her husband, what is ignored in the account is the simultaneous resistance of a woman to war. Compare Virginia Woolf's *Three Guineas.*

1224 *astonied* Astonished.

1233 *malicious* Here the readiness to believe that women are bad.

1236–73 *to be resident in hir owne house. . . . when their husbands came from the warres to visite them.* Warnings about the importance of women staying at home were pervasive during the sixteenth century. See, for example, Vives's *Instruction of a Christen Woman,* bk. 2, chap. 9, and bk. 3, chap. 6.

1242 *depelled* Dispelled.

1243–46 *the great excesse of apparell . . . as great wasters.* Tilney's text is remarkable for saying so little on this subject and embedding the advice within a longer sentence. Compare Vives's *Instruction,* bk. 1, chap. 9, and bk. 2, chap. 8; and Bullinger's *Christen State of Matrimonye,* chap. 23. Tilney was himself known for owning such an elaborate wardrobe "that he felt compelled to repent it in his will" (Streitberger, *Edmond Tyllney,* p. 14).

1244 *curious* Difficult to satisfy, particular, fastidious.

1248 *gadding* Roving, wandering, stopping here and there.

1252–54 *Seneca saith that his aunt . . . never went out of hir owne house.* Recounted in Seneca's *Consolation to Helvia* 19.6, in *Moral Essays,* vol. 2, pp. 486–87 (Johnson, pp. 232–33).

1254 *Faunus* "A *numen* anciently identified with Pan, whose festival . . . was kept in the *pagi* with dancing and merry-making. . . . He had female counterparts, Fauna . . . and Fatua" (*Oxford Classical Dictionary,* p. 432).

1256 *gate* Got, gained, acquired.

1258–62 *Licurgus commaunded. . . . at home to instruct hir children.* Although no such commandments appear in Plutarch's "Life of Lycurgus" or in his "Laconick Apophthegmes," Luxan discusses them in bk. 2 at fol. 61ᵛ and attributes them to Lycurgus.

1263–65 *My meaning is not . . . to have the maried wife continually lockt up, as a cloystred Nonne, or Ancres.* This qualification is similar to Bullinger's in *Christen State of Matrimonye* concerning daughters: "Nether wolde I not have them ever shut up as it were in Cage, never to speke nor to come forth but some tymes to see the good fasshions and honest behaviours of other for to kepe them ever in mewe is ynough ether to make them starke foles or els to make them naughtes, when they shall once come a brode into companye" (chap. 24, sig. K4, p. 75).

1265 *Ancres* Anchoress, a nun.

1267–73 *Lucretia the famous Romaine Ladye . . . when their husbands came from the warres to visite them.* Mention of Lucrece as an exemplary woman is ubiquitous in the sixteenth century, but this account of her virtue appears also in Vives's

Instruction, bk. 1, chap. 3, sig. C4ᵛ, and in Luxan, bk. 2, fol. 62ᵛ.

1278–82   *Plutarch telleth of a custome among the Numidians . . . should therefore lose his hand.*   This example appears in Luxan, bk. 2, fol. 63ᵛ.

1293   *curst*   Cursed, shrewish, cantankerous.

1295–98   *to looke well to hir huswifery . . . even in thinges of least importaunce.*   Similar advice was frequently given to women. For example, Xenophon's *Oeconomicus,* which was translated as the *Treatise of house holde* in 1532, stressed women's engagement with household management. In a middle portion of the dialogue, Isomachus explains to Socrates how he taught his wife to be a good housekeeper by advising that she work like the "maystres bee" of the hive: "For bicause sayde he, it bydeth alwaye in the hyve, and wyll not suffre no bees to be ydel: and they that shuld worke without, she sendeth them to their worke. And what so ever any of them bryngeth home, she marketh, receyvethe, and saveth it, untyll the tyme come that it must be occupied. And whan the tyme comethe, that it must be occupied, than she distributeth every thynge accordyng as equitie requireth. And she causeth them that do bide within, to weave and make the faire hony comes [combs] after the best wise" (from the 1537 edition, p. 24ᵛ; see also Vives's *Instruction,* bk. 1, chap. 3).

1300   *needle, and rocke*   Needlework and spinning. A "rocke" was a distaff (*OED,* sb. 2), used for spinning wool and flax.

1302–4   *Salomon commending a good woman . . . by the counsayle of hir handes.*   The same passage appears in Vives's *Instruction of a Christen Woman,* bk. 1, chap. 3, sigs. C4ᵛ–C5.

1306   *dressing of meate*   Preparing meat, which would include seasoning it, stuffing it, and making the gravy or sauce as necessary. The phrase was also used more generally to apply to other dishes prepared as part of a meal.

1311–14   *Stratomacha the wife of king Deiotarus . . . so esteemed of suche a noble Queene.*   Deiotarus was "tetrach of Galatia in Asia Minor. . . . He was a faithful friend of the Romans in their Asiatic Wars, and was rewarded by the senate, in 63 B.C., with the title of King" (Plutarch's *Lives,* vol. 5, ed. Perrin, p. 536). His wife is discussed as "Stratonice" in a section by that name in Plutarch's "Vertuous deeds of women" (*The Morals,* p. 501), but she is praised there for prevailing on her husband to have a child by another woman and passing it off as her own, since she had none herself, rather than for nursing him when he was sick (Johnson, p. 238).

1316–20   *whose face must be hir daylie looking glasse . . . wherto she must alwayes frame hir owne countenance.*   This passage is discussed in the introduction, pp. 61–63. Its most immediate source for Erasmus, Luxan, and Tilney is Plutarch's "Precepts of wedlocke," no. 12: "Like as a mirrour or looking glasse garnished with golde and precious stones, serveth to no purpose, if it doe not represent to the life the face of him or her that looketh into it; no more is a woman worth ought (be she otherwise never so rich) unlesse she conforme and frame her selfe, her life, her maners and conditions sutable in all respects to her husband. A false mirrour it is, and good for nothing, that sheweth a sad and heavie countenance to him who is merrie and jocund, and contrariwise, which resembleth a glad and smiling visage to one who is melancholike, angrie and discontent; even so, a bad woman is she, and a very untoward piece, who when her husband is desirous to solace himselfe and be merry in disporting with her, frowneth and looketh doggedly under the browes, and on the other side, when she seeth him amused in serious matters, and in a deepe study about his affaires, is set on a merrie pin, and given to mirth and laughter; for as the one is a signe of a sowre plumme and an unpleasant yoke-fellow, so the other bewraieth a woman that setteth light by the affections of her husband; whereas indeed befitting it were, that as (by the saying of Geometricians) the lines and superficers move not at all of themselves, but according to the motions of the bodies; even so a wife should have no proper passion or peculiar affection of her owne, but be a partaker of the sports, serious affaires, sad countenance, deepe thoughts, and smiling looks of her husband" (*The Morals*, pp. 317–18; no. 14 in *Moralia*, vol. 2, trans. Babbitt). In her discussion of the mirror metaphor in marriage in *The Currency of Eros*, pp. 26–27, Ann Rosalind Jones quotes from Robert Greene's *Penelope's Web* (1581), where the source for the metaphor is identified as Plato's *Androgina*. Erasmus's adaptation of the advice in *A mery Dialogue* is quoted in the introduction, pp. 60–61. Luxan has a similar passage in bk. 2 at fol. 66. Compare Virginia Woolf's remark in *A Room of One's Own* that women have for centuries functioned as "looking-glasses possessing the magic and delicious power of reflecting the figure of man at twice its natural size" (p. 35).

1321–22 *Why, quoth the Ladie Isabell, what if he bee mad, or dronke, must we then shew the like countenance.* Compare Xanthippe's response in Erasmus's *Mery Dialogue:* "O carefull state of wyves, when they must be gladde and fayne to followe their husbandes mindes, by thei eluyshe [elvish?], dronken or doyng what myschiefe they liste" (sig. A7–A7^v).

1324–26 *speake hym faire, and flatter him, till you get him to bed . . . with kissing and imbrasing.* What Julia recommends was called the bolster or curtain lecture, given when husband and wife were within the curtains of their own bed.

1328 *frowardly* Perversely, in an ill-humoured or refractory manner.

1330–34 *we are not much unlyke to wilde and savage beasts . . . and vexation of minde.* See note to ll. 650–52. In Plutarch's "Precepts of wedlocke," husbands are compared to elephants, bulls, and tigers (no. 40 in *The Morals*, 1603 ed.; no. 45 in *Moralia*, vol. 2, trans. Babbitt); in Erasmus's *Mery Dialogue* they are likened to elephants, lions, wild bulls, tigers, and horses (sig. A6). Luxan changes this list to lions, bulls, and bears (bk. 2, fol. 71), and Tilney alters it further to the lion and the unicorn.

1341–83 *There was, quoth he, a gentleman of good calling. . . . lived content with hir ever after.* This story, thought to be a folktale (see Heltzel, "Traces"), also appeared in Marguerite de Navarre's *Heptameron* as no. 38 (Miglior, "Edmund Tilney," p. 81), in Erasmus's *Conjugium*, Luxan's *Coloquios matrimoniales*, William Painter's *Palace of Pleasure* (1566), and William Warner's *Albion of England* (1586). In Marguerite's version, unlike that in Erasmus, Luxan, and Tilney, the wife is not explicitly praised for dissembling, and she does not pretend to be her husband's sister.

1343 *snowte fayre* Having a fair countenance; fair-faced, comely, handsome (*OED*, a). The disparaging implications of the word noted by the *OED* as applying to it in the sixteenth and early seventeenth centuries are supported by its appearance in Jane Anger, *Her Protection for Women*, where men who are "snout-fare" have faces that "look like a cream pot" (p. 180).

1358 *trust up* Trussed up, tied in a bundle, packed up.

1376–79 *He should. . . . in his unthriftinesse.* Compare Erasmus's character Xanthippe in *A mery Dialogue:* "She was one of goddes fooles. I would rather for a bed have layd under him a bundel of nettels: or a burden of thistels" (sig. B4). In response to a similar story, Xanthippe replies: "I would lever be slayne then I woulde be bawde unto myne owne husbande" (sig. B4ᵛ). The story appears in Luxan, chap. 2, fol. 69–69ᵛ.

1392–93 *it is a wise mans griefe, to beare the open reproofe of his wife.* That is, even a wise man grieves if his wife criticizes him when others are present. One function of the curtain lecture is to contain the reproofs of a wife within a private place.

1393–97 *The best place, is, as I sayde . . . but loving, kinde, gentle, merie, and pleasaunt.* Compare Erasmus in *A mery Dialogue:* "Be wyse of this especyall that thou never gyve hym foule wordes in the chambre, or inbed but be sure that all thynges there bee full of pastyme and pleasure. For yf that place which is ordeined to make amendes for all fautes and so to renew love, be polluted, eyther with strife or grugynges, then fayre wel al hope of love daies, or atonementes" (sig. B6).

1397–99 *For though the woman everie where, ought to be merie with hir mate: yet muste shee chiefely in bed.* This passage recalls the oft-repeated advice that wives were "to be bonere and buxom in bedde and at the borde," which the *OED*, (bonair[e], a) cites from a 1542 edition of *The prymer in Englysshe and in Latin after the use of Sarum. Bonair* meant courteous, gentle, or kind; *buxom* is defined as "blithe, jolly, well-favoured" (a, II) but also as "easily bowed or bent" (a, I). In Erasmus's *Mery Dialogue* Eulalia advises Xanthippe: "But Paule sayeth that wyves shoulde bee boner and buxume unto their husbandes with all humylytye" (sig. A3ᵛ).

1404–5 *being of hir selfe weake, and unable besides hir owne diligence.* The construction of women as weak is pervasive in the Renaissance. The Elizabethan homily on marriage explains that since "woman is a weake creature, not indued with like strength and constancie of minde" as man, she is "sooner disquieted" and "more prone to all weake affections and dispositions of mind" (*Certaine Sermons or Homilies,* p. 241). *The Book of Common Prayer* says wives should be honored "as unto the weaker vessel, and as heirs together of the grace of life" (p. 298). William Perkins, in *Christian Oeconomie,* advises a husband to bear patiently with his wife's infirmities "as anger, waywardness and such like, in respect of the weakness of her sex" (p. 125). The effect of these descriptions is to associate women's objections to their circumstances, which could take the form of anger, *with* their weakness, so their resistance was interpreted as a confirmation of their infirmity rather than a justifiable, even necessary response to personal and social constraints on their lives.

1417–21 *if either Medea, or Circe coulde have obtayned this Flower . . . nor Medea forgone hir welbeloved Jason.* Both women were famous for their abilities to charm men—Jason and Odysseus in particular—with their magical powers. They are mentioned in Luxan, bk. 2, fol. 47ᵛ, and the marital arts that Eulalia teaches Xanthippe are likened to Circe's in Erasmus's *Mery Dialogue,* sig. B7.

1428 *boren away* Sustained, carried off.

1428–29 *But the Ladie Isabella, who in this seconde debating fell to my lot* This remark probably refers to the formal seating arrangement of the participants, which resulted in an alignment or association on the second day of the pastime between the narrator Tilney and Isabella.

1429–31 *at our departing required me for hir sake, to penne the whole discourse of this flagrant Flower.* For the possibility that this passage conveys a request from Queen Elizabeth to Edmund Tilney that he write this text, see the introduction, pp. 6–7.

1432–36 *and therewith the rest of the ladies joyned with hir, at whose importunate request . . . I have adventured to publishe this Discourse.* These lines and those immediately preceding them characterize this text as specifically requested by women. For a discussion of women as generating and/or serving as the audience for symposia, see the introduction, pp. 71–75.

Bibliography

Adams, Joseph Quincy, ed. *The Dramatic Records of Sir Henry Herbert, Master of the Revels, 1623–1673.* Cornell Studies in English, no. 3. New Haven: Yale University Press, 1917.

Agrippa, Heinrich Cornelius. *Of the Nobilitie and Excellencie of Womankynde.* Trans. David Clapham. London, 1542 (*STC* 203); Ann Arbor: University Microfilms, Reel no. 71.

Allen, John William. *A History of Political Thought in the Sixteenth Century.* 1928; reprint, London: Methuen, 1957.

Althusser, Louis. "Ideology and Ideological State Apparatuses." In *Lenin and Philosophy and Other Essays.* Trans. Ben Brewster. New York: Monthly Review Press, 1971: 127–86.

Altman, Joel. *The Tudor Play of Mind: Rhetorical Inquiry and the Development of Elizabethan Drama.* Berkeley: University of California Press, 1978.

Amussen, Susan Dwyer. *An Ordered Society: Gender and Class in Early Modern England.* Oxford: Basil Blackwell, 1988.

Anger, Jane. *Her Protection for Women.* London, 1589 (*STC* 644). In *Half Humankind: Contexts and Texts of the Controversy about Women in England, 1540–1640.* Ed. Katherine Usher Henderson and Barbara F. McManus. Urbana: University of Illinois Press, 1985.

Anglo, Sydney. *The Courtier's Art: Systematic Immorality in the Renaissance.* Swansea: University College of Swansea, 1983.

Annals of English Drama, 975–1700, Ed. Alfred Harbage. 2d. ed., rev. S. Schoenbaum. Philadelphia: University of Pennsylvania Press, 1964.

Aquinas, Saint Thomas. *Commentary on the Nicomachean Ethics.* Vol. 2. Trans. C. I. Litzinger. Chicago: Henry Regnery, 1964.

[175]

———. *The Summa contra Gentiles*. Book 3. Trans. English Dominican Fathers. London: Burns Oates and Washbourne, 1923.

Arber, Edward, ed. *A Transcript of the Registers of the Company of Stationers of London, 1554–1640 A.D.* Vol. 1. London, 1875; reprint, New York: Peter Smith, 1950.

Aristotle. *The Works of Aristotle*. Trans. W. D. Ross. Vol. 9. *Ethica nicomachea, Magna moralia, Ethica eudemia.* 1915; reprint, London: Oxford University Press, 1963.

———. *The Works of Aristotle*. Trans. W. D. Ross. Vol. 10. *Politica, Oeconomica, Atheniensium respublica.* Oxford: Clarendon Press, 1921.

Armstrong, Nancy, and Leonard Tennenhouse, eds. *The Ideology of Conduct: Essays on Literature and the History of Sexuality.* London: Methuen, 1987.

Augustine, Saint. *Treatises on Marriage and Other Subjects.* Ed. Roy J. Deferrari. Washington, D.C.: Catholic University of America Press, 1955.

Aylmer, John. *An harborowe for faithfull and trewe subjectes.* London: J. Day, 1559 (*STC* 1005); Ann Arbor: University Microfilms, Pollard Reel no. 194.

Bal, Mieke. *Lethal Love: Feminist Literary Readings of Biblical Love Stories.* Bloomington: Indiana University Press, 1987.

———. "Sexuality, Sin, and Sorrow: The Emergence of Female Character (A Reading of *Genesis* 1–3)." In *The Female Body in Western Culture.* Ed. Susan Rubin Suleiman. Cambridge: Harvard University Press, 1986: 317–38.

Barnes, Harry Elmer. *A History of Historical Writing.* Norman: University of Oklahoma Press, 1937.

Barrett, Michèle. *Women's Oppression Today: Problems in Marxist Feminist Analysis.* London: Verso, 1980.

Barrett, Michèle, and Mary McIntosh. *The Anti-Social Family.* London: Verso, 1982.

Barrow, R. H. *Plutarch and His Times.* Bloomington: Indiana University Press, 1967.

Bataillon, Marcel. *Érasme et l'Espagne: Recherches sur l'histoire spirituelle du XVIe siècle.* Paris: Librairie E. Droz, 1937.

Beilin, Elaine V. *Redeeming Eve: Woman Writers of the English Renaissance.* Princeton: Princeton University Press, 1987.

Belsey, Catherine. "Disrupting Sexual Difference: Meaning and Gender in the Comedies." In *Alternative Shakespeares.* Ed. John Drakakis. London: Methuen, 1985: 166–90.

———. *The Subject of Tragedy: Identity and Difference in Renaissance Drama.* London: Methuen, 1985.

Benger, F. B. "Edmund Tylney, A Leatherhead Worthy: Master of the Revels to Queen Elizabeth I." *Proceedings of the Leatherhead and District Local History Society* 1:5 (1951): 16–21.

Benson, Larry D., ed. *The Riverside Chaucer.* 3d ed. Boston: Houghton Mifflin, 1987.

Bercher, William. *The Nobility of Women (1559).* Ed. R. Warwick Bond. London: Roxburghe Club, 1904.

Bergin, Thomas. *Boccaccio.* New York: Viking, 1981.

Bloch, R. Howard. "Medieval Misogyny." *Representations* 20 (Fall 1987): 1–24.

Bibliography

Boas, F. S. *The Revels Office and Edmund Tilney*. London: Oxford University Press, 1938.

Boccaccio, Giovanni. *Concerning Famous Women*. Trans. Guido A. Guarino. London: George Allen and Unwin, 1964.

——. *A pleasaunt disport of divers noble personages . . . entituled Philocopo*. Trans. H. G. London: H. Bynneman for Richard Smyth and Nicholas England, 1567 (*STC* 3180); reprint, New York: Da Capo Press, 1970.

The Book of Common Prayer, 1559: The Elizabeth Prayer Book. Ed. John E. Booty. Charlottesville: University Press of Virginia, 1976.

Boose, Lynda. "The Father's House and the Daughter in It." In *Daughters and Fathers*. Ed. Lynda Boose. Baltimore: Johns Hopkins University Press, 1989: 19–74.

Boylan, Michael. "The Galenic and Hippocratic Challenges to Aristotle's Conception Theory." *Journal of the History of Biology* 17:1 (Spring 1984): 83–112.

Brooke, Christopher N. L. "Marriage and Society in the Central Middle Ages." In *Marriage and Society: Studies in the Social History of Marriage*. Ed. R. B. Outhwaite. New York: St. Martin's, 1981: 17–34.

Bullinger, Heinrich. *The Christen State of Matrimonye*. Trans. Miles Coverdale. Antwerp: M. Crom, 1541 (*STC* 4045); reprint, Amsterdam: Theatrum Orbis Terrarum, 1974.

Butler, Alban. *Lives of the Saints*. Rev. ed. Ed. Herbert Thurston and Donald Attwater. New York: P. J. Kenedy and Sons, 1956.

Calendar of the Letters and State Papers Relating to English Affairs of the Reign of Elizabeth Preserved in, or originally Belonging to, the Archives of Simancas. Ed. Martin A. S. Hume. Vol. 1. 1892; reprint, Neudeln, Liechtenstein: Kraus, 1971.

Cambridge Italian Dictionary. Ed. Barbara Reynolds. Vol. 1. *Italian-English*. Cambridge: Cambridge University Press, 1981.

Camden, Carroll. *The Elizabethan Woman*. Rev. ed. Mamaroneck, N.Y.: Paul P. Appel, 1975.

Camden, William. *The History of the Most Renowned and Victorious Princess Elizabeth, Late Queen of England*. Ed. Wallace T. MacCaffrey. Abr. ed. Chicago: University of Chicago Press, 1970.

Canons and Decrees of the Council of Trent. Ed. and Trans. H. J. Schroeder. St. Louis: B. Herder, 1941.

Castiglione, Baldassare. *The Book of the Courtier*. Trans. Sir Thomas Hoby. 1561; reprint, Ed. J. H. Whitfield. New York: E. P. Dutton, 1975.

——. *The courtyer of count Baldessar Castilio divided into foure bookes*. Trans. Thomas Hoby. London: William Seres, 1561 (*STC* 4778).

Certaine Sermons or Homilies Appointed to be read in Churches in the Time of Queen Elizabeth I (1547–1571): A Facsimile of Reproduction of the Edition of 1623. Ed. Mary Ellen Rickey and Thomas B. Stroup. Gainesville, Fla.: Scholars' Facsimiles and Reprints, 1968.

Chambers, E. K. *The Elizabethan Stage*. Vols. 1 and 4. Oxford: Clarendon, 1923.

Christine de Pizan. *The Book of the City of Ladies.* Trans. Earl Jeffrey Richards. New York: Persea Books, 1982.

Cicero. *De inventione, De optimo genere oratorum, Topica.* Trans. H. M. Hubbell. Cambridge: Harvard University Press, 1949.

——. *De senectute, De amicitia, De divinatione.* Trans. William Armstead Falconer. Cambridge: Harvard University Press, 1964.

Clark, Elizabeth A. *Jerome, Chrysostom, and Friends: Essays and Translations.* Studies in Women and Religion, vol. 1. New York: Edwin Mellen Press, 1979.

Crane, Thomas Frederick. *Italian Social Customs of the Sixteenth Century and Their Influence on the Literatures of Europe.* Cornell Studies in English, no. 5. New Haven: Yale University Press, 1920.

Cressy, David. "Describing the Social Order of Elizabethan and Stuart England." *Literature and History* 3 (1976): 29–44.

Davies, Kathleen M. "Continuity and Change in Literary Advice on Marriage." In *Marriage and Society: Studies in the Social History of Marriage.* Ed. R. B. Outhwaite. New York: St. Martin's, 1981: 58–80.

Davis, Natalie Zemon. "Women on Top: Symbolic Sexual Inversion and Political Disorder in Early Modern England." In *The Reversible World: Symbolic Inversion in Art and Society.* Ed. Barbara A. Babcock. Ithaca: Cornell University Press, 1978: 147–90.

de Lorris, Guillaume, and Jean de Meun. *The Romance of the Rose.* Trans. Charles Dahlberg. Princeton: Princeton University Press, 1971.

Devereux, E. J. *A Checklist of English Translations of Erasmus to 1700.* Oxford: Oxford Bibliographical Society, 1968.

de Vocht, Henry. *The Earliest English Translations of Erasmus' "Colloquia," 1536–1566.* Louvain: Uystpruyst, 1928.

Dod, John, and Richard Cleaver. *A Godlie Forme of Householde Government: For the Ordering of Private Families, according to the direction of Gods Word.* London: F. Kingston for T. Man, 1598 (*STC* 5383).

Dollimore, Jonathan. *Radical Tragedy: Religion, Ideology, and Power in the Drama of Shakespeare and His Contemporaries.* Chicago: University of Chicago Press, 1984.

Dollimore, Jonathan, and Alan Sinfield, eds. *Political Shakespeare: New Essays in Cultural Materialism.* Manchester: Manchester University Press, 1985.

Drakakis, John, ed. *Alternative Shakespeares.* London: Methuen, 1985.

Dronke, Peter. *Abelard and Heloise in Medieval Testimonies.* Glasgow: University of Glasgow Press, 1976.

Dubrow, Heather. *A Happier Eden: The Politics of Marriage in the Stuart Epithalamium.* Ithaca: Cornell University Press, 1990.

Dusinberre, Juliet. *Shakespeare and the Nature of Women.* London: Macmillan, 1975.

E., T. *The Lawes Resolutions of Women's Rights.* London: J. More for J. Grove, 1632 (*STC* 7437); Ann Arbor: University Microfilms, Reel no. 883.

Bibliography

Eagleton, Terry. *Literary Theory: An Introduction*. Oxford: Basil Blackwell, 1983.

Eccles, Mark. "Sir George Buc, Master of the Revels." In *Thomas Lodge and Other Elizabethans*. Ed. Charles J. Sisson. Cambridge: Harvard University Press, 1933.

Elyot, Sir Thomas. *The Defence of Good Women* (*STC* 7658). Ed. Edwin Johnston Howard. Oxford, Ohio: Anchor Press, 1940.

Engels, Friedrich. *The Origin of the Family, Private Property, and the State*. 1884; reprint, Middlesex: Penguin Books, 1985.

Erasmus, Desiderius. *The Colloquies of Erasmus*. Trans. Craig R. Thompson. Chicago: University of Chicago Press, 1965.

——. "An Epistle to perswade a young jentleman to Marriage." [*Encomium matrimonii*] (*STC* 25799). In Thomas Wilson, *Arte of Rhetorique*. Ed. Thomas J. Derrick. New York: Garland, 1982.

——. *A mery Dialogue, declaringe the propertyes of shrowde shrews, and honest wives* [1557]. [*Conjugium*] (*STC* 10455). In *Tudor Translations of the Colloquies of Erasmus (1536–1584)*. Facsimile ed. with introduction by Dickie A. Spurgeon. Delmar, N.Y.: Scholars' Facsimiles and Reprints, 1972.

——. *Seven Dialogues both pithie and profitable*. Trans. William Burton. London: V. Simmes for N. Ling, 1606 (*STC* 10457).

Erickson, Carolly. *Mistress Anne*. New York: Summit Books, 1984.

Ezell, Margaret J. *The Patriarch's Wife: Literary Evidence and the History of the Family*. Chapel Hill: University of North Carolina Press, 1987.

Fehrenbach, Robert J. "When Lord Cobham and Edmund Tilney 'were att odds': Oldcastle, Falstaff, and the Date of *I Henry IV*." *Shakespeare Studies* 18 (1985): 87–101.

Ferguson, Margaret W., Maureen Quilligan, and Nancy J. Vickers, eds. *Rewriting the Renaissance: The Discourses of Sexual Difference in Early Modern Europe*. Chicago: University of Chicago Press, 1986.

Ferguson, Moira, ed. *First Feminists: British Women Writers, 1578–1799*. Bloomington: Indiana University Press, 1985.

Fitz, Linda. See Linda Woodbridge.

Foucault, Michel. *The History of Sexuality*. Trans. Robert Hurley. Vol. 1. *An Introduction*. New York: Vintage Books, 1980. Vol. 2. *The Uses of Pleasure*. New York: Vintage Books, 1990. Vol. 3. *The Care of the Self*. New York: Vintage Books, 1988.

Gallagher, Catherine. "Embracing the Absolute: The Politics of the Female Subject in Seventeenth-Century England." *Genders* 1 (Spring 1988): 24–39.

The Geneva Bible: A Facsimile of the 1560 Edition. Introduction by Lloyd E. Berry. Madison: University of Wisconsin Press, 1969.

Gillis, John R. *For Better, For Worse: British Marriages, 1600 to the Present*. Oxford: Oxford University Press, 1985.

Goedeke, Karl. *Grundrisz zur Geschichte der deutschen Dichtung*. Vol. 2. Dresden: LS. Ehlermann, 1886.

Goody, Jack. *The Development of the Family and Marriage in Europe.* Cambridge: Cambridge University Press, 1913.

Gouge, William. *Of Domesticall Duties.* London: John Haviland for William Bladen, 1622 (*STC* 12119); reprint, Amsterdam: Theatrum Orbis Terrarum, 1976.

Graham, Elspeth, Hilary Hinds, Elaine Hobby, and Helen Wilcox, eds. *Her Own Life: Autobiographical Writings by Seventeenth-Century English Women.* London: Routledge, 1989.

Greenblatt, Stephen. *Renaissance Self-Fashioning: From More to Shakespeare.* Chicago: University of Chicago Press, 1980.

Guttentag, Marcia, and Paul F. Secord. *Too Many Women?: The Sex Ratio Question.* Beverly Hills: Sage, 1983.

Haec Vir: or, the Womanish Man: Being an Answere to a late Book intitled 'Hic Mulier' (*STC* 12599). In Katherine Usher Henderson and Barbara F. McManus. *Half Humankind: Contexts and Texts of the Controversy about Women in England, 1540–1640.* Urbana: University of Illinois Press, 1985.

Hagstrum, Jean. *Sex and Sensibility: Ideal and Erotic Love from Milton to Mozart.* Chicago: University of Chicago Press, 1980.

Halkett, John. *Milton and the Idea of Matrimony: A Study of the Divorce Tracts and Paradise Lost.* New Haven: Yale University Press, 1970.

Haller, William. "Hail Wedded Love." *ELH* 13 (1946): 79–97.

Haller, William, and Malleville Haller. "The Puritan Art of Love." *Huntington Library Quarterly* 5 (1941–42): 235–72.

Hamilton, Roberta. *The Liberation of Women: A Study of Patriarchy and Capitalism.* London: George Allen and Unwin, 1978.

Heale, William. *An Apologie for Women, or, An opposition to Mr. Dr. G. his assertion, who held in the Act at Oxford. Anno. 1608. that it was lawfull for husbands to beate their wives.* Oxford: Joseph Barnes, 1609 (*STC* 13014).

Heltzel, Virgil B. "Traces of a *Wildfrau* Story in Erasmus." *Philological Quarterly* 8:4 (October 1929): 348–54.

Henderson, Katherine Usher, and Barbara F. McManus. *Half Humankind: Contexts and Texts of the Controversy about Women in England, 1540–1640.* Urbana: University of Illinois Press, 1985.

Henze, Catherine. "Author and Source of 'A Dyalogue Defensyve for Women.' " *Notes and Queries* 221 (1976): 537–39.

Herford, Charles E. *Studies in the Literary Relations of England and Germany in the Sixteenth Century.* 1886; reprint, London: Frank Cass, 1966.

Herodotus. *The History of Herodotus.* Trans. George Rawlinson. Great Books of the Western World, vol. 6. Chicago: Encyclopedia Britannica, 1952.

Hesiod. *The Works of Hesiod.* Trans. R. M. Frazer. Norman: University of Oklahoma Press, 1983.

Bibliography

Heywood, John. *A Dialogue of Proverbs*. Ed. Rudolph E. Habenicht. Berkeley: University of California Press, 1963.

Hill, Christopher. *Society and Puritanism in Pre-Revolutionary England*. 2d ed. New York: Schocken Books, 1967.

Hooker, Richard. *Of the Laws of Ecclesiastical Polity. Book V. The Folger Library Edition of the Works of Richard Hooker*, vol. 2. Ed. W. Speed Hill. Cambridge: Belknap Press of Harvard University Press, 1977.

Horowitz, Maryanne Cline. "Aristotle and Woman." *Journal of the History of Biology* 9:2 (Fall 1976): 183–213.

Howard, George Elliot. *A History of Matrimonial Institutions*. Vols. 1 and 2. New York: Humanities Press, 1964.

Irigaray, Luce. *This Sex Which Is Not One*. Trans. Catherine Porter. 1977; reprint, Ithaca: Cornell University Press, 1985.

Jameson, Fredric. *The Political Unconscious: Narrative as a Socially Symbolic Act*. Ithaca: Cornell University Press, 1981.

Johnson, James T. "The Ends of Marriage." *Church History* 30 (1969): 429–36.

Johnson, Ralph Glassgow, ed. "A Critical Third Edition of Edmund Tilney's *The Flower of Friendshippe*, published in 1577." Ph.D. diss., University of Pittsburgh, 1960.

Jones, Ann Rosalind. *The Currency of Eros: Women's Love Lyric in Europe, 1540–1620*. Bloomington: Indiana University Press, 1990.

Jonson, Ben. *Epicoene, or The Silent Woman*. In *Drama of the English Renaissance*. Vol. 2. *The Stuart Period*. Ed. Russell A. Fraser and Norman Rabkin. New York: Macmillan, 1976.

Jordan, Constance. *Renaissance Feminism: Literary Texts and Political Models*. Ithaca: Cornell University Press, 1990.

Kelly, Henry Ansgar. *Love and Marriage in the Age of Chaucer*. Ithaca: Cornell University Press, 1975.

Kelly, Joan. *Women, History, and Theory: The Essays of Joan Kelly*. Chicago: University of Chicago Press, 1984.

Kelso, Ruth. *Doctrine for the Lady of the Renaissance*. Urbana: University of Illinois Press, 1956.

Kinney, Arthur F. *Humanist Poetics: Thought, Rhetoric, and Fiction in Sixteenth-Century England*. Amherst: University of Massachusetts Press, 1986.

Kirkham, Victoria. "Reckoning with Boccaccio's *Questioni d'Amore*." *Modern Language Notes* 89:1 (January 1974): 47–59.

Klein, Joan Larsen. *Daughters, Wives, and Widows: Writings by Men about Women and Marriage in England, 1500–1640*. Urbana: University of Illinois Press, 1992.

Knight, Philip. *Flower Poetics in Nineteenth-Century France*. Oxford: Clarendon, 1986.

Knox, John. *The First Blast of the Trumpet against the Monstrous Regiment of Women, 1558* (*STC* 15070). Ed. Edward Arber. Westminster: Archibald Constable, 1895.

Koeppel, Emil. *Studien zur Geschichte der italienischen Novelle in der englischen Litteratur des sechzehnten Jahrhunderts*. Strassburg: Karl J. Trübner, 1892.

Kristeva, Julia. "A Holy Madness: She and He." In *Tales of Love*. Trans. Leon S. Roudiez. New York: Columbia University Press, 1987.

Lamb, Mary Ellen. "The Countess of Pembroke and the Art of Dying." In *Women in the Middle Ages and Renaissance: Literary and Historical Perspectives*. Ed. Mary Beth Rose. New York: Syracuse University Press, 1986: 207–26.

Lanyer, Aemilia. *Salve Deux Rex Judaeorum* (*STC* 15227). Selections in *The Paradise of Women: Writings by Englishwomen of the Renaissance*. Ed. Betty Travitsky. Westport, Conn.: Greenwood Press, 1981.

Laqueur, Thomas. "Orgasm, Generation, and the Politics of Reproductive Biology." *Representations* 14 (Spring 1986): 1–41.

Leclercq, Jean. *Monks on Marriage: A Twelfth-Century View*. New York: Seabury Press, 1982.

Leites, Edmund. *The Puritan Conscience and Modern Sexuality*. New Haven: Yale University Press, 1986.

Lerner, Gerda. *The Creation of Patriarchy*. New York: Oxford University Press, 1986.

Letters of Abelard and Heloise. Trans. Betty Radice. Middlesex: Penguin Books, 1974.

Levin, Carole. "Queens and Claimants: Political Insecurity in Sixteenth-Century England." In *Gender, Ideology, Action: Historical Perspectives on Women's Public Lives*. Ed. Janet Sharistanian. Westport, Conn.: Greenwood Press, 1986: 41–66.

Lewalski, Barbara K. "Of God and Good Women: The Poems of Aemilia Lanyer." In *Silent But for the Word: Tudor Women as Patrons, Translators, and Writers of Religious Words*. Ed. Margaret P. Hannay. Kent: Kent State University Press, 1985: 203–24.

Lewis, C. S. *The Allegory of Love: A Study in Medieval Tradition*. New York: Oxford University Press, 1950.

———. *English Literature in the Sixteenth Century Excluding Drama*. London: Oxford University Press, 1954.

Lindelbaum, Peter. "Lovemaking in Milton's Paradise." *Milton Studies* 6 (1974): 277–306.

Luxan, Pedro de. *Coloquios matrimoniales*. Madrid: Ediciones Atlas, 1943.

———. *Coloquios matrimoniales del licenciado Pedro de Luxan*. N.p. [Seville]: Dominico de Robertis, 1550.

McCutcheon, Elizabeth. "Margaret More Roper: The Learned Woman of Tudor England." In *Women Writers of the Renaissance and Reformation*. Ed. Katharina M. Wilson. Athens: University of Georgia Press, 1987: 449–80.

Macfarlane, Alan. *Marriage and Love in England: Modes of Reproduction, 1300–1840*. Oxford: Basil Blackwell, 1986.

McKerrow, R. B. *Printers' and Publishers' Devices in England and Scotland, 1485–1640*. London: Bibliographical Society, 1949.

——, ed. *A Dictionary of Printers and Booksellers in England, Scotland, and Ireland, and of Foreign Printers of English Books, 1557–1640*. London: Bibliographical Society, 1968.

McLaren, Dorothy. "Marital Fertility and Lactation, 1570–1720." In *Women in English Society, 1500–1800*. Ed. Mary Prior. London: Methuen, 1985: 22–53.

McLaughlin, Eleanor Como. "Equality of Souls, Inequality of Sexes: Woman in Medieval Theology." In *Religion and Sexism: Images of Woman in the Jewish and Christian Traditions*. Ed. Rosemary Radford Ruether. New York: Simon and Schuster, 1974: 213–66.

McLean, Andrew. "Another English Translation of Erasmus' *Coniugium:* Snawsel's *Looking Glasse for Maried Folkes* (1610)." *Moreana* 11 (1974): 55–64.

Maclean, Ian. *The Renaissance Notion of Woman: A Study in the Fortunes of Scholasticism and Medical Science in European Intellectual Life*. Cambridge: Cambridge University Press, 1980.

Marcus, Leah S. *Puzzling Shakespeare: Local Reading and Its Discontents*. Berkeley: University of California Press, 1988.

——. "Shakespeare's Comic Heroines, Elizabeth I, and the Political Uses of Androgyny." In *Women in the Middle Ages and the Renaissance: Literary and Historical Perspectives*. Ed. Mary Beth Rose. New York: Syracuse University Press, 1986: 135–53.

Margaret of Angoulême. *A godly medytacyon of the christen sowle*. Trans. Elizabeth I. London: H. Denham, [1568?] (*STC* 17320.5).

Martial. *Epigrams*. 2 vols. New York: G. P. Putnam's Sons, 1925.

Meagher, John D. "Robert Copland's *The Seven Sorrows,*" *English Literary Renaissance* 7:1 (Winter 1977): 17–50.

Menander. *The Principal Fragments*. New York: G. P. Putnam's Sons, 1921.

Miglior, G. "Edmund Tilney, prosatore elisabettiano." *Annali della Facoltá di Lingue e Letterature Straniere di Cá Foscari* 8:1 (1969): 68–90.

Miller, Robert P., ed. *Chaucer: Sources and Backgrounds*. New York: Oxford University Press, 1977.

Moncada, Ernest J. "The Spanish Source of Edmund Tilney's 'Flower of Friendshippe.'" *Modern Language Review* 65 (1970): 241–47.

Montaigne, Michel de. *The Essayes or Morall, Politike and Millitarie Discourses*. Trans. John Florio. London: Valentine Sims for Edward Blount, 1603 (*STC* 18041).

Montrose, Louis Adrian. "The Elizabethan Subject and the Spenserian Text." In *Literary Theory/Renaissance Texts*. Ed. Patricia Parker and David Quint. Baltimore: Johns Hopkins University Press, 1986: 303–40.

More, Thomas. *Utopia*. Trans. and ed. H. V. S. Ogden. New York: Appleton-Century Crofts, 1949.

Mountaine, Dydymus [Thomas Hill]. *The Gardeners Labyrinth*. London: Henry Bynneman, 1577 (*STC* 13485).

Neale, J. E. *Elizabeth I and Her Parliaments, 1559–1581.* London: Jonathan Cape, 1953.
——. *Queen Elizabeth I: A Biography.* 1934; reprint, New York: Doubleday, 1957.
Noonan, John T., Jr. *Contraception: A History of Its Treatment by the Catholic Theologians and Canonists.* Enl. ed. Cambridge: Belknap Press of Harvard University Press, 1986.
Noreña, Carlos G. *Juan Luis Vives and the Emotions.* Carbondale: Southern Illinois University Press, 1989.
Offen, Karen. "Defining Feminism: A Comparative Historical Approach." *Signs: A Journal of Women in Culture and Society* 14:1 (Autumn 1988): 119–57.
Outhwaite, R. B. "Introduction: Problems and Perspectives in the History of Marriage." In *Marriage and Society: Studies in the Social History of Marriage.* Ed. R. B. Outhwaite. New York: St. Martin's, 1981: 1–16.
Oxford Classical Dictionary. 2d ed. Ed. N. G. L. Hammond and H. H. Scullard. Oxford: Clarendon Press, 1970.
Oxford English Dictionary. 2d ed. Ed. J. A. Simpson and E. S. C. Weiner. Oxford: Clarendon Press, 1989. Cited herein as *OED.*
Ozment, Steven. *When Fathers Ruled: Family Life in Reformation Europe.* Cambridge: Harvard University Press, 1983.
Partridge, Eric. *Shakespeare's Bawdy.* New York: E. P. Dutton, 1969.
Perkins, William. *Christian Economie: Or, a short survey of the right manner of ordering a familie according to the Scriptures.* Trans. T. Pickering. 1609 (*STC* 19677); reprint, Ann Arbor: University Microfilms, Pollard Reel no. 1113.
——. *Christian Oeconomie: Or, a Short Survey of the Right Manner of Erecting and Ordering a Family.* Trans. Thomas Pickering. London: Leonard Green and Felix Kingstone, 1618. In Perkins's *Works.* Vol. 3. Cambridge: Cantrell Legge, 1618 (*STC* 19651).
——. *Works.* Ed. Ian Breward. Vol. 3. Appleford, England: Sutton Courtenay Press, 1970.
Perlette, John M. "Anthony Ascham's 'Of Marriage.'" *English Literary Renaissance* 3:2 (Spring 1973): 284–305.
Pettie, George. *A Petite Pallace of Pettie His Pleasure.* Ed. Herbert Hartman. London: Oxford University Press, 1938.
Phillips, Margaret Mann. "The Xanthippe of Desiderius Erasmus." *Thomas More Gazette* 2 (1980): 51–52.
Pliny. *Letters and Panegyricus.* 2 vols. Trans. Betty Radice. Cambridge: Harvard University Press, 1969.
Plutarch. *The Education or Bringinge Up of Children.* Trans. Sir Thomas Elyot. [1532?] (*STC* 20057); reprint, Amsterdam: Theatrum Orbis Terrarum, 1969.
——. *Lives.* 11 vols. Trans. Bernadotte Perrin. Cambridge: Harvard University Press, 1914.

——. *The Lives of the Noble Grecians and Romanes.* 5 vols. Trans. from Greek to French by James Amyot; trans. from French to English by Thomas North. 1579 ed. with addition of fifteen lives from the third edition of 1603. London: Nonesuch Press, 1930.

——. *Moralia.* Vol. 2. Trans. Frank Cole Babbitt. New York: G. P. Putnam's Sons, 1928.

——. *Moralia.* Vol. 9. Trans. E. L. Minar, Jr., F. H. Sandbach, and W. C. Helmbold. Cambridge: Harvard University Press, 1961.

——. *The Philosophie, commonlie called, The Morals.* Trans. Philemon Holland. London: Arnold Hatfield, 1603 (*STC* 20063).

Powell, Chilton Latham. *English Domestic Relations, 1487–1653.* New York: Columbia University Press, 1917; reprint, New York: Russell and Russell, 1972.

Rebhorn, Wayne A. *Courtly Performances: Masking and Festivity in Castiglione's "Book of the Courtier."* Detroit: Wayne State University Press, 1978.

Robertson, D. W., Jr. *Abelard and Heloise.* New York: Dial, 1972.

——. "The Doctrine of Charity in Medieval Literary Gardens." In *Essays in Medieval Culture.* Princeton: Princeton University Press, 1980: 21–50.

Robinson, F. N., ed. *The Works of Geoffrey Chaucer.* 2d ed. Boston: Houghton Mifflin, 1957.

Robinson, Lillian S. "Woman under Capitalism: The Renaissance Lady." In *Sex, Class, and Culture.* 1978; reprint, New York: Methuen, 1986.

Rose, Mark. *Heroic Love: Studies in Sidney and Spenser.* Cambridge: Harvard University Press, 1968.

Rose, Mary Beth. *The Expense of Spirit: Love and Sexuality in English Renaissance Drama.* Ithaca: Cornell University Press, 1988.

Russell, D. A. *Plutarch.* London: Duckworth, 1972.

Safley, Thomas Max. *Let No Man Put Asunder: The Control of Marriage in the German Southwest: A Comparative Study, 1550–1600.* Kirksville, Mo.: Sixteenth-Century Journal Publishers, 1984.

Schochet, Gordon. *Patriarchalism in Political Thought: The Authoritarian Family and Political Speculation and Attitudes.* Oxford: Basil Blackwell, 1975.

Schüking, Levin L. *The Puritan Family: A Social Study from the Literary Sources.* Trans. Brian Battershaw. London: Routledge and Kegan Paul, 1969.

Scott, Mary Augusta. *Elizabethan Translations from the Italian.* Boston: Houghton Mifflin, 1916.

Seneca. *Moral Essays.* 3 vols. Trans. John W. Basore. New York: G. P. Putnam's Sons, 1928.

Shakespeare, William. *The Riverside Shakespeare.* Gen. ed. G. Blakemore Evans. Boston: Houghton Mifflin, 1974.

Shakespeare's Plutarch. 2 vols. Ed. Tucker Brooke. New York: Haskell House, 1966.

Short-Title Catalogue of Books Printed in England, Scotland, and Ireland and of English Books Printed Abroad, 1475–1640. 2d ed. 2 vols. Ed. W. A. Jackson, F. S. Ferguson, and Katharine F. Pantzer. London: Bibliographical Society, 1976, 1986.

Short-Title Catalogue of Books Printed in the German-Speaking Countries and German Books Printed in Other Countries from 1455 to 1600 Now in the British Museum. London: Trustees of the British Museum, 1962.

Smith, D. Nichol. "Authors and Patrons." In *Shakespeare's England: An Account of the Life and Manners of His Age.* Vol. 2. Oxford: Clarendon Press, 1916: 182–211.

Smith, Hilda L. *Reason's Disciples: Seventeenth-Century English Feminists.* Urbana: University of Illinois Press, 1982.

Smith, William. *A Classical Dictionary of Biography, Mythology, and Geography.* London: J. Murray, 1889.

Snawsel, Robert. *A Looking Glasse for Maried Folkes.* London: 1610 (*STC* 22886); reprint, Ann Arbor: University Microfilms, Reel no. 728.

Somerset, Anne. *Elizabeth I.* London: Fontana, 1992.

Spenser, Edmund. *The Faerie Queene.* Ed. Thomas P. Roche, Jr. Middlesex: Penguin Books, 1978.

Stallybrass, Peter. "The World Turned Upside Down: Inversion, Gender, and the State." In *The Matter of Difference: Materialist Feminist Criticism of Shakespeare.* Ed. Valerie Wayne. Ithaca: Cornell University Press, 1991: 201–20.

Staves, Susan. "Where Is History but in Texts?: Reading the History of Marriage." In *The Golden and the Brazen World: Papers in Literature and History, 1650–1800.* Ed. John M. Wallace. Berkeley: University of California Press, 1985: 125–43.

Stone, Lawrence. *The Family, Sex, and Marriage in England, 1500–1800.* New York: Harper and Row, 1977.

——. "Social Mobility in England, 1500–1700." *Past & Present* 33 (April 1966): 16–55.

Streitberger, W. R. *Edmond Tyllney, Master of the Revels and Censor of Plays: A Descriptive Index to His Diplomatic Manual on Europe.* New York: AMS Press, 1986.

——. "Edmond Tyllney's 'Topographical Descriptions, Regiments, and Policies' of England and Wales: A Critical Edition." Ph.D. diss., University of Illinois, 1973.

——. "On Edmond Tyllney's Biography." *Review of English Studies.* N.s. 29 (February 1978): 11–35.

——, ed. *Jacobean and Caroline Revels Accounts, 1603–1642.* In *Malone Society Collections.* Vol. 13. Oxford: Oxford University Press, 1986.

Strong, Roy. *The Cult of Elizabeth: Elizabethan Portraiture and Pageantry.* New York: Thames and Hudson, 1977.

Sugden, Edward H. *A Topographical Dictionary to the Works of Shakespeare and His Fellow Dramatists.* Manchester: University Press, 1925.

Surtz, Edward L. *The Praise of Wisdom: A Commentary on the Religious and Moral*

Bibliography

Problems and Backgrounds of St. Thomas More's 'Utopia.' Chicago: Loyola University Press, 1957.

Telle, Emile V. *Érasme de Rotterdam et le septième sacrement: Étude d'evangelisme matrimonial au XVIᵉ siècle et contribution à la biographie intellectuelle d'Érasme.* Geneva: Librairie E. Droz, 1954.

Therborn, Göran. *The Ideology of Power and the Power of Ideology.* London: Verso, 1980.

Thevet, Andrewe. *The New found worlde, or Antarctike.* Trans. [Thomas Hacket?]. London: Henrie Bynneman for Thomas Hacket, 1568 (*STC* 23950).

Thomas, Keith. "The Double Standard." *Journal of the History of Ideas* 20 (1959): 195–216.

Tilley, Morris. *A Dictionary of Elizabethan Proverbs.* Ann Arbor: University of Michigan Press, 1950.

Tilney-Bassett, J. G. "Edmund Tilney's *The Flower of Friendshippe.*" *The Library,* 4th ser., 26 (1946): 175–81.

Todd, Margo. *Christian Humanism and the Puritan Social Order.* Cambridge: Cambridge University Press, 1987.

——. "Humanists, Puritans, and the Spiritualized Household." *Church History* 49 (March 1980): 18–34.

Traub, Valerie. "Jewels, Statues, and Corpses: Containment of Female Erotic Power in Shakespeare's Plays." *Shakespeare Studies* 20 (1988): 215–38.

Turner, James Grantham. *One Flesh: Paradisal Marriage and Sexual Relations in the Age of Milton.* Oxford: Clarendon Press, 1987.

Utley, Francis Lee. *The Crooked Rib: An Analytical Index to the Argument about Women in English and Scots Literature to the End of the Year 1568.* 1944; reprint, New York: Octagon, 1970.

Vaghane, Robert, or Robert Burdet. "A dyalogue defensyve for women." 1542 (*STC* 24601); reprint, Ann Arbor: University Microfilms, Reel no. 157.

Vives, Juan Luis. *The Instruction of a Christen Woman.* Trans. Richard Hyrde. London: T. Berthelet, [1529?] (*STC* 24856). Facsimile in *Distaves and Dames: Renaissance Treatises For and About Women.* Ed. Diane Bornstein. Delmar, N.Y.: Scholars' Facsimiles and Reprints, 1978.

——. *The Office and Duetie of an Husband.* Trans. Thomas Paynell. London: John Cawood, [1555?] (*STC* 24855).

Watson, Foster. *Vives and the Renascence Education of Women.* London: Edward Arnold, 1912.

Wayne, Valerie. "Historical Differences: Misogyny and *Othello.*" In *The Matter of Difference: Materialist Feminist Criticism of Shakespeare.* Ed. Valerie Wayne. Ithaca: Cornell University Press, 1991: 153–79.

——. "Refashioning the Shrew." *Shakespeare Studies* 17 (1985): 159–87.

———. "Some Sad Sentence: Vives' *Instruction of a Christian Woman*." In *Silent But for the Word: Tudor Women as Patrons, Translators, and Writers of Religious Works*. Ed. Margaret P. Hannay. Kent: Kent State University Press, 1985: 15–29.

Whetstone, George. *An Heptameron of Civill Discourses*. London: Richard Jones, 1582 (*STC* 25337).

Whigham, Frank. *Ambition and Privilege: The Social Tropes of Elizabethan Courtesy Theory*. Berkeley: University of California Press, 1984.

Williams, E. Carleton. *Bess of Hardwick*. London: Longman's, 1959.

Williams, Neville. *All the Queen's Men: Elizabeth I and Her Courtiers*. 1972; reprint, London: Sphere Books, 1974.

Williams, Raymond. *Marxism and Literature*. Oxford: Oxford University Press, 1977.

Wilson, Thomas. *Arte of Rhetorique*. Ed. Thomas J. Derrick. New York: Garland, 1982.

Woodbridge, Linda [Linda T. Fitz]. " 'What Says the Married Woman?': Marriage Theory and Feminism in the English Renaissance." *Mosaic* 13:2 (Winter 1980): 1–22.

———. *Women and the English Renaissance: Literature and the Nature of Womankind, 1540–1620*. Urbana: University of Illinois Press, 1984.

Woolf, Virginia. *A Room of One's Own*. London: Harcourt Brace Jovanovich, 1929.

Wrightson, Keith. *English Society, 1580–1680*. New Brunswick, N.J.: Rutgers University Press, 1982.

Xenophon. *Cyropaedia*. 2 vols. Trans. Walter Miller. Cambridge: Harvard University Press, 1914.

———. *Treatise of house holde*. Trans. Gentian Hervet. London: T. Berthelet, 1537 (*STC* 26071).

Index

References to Tilney's text appear here by line number in roman; italicized references are either to pages in the editorial material or to line numbers in the Explanatory Notes, the latter designated as "n." Where line numbers in Tilney's text and an Explanatory Note are identical, only the note reference has been provided.

Index

Armstrong, Nancy, *6, 726–40n*

Arraignment of Lewde, Idle, Froward, and Unconstant Women (Swetnam), *40*

Arte of Rhetorique (Wilson), *5–6, 21*

Ascham, Roger, *50*

Audiences: for conduct books, *73–74, 82, 1432–36n*

Augustine, *14, 19–20, 22, 26, 68, 184–86n*

Authority: male, *4, 36–37, 56, 63, 68, 73, 75–78,* 100–104, *124–28, 1175–88n. See also* Patriarchy; Power

Aylmer, John, *45, 76, 79*

Babylonians, *226–35n, 273n*

Bal, Mieke, *14*

Baptista Fulgosa, *482–93n*

Barcina, *51, 57,* 313, 325, 328

Barrett, Michèle, *12*

Bataillon, Marcel, *33, 726–40n*

Bawcutt, Nigel, *9*

Beating (of spouses), *27, 789–92n, 794–95n, 1146–47n*

Becon, Thomas, *5*

Beds: as place for merriment, *1393–97n, 1397–99n;* tale of, *1341–83. See also* Curtain lecture

Beilin, Elaine V., *88*

Belsey, Catherine, *43, 66, 962–66n*

Bergin, Thomas, *73*

Bess of Hardwick (Carleton), *12*

Bible: as basis for companionate marriage, *13–15, 19, 85;* on spiritual equality, *69;* Tilney's use of, *95, 367n. See also* Names of biblical figures

Bloch, R. Howard, *18, 40*

Boccaccio, Giovanni, *63;* influence of, on *Flower, 6, 7, 70–72, 73, 91n, 165–67n, 1020–77nn, 1185–86n*

Boleyn, Anne, *9, 58, 59*

Book of the Courtier, The. See Courtier, The

Boose, Lynda, *216–25n*

Bray, Mary (Dame), *10–12*

Bride-Bush (Whately), *5*

Brutus, 1053–54

Bullinger, Heinrich, *5, 24–26, 36, 182–83n, 184–86n, 504n, 1243–46n, 1263–65n*

Burckhardt, Jacob, *84, 85, 92*

Burdet, Robert, *87*

Burton, William, *24, 31*

Camden, William, *46*

Campofulgosus, Baptista, *482–93n*

Canary Islands, *259–61, 212–82n, 253–61n, 259n*

Candia, *578n*

Castiglione, Baldassare, *66, 91n;* influence of, on *Flower, 6, 39, 70–71, 75, 165–67n. See also Courtier, The*

Catherine of Aragon, *247n*

Catholic Church: marital doctrine of, *1, 13–14, 17–21, 40, 179n;* separation of, from humanism, *27–29. See also* Council of Trent

Cato, *683–87n*

Cecil, William, *48–49, 79*

Chadwick, Joseph, *33*

Chaldeans, *212–82n, 273n*

Charles (archduke of Austria), *46, 47, 79*

Chastity: female, *19, 52–53, 60, 65, 92, 969–73,* 1283; male, *54. See also* "Shamefastnesse"; Virginity; Virtue

Chaucer, Geoffrey, *18, 19, 39, 40, 63, 247n, 386–98n*

Chaucer: Sources and Backgrounds (Miller), *18*

Chiding, *1387–93n, 1201–2n, 1324–26n*

Children: education of, *818–42, 1249–50, 1262, 843–47n. See also* Procreation

Christ, *191–92n, 197–99n*

Christen State of Matrimonye (Bullinger), *5, 24–25, 182–83n, 504n, 1243–46n, 1263–65n*

Christian Humanism and the Puritan Social Order (Todd), *2, 27–28*

Christian Oeconomie (Perkins), *5–6, 28, 179n*

Christine de Pizan, *85, 1020–24n*

Chrysostom, *15*

Cicero, *216–25n, 288–89n*

Circe, *1417–21n*

City of God, The (Augustine), *20, 68, 184–86n*

Civil Conversations (Guazzo), *6*

Clark, Elizabeth A., *15*

Class: consideration of, in choice of a mate, *11, 13, 50–57;* gendered criteria of, in Renaissance England, *4, 53–59;* hierarchies of, *74–75. See also* Virtue

Cleaver, Richard, *5, 36, 295–99n, 442–44n, 726–40n*

Cleopatra, *599–602n*

Clerk's Tale, The, 39, 63, 247n

Clifford, Anne, *12*

Colloquies, The (Erasmus), *6, 21, 23, 29. See also individual titles*

[190]

Index

Index

Guevara, Antony, *726–40n*
Guttentag, Marcia, *253–61n*
Guzman de Silva (ambassador), *46*

Haec Vir; or, The Womanish Man, 88, *91*
Hageman, Elizabeth, *9*
Hannay, Margaret, *27,* 88
Harrington, William, *5*
Hayward, John, *9*
Heale, William, *1146–47n*
Hegemony, 2, 38. *See also* Dominant ideologies (of marriage)
Heloise, *40–42, 71n*
Henderson, Katherine Usher, 88
Henry VIII (king of England), *50, 58–59, 247n*
Henze, Catherine, *87*
Heptameron of Civill Discourses, An (Whetstone), *5*
Herbs: in Luxan's book, *35, 609–847n;* Tilney's use of, *142, 500–501, 610–819, 609–847n*
Herford, Charles E., *30*
Herodotus, *571n, 1139–45n*
Hesiod [Hesiodus], *346–51n*
Heywood, John, *789–92n*
Hic Mulier, 88, *91*
Hierarchy. *See* Authority; Equality; Power
Hill, Christopher, *3, 69*
Hoby, Thomas (Sir), *66. See also Courtier, The*
Hoffmann, George, *9*
Holm, Janis Butler, *15*
Hooker, Richard, *35, 78, 179n*
Horowitz, Maryanne Cline, *15*
Howard, Catherine, *9, 58*
Hubbell, H. M., *216–25n*
Humanists: on marriage, *2, 3, 4, 11, 17, 21–25, 26–38, 43, 83, 92;* views of, compared to Catholic ideologies, *28–29,* to Protestant ideologies, *26, 27–28, 31, 32–33, 36, 83;* on women, *49–50, 69, 76–77. See also* Erasmus, Desiderius; Equality; Tilney, Edmund
Hundreth Sundrie Flowers, A (Gasgoigne), *66*
Husbands: abusive, *27;* choosing of, *946–66;* duties of, *39, 419–861;* examples of loving, *35, 64–65, 450–68, 482–99;* reforming of, *29, 1323–85;* as thieves of their wives' will, *62–65, 442–44n;* unpleasant, *1010–20, 650–52n, 1330–34n. See also* Beating; Men
Hutchinson, Anne, *83*

Ideology(ies): in *Conjugium, 36–37;* defined, *12;* in *Flower, 35, 38–93;* of marriage, *2, 3–4;* origins of companionate, *13–29;* significance of, *90. See also* Dominant ideologies; Emergent ideologies; Residual ideologies
Ideology of Conduct (Armstrong and Tennenhouse), *6, 726–40n*
Immortality: and marriage, *204–6n*
Index of Prohibited Books, 21
Institutio christiani matrimonii (Erasmus), 23
Instruction of a Christen Woman (Vives), *6, 26, 47, 52–53, 73n, 290–95n, 374n, 386–98n, 1110–21n, 1236–73n, 1243–46n*
Inversion (of sex roles): in marriage, *18, 51;* in symposia, *71–75*
Irigaray, Luce, *61, 62–63*
Irving, Harold, *33*
Isabella (character), *70;* asks Tilney to record this discourse, *7, 1429–31n;* association of, with Elizabeth I, *4, 6–7, 45, 47, 49, 70n;* emergent marital ideology associated with, *4, 39, 42–45, 49–50, 76–82, 83, 86, 88;* speeches by, *354–57, 1007–9, 1131–45, 1151–52, 1160–63, 1321–22*

James I (king of England), *57*
Jameson, Frederic, *12*
Jason, *1417–21n*
Jealousy, *796–817*
Jeffs, Abel, *7, 95*
Jerome, *15, 17–19,* 21
Job (biblical figure), *764–65n*
Johnson, Ralph Glasgow, *95, 146*
Jones, Ann Rosalind, *61, 92, 1316–20n*
Jonson, Ben, *386–98n*
Jordan, Constance, *24, 84, 85,* 88
Jovinian, *17, 19,* 20
Julia (character), *51, 64, 65, 69, 81, 64, 70, 80, 1422–23, 1427;* on duties of a wife, *61, 934–1416;* marital status of, *471–72n;* as overseer of symposium, *71–75, 129–37, 150–64;* as proponent of dominant marital ideology, *39, 43, 50, 77–78, 64n;* speeches by, *150–64, 238–42, 270–71, 316–26, 469–70, 565–67, 853–55, 862–73, 934–1006, 1010–99, 1104–30, 1153–59, 1166–74, 1178–88, 1196–1320, 1323–29, 1339–40, 1384–1416*
Julia (Pompey's wife), *63, 1020–24n, 1077–85n*
Julius Caesar (Shakespeare), *1053–54n*

Kelly, Joan, *85–86, 91–92*

Index

Miller, Robert P., *18*

Milton, John, *14, 54*

Mimians, *63, 1025–47n*

Misogyny, *86;* in Catholic discussions of marriage, *18–20, 28;* humanists' views of, *22–23, 49, 74–75, 76, 403n;* role of, in *Flower, 39–40, 74–75, 478–79n;* views associated with, *76, 386–98n, 1100–1103n, 1189–95n.* *See also* Gualter of Cawne

Mithridates, *1215–27n*

Moncada, Ernest J., *33, 35, 45, 577n*

Montaigne, Michel de, *589–93n, 675–77n*

Montrose, Louis Adrian, *48, 49, 79*

Morals, The (Plutarch), *16–17, 571n, 645–48n, 675–77n, 687–93n, 1025–47n, 1311–14n. See also* "Precepts of Wedlocke"

More, Thomas (Sir), *49, 76, 362–63n*

Moriae encomium (Erasmus), *21*

Morse, Charlotte, *63, 247n*

Mountaine, Dydymus, *70, 96*

Mountjoy, Baron, *23, 34*

Names (of characters): and ideology in *Flower, 38–40*

Neale, J. E., *49, 79, 81*

Nero, *63, 1067*

New Mother, The (Erasmus), *34, 69, 76, 86–87*

Niccholes, Alexander, *5*

Nice Wanton (play), *37*

Nicomachean Ethics (Aristotle), *15–16, 20, 288–89n, 295–99n*

Noah [Noe], *575n, 593–95n*

Nobility, *51–52, 81–82. See also* Class; Virtue

Noonan, John T., Jr., *19, 20*

Noreña, Carlos G., *26*

Numidians, *1160–63n, 1278–82n*

Obedience: in dialogue, *100–104, 124–28, 152, 169–71, 915–17;* in marriage, *44, 74, 76–78;* in women, *937–38, 1128–88, 1198–1213*

Octavius Caesar, *599–602n*

Oeconomicus (Xenophon), *15*

Of Domesticall Duties (Gouge), *5, 12–13, 78–79, 525–26n*

Offen, Karen, *82*

Office and Duetie of an Husband (Vives), *5, 27, 73n, 143–45n, 316–19n, 504n*

"Of Love" (Plutarch), *16–17. See also Morals, The*

Othello (Shakespeare), *386–98n, 778n*

Panthea, *63, 1048–53n*

Paradise, *71, 185, 119n, 184–86n*

Parents: forsaking, *198, 983–84n;* love toward, *200–201n*

Parr, Catherine, *50*

Parthians, *990, 1155–59n*

Partridge, Eric, *67*

Patient Grissil (Dekker, Chettle, and Haughton), *247n*

Patriarchy, *53–54, 66, 68, 281–82n. See also* Authority; Feminism; Women: alleged inferiority of

Paul (biblical figure), *20, 583–85n*

Paul IV (pope), *28*

Paulina (wife of Seneca), *63, 1065–70n*

Paynell, Thomas, *316–19n*

Peake, Robert (the Elder), *9*

Pedro (character), *6, 11, 67, 121, 1427, 54–55n; as apparent advocate of women, 74, 75, 89–90, 406–9;* origins of, *33–35;* as proponent of dominant marital ideology, *50–57, 64–65;* as representative of humanists, *39–40, 43;* speeches by, *90–97, 103–4, 124—47, 165–237, 243–45, 249–61, 266–69, 272–315, 327–53, 358–76, 379–82, 406–68, 478–564, 568–618, 704–72, 776–79, 783–842, 848–52, 856–61, 874–81, 1330–38, 1341–75, 1380–83. See also* Luxan, Pedro di

Peel, J. D. Y., *7, 9*

Perkins, William, *5, 6, 28–29, 179n*

Pettie, George, *801–2n*

Philip II (king of Spain), *46, 47*

Phillip, John, *247n*

Phoebus, *52n*

Pietas puerilis (Erasmus), *34*

Pitachus Mityleneus, *290–95n*

Plato, *716, 589–93n, 1055–64n, 1316–20n*

Play of Patient Grissel (Phillip), *247n*

Pliny, *64, 140–41n, 1086–93n*

Plutarch, *22, 596–99n, 599–602n, 683–87n, 830–33n;* on marriage, *16–17, 51, 1141, 295–99n, 302–6n, 310–15n, 351–53n, 455–60n, 461–68n, 962–66n, 1053–54n, 1278–82n. See also Morals, The;* "Precepts of Wedlocke"

Polygamy, *288–89n. See also* Marriage: customs of; Sex ratios

Pompey, *63, 1020–24n, 1077–85n*

Porcia (Brutus's wife), *63, 1053–54n*

Power: in companionate marriages, *14–15, 27, 82–83;* granted to women by men, *73, 75, 129–37, 149–57, 866–67, 876–81;* and

Library of Congress Cataloging-in-Publication Data

Tilney, Edmund, d. 1610.
  [Briefe and pleasant discourse of duties in mariage, called the flower of friendshippe]
  The flower of friendship : a Renaissance dialogue contesting marriage / by Edmund Tilney ;
edited and with an introduction by Valerie Wayne.
      p.   cm.
  Originally published: A briefe and pleasant discourse of duties in mariage, called the flower
of friendshippe. London : Henrie Denham, 1568.
  Includes bibliographical references (p.   ) and index.
  ISBN 0-8014-2454-2 (cloth : alk. paper). — ISBN 0-8014-9705-1 (paper : alk. paper)
    1. Marriage—Early works to 1800.   2. Sex role—Early works to 1800.   3. Women—
Early works to 1800.   4. Dialogues, English.   I. Wayne, Valerie.   II. Title.
PR2384.T45B75   1992
306.81—dc20   92-52776